Before and Beyond the Global Economic Crisis

Before and Beyond the Global Economic Crisis

Economics, Politics and Settlement

Edited by

Mats Benner

Lund University, Sweden

Edward Elgar

Cheltenham, UK • Northampton, MA, USA

Published by
Edward Elgar Publishing Limited
The Lypiatts
15 Lansdown Road
Cheltenham
Glos GL50 2JA
UK

Edward Elgar Publishing, Inc.
William Pratt House
9 Dewey Court
Northampton
Massachusetts 01060
USA

A catalogue record for this book
is available from the British Library

Library of Congress Control Number: 2012946684

This book is available electronically in the ElgarOnline.com
Economics Subject Collection, E-ISBN 978 1 78195 201 6

ISBN 978 1 78195 200 9

Typeset by Servis Filmsetting Ltd, Stockport, Cheshire
Printed by MPG PRINTGROUP, UK

Contents

Figures

Tables

Contributors

Roger E. Backhouse is at the Department of Economics, Birmingham University, UK and at the Erasmus Institute for Philosophy and Economics, Erasmus University, Rotterdam, Netherlands.

Mats Benner is at the Research Policy Institute, Lund University, Sweden.

Robert Boyer is at the Institut des Amériques, Paris.

Anna W. Gustafsson is at the Centre for Languages and Literature, Lund University, Sweden.

Fredrik Hansen is at the Department of Economics, Lund University, Sweden.

Bob Jessop is at the Department of Sociology, Lancaster University, UK.

Lars Jonung is at the Knut Wicksell Centre for Financial Economics, Lund University, Sweden.

Johannes Lindvall is at the Department of Political Science, Lund University, Sweden.

Åsa Lundqvist is at the Department of Sociology, Lund University, Sweden.

Bengt-Åke Lundvall is in the Department of Business and Management, Aalborg University, Denmark.

Lennart Schön is at the Department of Economic History, Lund University, Sweden.

Ngai-Ling Sum is at the Department of Politics, Philosophy and Religion, Lancaster University, UK.

Jan Svensson is at the Centre for Languages and Literature, Lund University, Sweden.

Acknowledgements

This book concludes the project 'After the Crisis – a research programme on the political economy of the future', conducted at the Pufendorf Institute at Lund University between August 2009 and May 2011. The Institute provided a congenial and supportive environment for our collective endeavour and we have had numerous interactions within the group and with invited guests, some of whom generously contributed to this book. Financial support from the Institute is gratefully acknowledged. On a personal note, I thank Sture Forsén, the former Director of the Institute, and Eva Persson, the Institute's Administrative Director, for their unfailing support and encouragement, from the very beginning to the very end of the project. At a late stage, the manuscript was scrutinized by Mats Börjesson and Robert Östling who provided insightful and incisive questions and appraisal.

Mats Benner
Lund, May 2012

Before and beyond the global economic crisis: an introduction

Mats Benner

In his presidential address to the annual meeting of the American Economic Association in 2003, Nobel laureate Robert Lucas declared that the problem of depression-prevention – the elusive goal of virtually all social and political projects of the twentieth century – had now been solved 'for all practical purposes' (Lucas 2003, p.1). Substantive reforms of financial regulation and of fiscal and monetary policies had finally achieved the synchronization of markets and politics that had eluded capitalist societies throughout the last century. As a consequence, the need for an interventionist state – except to perform the most basic of functions – had ceased to exist. Society and markets would and could instead continue to exist in harmonious interplay, shaped and reinforced by ideologies, norms and attitudes cherishing the values of individual self-determination and political restraint (Rodgers 2010).

Lucas's vision of a seamless integration of markets and society had spread widely by the mid-2000s, and taken up in notions like 'capitalism unleashed' in a finance-led economic growth model of remarkable stability and vitality (cf. Glyn 2007). Even more critical voices took the relative stability of the growth model more or less for granted and instead critiqued its articulation with global cultural and political processes (Hardt and Negri 2000). The stability of the growth model itself was never or only rarely questioned.

The collapse of the financial system that began in 2007 and that culminated in the fall of 2008 undermined the harbingers of a new era of crisis-free capitalism. The state re-entered the economy very hastily, rapidly crafting a combination of rescue packages and new sets of regulations, often at the behest of the financial actors themselves. In the process, financial markets moved from being perceived as the engines of economic growth and social relations into being seen as dangerous liabilities, and financial actors were transformed from heroes to villains. The question that this book deals with is the long-term impact of the 2007–08 financial crisis: are we about to enter a new era in state–society–market interaction and will the finance-led economic growth model be transformed?

The topic of this book has been a moving target. The work began in 2009 and was finalized in the spring of 2012. It has been surrounded by turbulence and even more crises of various kinds, to the extent that the title of the entire undertaking ('After the Crisis?') eventually seemed like a misnomer. Instead of having a distinct beginning and a similarly discrete end, the crisis of the financial system in 2007 and 2008 mutated into a phase of rapid political redeployment later followed by a sovereign debt crisis and a currency crisis which has triggered massive political responses and a recalibration of political relations and institutions not only in Europe but also in other regions of the world. Hence, and not surprisingly, the financial crisis has led to a political crisis, and will undoubtedly continue to trigger transformations in the social, political and economic fabric. Whether or not the crisis (and the crisis that it has triggered) will lead to a new socio-economic compact and a new economic growth model – and a parallel refurbishment of the political and institutional landscape – is more uncertain.

Furthermore, as the ensuing events have clearly shown, the crisis in 2008 had deep roots and followed a certain historical pattern (including the pretentious assumptions of this time being different and not prone to the same instabilities as others periods in time; cf. Reinhart and Rogoff 2009). This was no isolated crisis of the financial system – it was instead a crisis of an entire socio-economic model, following a path of systemic development, breakdown and restructuring well known in history, partially but not exclusively evolving in tandem with the rise and spread of new technologies. Hence, it gradually became clear that it would be difficult to locate the 'after' in our initial formulation of 'after the crisis'. What we could do was to locate a 'before', that is, the events that preceded the immediate crisis in 2007–08, and a 'beyond' the financial crisis – that is, how the crisis has played out and continues to influence ideas, policies and practices. After the apocalyptic events of the autumn of 2008 have faded away in memory, and with them some of the more drastic expectations and fears (and hopes) of a total breakdown of global economic relations, the long-term challenges that they highlighted are becoming increasingly clear, even though the resolution of the crisis and the socio-economic models that emerge remain open issues. There are only weak signs of a transformation of the neo-liberal agenda encapsulated in Lucas's 2003 speech. The crisis also, as several of the contributions to this book highlight, follows a familiar pattern of socio-economic development, and in this sense the crisis did not come unexpectedly. Nor does it surprise that the financial crisis has mutated into a sovereign debt crisis which has developed into a political crisis. However, the forms of 'crisis resolution', and the shape and form of a post-crisis compact are still open and no coherent alternatives to the policy models that have shaped the last three decades have yet crystallized.

The long-term impact and the impact of the various forms of crisis management therefore remain to be seen – indeed, the repercussions, in politics and economics, continue to move back and forth and will continue to do so over an extended period of time. The crisis remains one that both reinforces and challenges the socio-economic model that has been dominant since the 1980s – and it is therefore of major interest to those (like the group represented in this volume) that engage in the long-run dynamics of capitalist economies and their social, political and economic institutions.

The uncertainties notwithstanding, it has been a crisis of many of the established dogmas of the recent decades:

- The focus on fiscal policy restraint turned into the opposite with radical increases in state expenditure and ensuing spikes in sovereign debt – which in their turn have triggered imbalances in global economic relations and cooperation, and the sharing of risks between states, financial institutions and global organizations. The placid and passive state that Lucas envisaged has instead become enmeshed in fundamental economic instability, with profound social and political repercussions.
- Privatizations and public withdrawal from the regulation, management and ownership of vital parts of the economy were (temporarily?) replaced by bailouts and widespread nationalizations of the finance sector and, in some cases, also injections of state support into key industrial sectors and firms.
- This may pave the way for a transformed role of the state in the economy, from reactive partnering with the market to enforcer not just of new sectors but also of new economic relations. This includes re-regulating corporate strategies and financial services, adjusting regulation to the psychology of economic crises and how they can be tamed and contained (Akerlof and Shiller 2009). Regulating and curtailing incentives in the financial sectors, partly as a result of nationalizations and/or public bailouts, is another expression.
- There has been a move away from retrenchment of welfare policies in the form of cost-cutting and market-conforming towards sheltering and reducing the strains of unemployment ('social investments'; Morel et al. 2011); and possibly also towards enhancing welfare policies to create a stable ground for long-term growth, for instance in relation to immigration and families, but also to the elderly, education etc.
- The search is on for a new socio-economic discourse and new and more realistic macroeconomic models, viewing the market as shaped by recurrent instability and by volatile relations between markets,

governments and citizens within a finance-led economic growth model (Sachs 2011; Skidelsky 2009; Wolf 2008; Boyer, this volume, Chapter 4).

- We may also envisage not only transformations in economic interaction as an outcome of crisis strategies (which may vary from protectionism to enhanced self-sufficiency), but also new types of geopolitical relations, enhancing the steering capacity of nation states and other political entities to absorb the impact of a volatile global economy (Cohen and DeLong 2010; Rodrik 2011; Sum, this volume, Chapter 9).
- More generally, a new understanding of the mechanisms of economic growth might be emerging, based less on reliance on reinforced market mechanisms and more on societal resilience and the capacity to formulate 'societal goals' for the economy rather than the other way around (Hull Kristensen and Lilja 2011; Hutton 2010; McDonough et al. 2010; Lundvall, this volume, Chapter 8).

All of the above points indicate that the crisis may turn out to be a watershed in the regulation of social, political and economic affairs. However, we need to be cautious as some of the dogmas that shaped economic and social policies in the last three decades have returned in full force after a brief hiatus of state-led crisis management (Crouch 2011; Jessop, this volume, Chapter 12). Hence, it would be far too early to assume that a systemic change is underway; it may instead turn out to be a continuation and deepening of the socio-economic model of the last decades. It may however also be a phase in which we will see divergent responses to the challenges of the crisis, where some countries and regions venture into the construction of new institutional responses whereas others recede to older patterns, in roughly the same vein as countries varied in their response to the political and economic crisis of the 1970s (Lindvall 2010).

Whether or not the crisis will lead to a broader restructuring of economic relations and market regulations, as the crises of the 1930s and the 1970s did, is therefore an open issue. In our work, we have striven to integrate different perspectives in the analysis of potential ways out of the crisis – from path-dependency ('more of the same') to the emergence of novel ways of regulating the economy and embedding economic relations. By stressing the temporal dimension – 'before and beyond' – we point out that our emphasis is on the historical roots of financial crisis and the particular features that shaped the current one: this pertains to the regulation of the financial system and to markets in general but also to the complex relationship between public policy, social relations and economic organization. The direction of the renewal ('beyond the crisis') cannot be ascertained at present; a multitude of paths beyond it are possible. The tendencies are all but clear and already now we find a bewildering variety of responses – from radically (if highly contested) fiscal expansion in the US to (equally contested) austerity policies in the EU, most prominently in Southern Europe, Ireland and the UK. Outside the confines of Europe and North America, we find a similar complex variety of responses, where short-term crisis responses have been complemented by structural measures to reduce the dependency on exports of manufactured goods for the volatile markets of Europe and North America (see Schön and Sum, this volume, Chapters 1 and 9). We find a similarly bewildering variety of social responses to the crisis – ranging from xenophobia to radicalization, from fatalism to social protest. However, so far, these responses have not triggered any major changes in the political or ideological landscape or the rise of new major social movements. Instead, the dogmas and recipes that dominated prior to the crisis still dominate the political landscape and genuine political alternatives seem distant.

The crisis has nonetheless fostered some discursive combats and some seeds of a potential political upheaval – this would include the intense debates in the US on the stimulus packages and the causes and remedies of the economic recession (Krugman 2012; see also Gustafsson, Hansen and Svensson in this volume, Chapters 10, 3 and 5). European debates have been more placid, with fewer direct confrontations between policy stances. The austerity policy that has followed the financial breakdown in the EU has not to the same extent fostered political debates and alternatives (except among the far right and some smaller left-leaning movements). China and the BRIC countries are portrayed as models of stability in a global roaring sea, but these accounts overstate the degree of social and political consensus (Sum, this volume, Chapter 9). Academic accounts also stumble over the interpretations of the crisis and the ways out of it. The sum of all these events might foster a watershed in the evolution of macroeconomic theorizing and doubt if such a change is underway (Backhouse 2010 and this volume, Chapter 2).

Nevertheless, it is noteworthy that economics has become a field shaped by slightly less uniformity after decades of at least overt consensus, as witnessed in the sharp debates on crisis analysis and crisis diagnosis being pursued on blogs and in popular debates (Cohen and DeLong 2010). The crisis has had the impact of revealing and provoking real controversies, not only between academic interpretations but also between crisis-management models. The neo-liberal sense of victory captured by Lucas's statement in 2003 seems less strong now and more open to fundamental critique, even though Lucas himself and others cling to a belief in the self-regulating market. The political debate in the US on the economy indicates a sharp diversion of standpoints focused around the recovery package. In other instances, the response is more path-dependent, building on rather than diverging from the policies and rhetoric pursued prior to the financial debacle. In the UK, it seems to have resulted in an even more conscientious implementation of some of the basic principles of the neo-liberal agenda – tight lids on public expenditure, cutbacks in social services, and a dedicated redistribution between the citizenry and industry, seemingly reflecting a lack of ability or willingness to depart from the finance-dominated economic growth path (Jessop, this volume, Chapter 12). However, it has also triggered etatist responses, and even some more far-reaching proposals as to the viability of the economic growth model of the last three decades (cf. Harvey 2010).

THE EVOLUTION OF SOCIETAL MODELS IN THE POSTWAR PERIOD

As an introduction to the volume, we now turn to a brief outline of the way into the crisis, and the alternative ways out of or through it. The first issue is therefore a stocktaking of the socio-economic experience in the postwar period, with a particular focus on the conditions in western Europe and North America: how relatively stable models of accumulation have developed and how they have been institutionally embedded and socially and politically supported, but also how they have been increasingly plagued by contradictions and weaknesses, and how these weaknesses have been addressed and dealt with.

After the first turbulent period following the Second World War, the world seemed to be moving towards a new socio-economic-political equilibrium. Europe has been singled out as a model of parallel social cohesion and economic dynamics (cf. Anderson 2009). In a classic study, *Modern Capitalism*, Andrew Shonfield (1965) highlighted the converging tendencies of developed countries in the postwar period, where various forms of state–market interactions had been established to even out economic fluctuations and to ensure the smooth introduction of new technology and rational corporate planning. Europe led the way towards this 'mixed economy' by virtue of its historical traditions of state planning, but similar tendencies were evident in North America.

As a result of erratic economic growth in the 1970s and 1980s, the model came under immense strain, and was a battleground for a wide variety of political-economic recipes, from neo-liberalism to etatism. Europe became, in the words of a famous analysis, the scene of a confrontation of '*capitalisme contre capitalisme*' (Albert 1998), or between different versions of an emerging mode of regulation, all emphasizing increasing work supply and the flexible adaptation of firms and labour markets to technological opportunities and market fluctuations (Scharpf 1987). The US and UK had already ventured on a post-compromise pattern, releasing the forces of their financial industries and deregulating previously controlled markets for labour, infrastructure and services (Hall 1986; Gamble 1994). Some argued that a few European countries, primarily Germany, had squared the circle of economic globalization by developing models of 'diversified quality production' that could withstand the competition on increasingly open markets (Streeck 1992); more pessimistic observers instead argued that Europe was poorly adapted for the very same global challenges and had to couple a declining industrial sector with a growing service economy to retain the commitment to full employment (Scharpf and Schmidt 2000). Europe at this time (circa 2000) seemed to be confronted by the rise and seemingly better fit of a 'thinner' capitalism, with market-conforming institutions regulating labour markets and the service sector and with denser networks around finance and knowledge dissemination and innovation (Crouch and Streeck 1997). The organized and coordinated Social Democratic–Christian Democratic experience in all its varied forms seemed poorly equipped to deal with the emerging conditions of an open and knowledge-based economy. While the US at the time appeared as an unflappable system, it too underwent dramatic changes in the postwar period, when a fairly detailed system of state economic planning, combined with ambitious if patchy developments of welfare programmes and commitments in areas like education, health care and environmental protection, was gradually dismantled (Graham 1976). Furthermore, a gradual liberalization of financial services (which triggered increasingly adventurous financial innovations) together with an increasingly lax monetary policy underpinned US growth. High-technology industries could thrive on the dynamic research systems and the rich supply of venture capital, while increased liquidity of the US households sustained a long period of growing prosperity and employment (Nocera 1994; Rivlin 2010; Lowenstein 2001).

After the European postwar model was declared obsolete by observers like Crouch and Streeck (1997), deemed unfit for the emerging innovation-led and finance-driven economy, the first decade of the third millennium saw the focus shifting decisively to an emulation of the US examplar, with the financial system and high-technology clusters reinforcing one another, accompanied by positive spillover effects to the entire economy. European countries, herded by the European Union, tried to mimic the US growth model by pursuing a soft monetary policy, support schemes to spur European high-tech clusters and networks, and deregulations of the

European finance sector. An important driver in this development was the EU, capitalizing on the perceived weakness of the nation states to bring about institutional reforms, primarily in the areas of research, innovation and education (Borrás 2003).

The period of 'capitalism unleashed' (circa 1995–2008; Glyn 2007) therefore highlighted the difficulties of the coordinated European economies in adapting to the new 'rules of the game', and the growing interrelation between the US and China further stressed the interpretation that Europe was losing its role as a distinct and productive 'institutional alternative' in the 'global knowledge-based economy'. The EU and the European nations seemed unable to produce a coherent or viable alternative to US hegemony and to the growing mutual interpenetration of the US and Chinese economies ('Chimerica' – Ferguson 2008). Instead, the US growth machine seemed unparalleled, at least among the 'developed' economies, and the successful integration of a vibrant financial sector with dynamic and fast-growing industries like biotechnology and information technology triggered intense policy debates on the institutional preconditions for a durable socio-economic compact. Debates centred around activation policies to manage social exclusion and limit public welfare expenditure, relaxations of financial services regulation to lubricate the economic machinery and shifts of responsibility for certain social services from state to market. The entire package was encapsulated in a centrist programme of aligning market liberalism with modest ambitions of social inclusion and redistribution, for a European way into the future (the 'Third Way' – Giddens 1998).

Hence, the decade before the 2007–08 crisis erupted was perceived as one of a virtuous circle between finance-dominated growth and docile if sometimes mildly redistributive public policies as shown in, for instance, the 'Third Way' debate and the design of various kinds of pan-European growth strategy. In this period, a recurrent theme was that the welfare state had to be curtailed to contain costs and to support the mechanisms of the emerging globalized economy (Jessop 2002). In the run-up to the financial crisis, there seemed to be few alternatives to 'private Keynesianism' and financialization as drivers of economic growth and social cohesion; indeed, the political and discursive landscape seemed to become increasingly narrow, with prominent political and intellectual leaders arguing for a 'new middle' in politics, inhabited by market-conforming but socially ambitious political leaders, who on the one hand removed the fetters from market forces – in particular those within the financial system – and on the other hand carried through a selective number of policies for social redistribution and social services.

The linchpin of the 'new middle' was an acceptance of the productivity and capacity for self-organization in the financial sector, also among parties and organizations of the political left, which have been traditionally sceptical about the long-term capacity of markets to secure their own reproduction (and even more sceptical of their capacity to ascertain social redistribution). Instead, a liberalization of markets seemed to secure not only economic growth in a much less erratic way than in the long aftermath of Keynesianism: it could also serve as a foundation for a new wave of social reforms, in what could be called an 'inverted embeddedness' (Blyth 2002). First, more stable growth seemed to create more employment, thereby lessening the dependence on public welfare. Second, financialization functioned also as a redistributive mechanism, for instance by allowing new groups into the housing market and by transforming owned property into 'cash machines' for households. Third, to a lesser extent, the long wave of high growth enabled the construction of some expansions of public commitments in welfare, primarily in education (UK) and in social security and/or health care (US).

All of this made what seemed a new historical compromise possible, navigating between popular interests and market dynamics, as they now seemed to enjoy a productive relationship. A new pragmatic centre-left made aggressive interventions to reduce state regulation of the financial sector, seemingly not as a response to the political interests of the financial sector but rather to serve their own political self-interest. Markets were not to be contained and embedded; if properly and responsibly disembedded, they were powerful allies for a new progressive political bloc of progressive political leaders.

Everything seemed indeed to work smoothly in this alleged depression-free economy. Then in 2007 the stability began to crack. It began in the UK with the run on the Northern Rock bank. In parallel, signs were becoming increasingly troubling concerning the state of the US housing market. The events that then unfolded, culminating with Lehman Brothers filing for bankruptcy protection on 15 September 2008, have been thoroughly described in several journalistic accounts, depicting the behaviour of leading actors during the crisis and showcasing the stress, even panic, under which policies were pursued (Sorkin 2009; Lowenstein 2010). In such accounts, the crisis and its aftermath emerge as a series of actions, beginning with the government-orchestrated take-over of Bear Sterns by JP Morgan in March 2008, followed by the failed reorganization and eventual bankruptcy of Lehman Brothers in the spring and summer of 2008 and then the panicked introduction of the Troubled Assets Rescue Package (TARP) to circumvent any further falls of giant financial firms. In such accounts, events culminate with the de facto nationalization of the world's largest insurance company AIG and the massive insertions of capital into the troubled financial system, where even such megafirms as JP Morgan and Goldman Sachs were affected (a similar account has been given of the financial crisis in the UK in Brummer 2008).

Hence, while the dramatic events in 2007 and 2008 forced through radical policy measures – measures that deviated from the orthodoxies of the last two decades – the basic premise was that the crisis should not lead to a radical change in the regulation of the financial sector, because of the strength of the institutional set-up and the general mechanisms of economic growth ('financialization'). Crisis policies were pursued not to transform the financial system, but rather to rescue it.

In parallel, welfare policies were mobilized in the short term to mitigate the consequences of the rapid economic downfall. Prior to the 2008 crisis, European welfare policy had been geared towards adapting to the 'new' conditions of the globalized economy, with cost restraints but also new social relations and network-based welfare models – including the devolution of state authority and the introduction of 'private Keynesianism' in the form of market-based provision of resources to households and families (Crouch 2004). This reflected the remarkable belief in, and presupposition of, the efficiency of market-mediated mechanisms to manage private and social risk, also in a long-term perspective. It thereby also served the economic policy goal of shifting responsibilities from the public purse to private sources. However, the current issue is the impact of the financial crisis and its aftermath on social policy: will it trigger a further devolution of responsibilities from the state to civil society and to families for social reproduction? This is clearly the case in the UK where the notion of a 'Big Society' has been conjured up as a response to the fiscal hardship of the British state. As a contrast, the debates on a 'social investment state' envisage a more activist approach of the state to pave the way for a return to employment via social protection. The most viable model may include a combination of both, as the Scandinavian experience in the 1990s crisis indicates. As Åsa Lundqvist argues in her contribution, the cost-cutting and market-shifting ambitions paid off in the short term, protecting advanced welfare states (like the Swedish) from the pressure of sovereign debt and international economic exposure, but it simultaneously exposed them to the more creeping challenges of social reproduction. As a response, austerity was transformed rather rapidly into a return to some if not all of the social policy measures of the pre-crisis period. The Swedish case might give some lessons for the European countries which are now shifting from generosity in the face of the financial crisis to austerity as a response to the debt crisis. The Swedish case actually shows a family policy renaissance after the period of austerity, even though the marginalization of certain families seems to remain, despite the improved conditions. A crisis of the welfare state now plagues the Southern European states, which are in dire need of reformed family policies to enhance labour market participation and to decrease the dependence on male breadwinners as the sole providers, but which cannot both afford them *and* comply with the demands of international lenders and creditors.

The Asian countries, which have weathered the crisis well this time, face similar challenges to reform and expand their social policies, especially those relevant to families, as they face declining fertility and ageing populations. Hence, one of the more prominent trends in social policy must be expected to take place in family policy, which currently impedes growth patterns in countries both affected and not affected by the financial crisis. As Lundqvist's analysis shows, family policy is a field dominated by entrenched beliefs and interests, and any attempt to adopt a gender-equal regime is likely to meet with much resistance.

The evolution of social policies is also mixed. In the short-term perspective, the economic crisis triggered a reversal of the pattern of cost-cutting and market-based solutions of the past decades: social policy measures have been mobilized to contain some of the turbulence of the contraction, primarily through unemployment support but also through labour market policy measures, notably in the US but also in many EU countries and perhaps most spectacularly in China with massive infrastructural projects. There is also an intertwining with welfare policies and the crisis measures for the financial sector: rescue packages for the financial sector were motivated by the detrimental effects of a financial collapse on the housing market. Similarly, the rapid decline in employment in some vulnerable regions and industrial sectors forced through policies for employment-sheltering and corporate support, and even bailouts and government takeovers of critical firms including global giants like General Motors (cf. Rattner 2010). Similar initiatives to shelter economic actors and social interests were taken in Europe, where public interventions in several manufacturing sectors, in particular the automotive industry, were incepted to counteract the impact of the rapid decline in economic activity following the financial debacle. In this sense, welfare policies, labour market measures and crisis management reinforced one another at the onset of the crisis.

However, as governments have been abdicating from the state of siege, they have sought increasingly for ways out of their public obligations to provide support for employment and corporate survival; in this they have been driven partly by concerns for sovereign debt, partly by political path-dependency and a return to the political dogmas of the pre-crisis period. The 'great transformation' of market-based solutions still shapes social and political interests, and new interests and models of economic governance are not discernable yet (Blyth 2002; Backhouse, this volume, Chapter 2). Some attempts have, arguably, been made to afford alternative visions for growth, employment and inclusion. Lundvall's contribution to this volume (Chapter 8) is an example, envisaging a new deal where major investments in education and training serve the purpose of enhancing both social inclusion and economic efficiency. Other contributions discuss the preconditions for a 'green new deal' with the transformation of society and economy driven by the inclusion of ecological concerns regarding social and economic reproduction (Schön, this volume, Chapter 1; cf. Friedman 2008). Mild versions of such a growth programme have been incepted in the US and Germany, with government-sponsored schemes for solar energy and wind technology. On the basis of a long-term analysis of patterns of structural economic change, and highlighting the complex interplay between demand, prices and supply, Schön's contribution outlines the structural contractions but also the opportunities released in the crisis, and in particular how different regional blocs may capitalize on the rise and continued deployment of new technologies and new patterns of demand (including the search for new sources of energy). In Schön's interpretation, Europe somewhat surprisingly emerges as the potentially leading region in the introduction and generalization of a new growth paradigm based on energy and climate constraints; Lundvall's contribution also points to the social and organizational capacity of Europe, even though the structure of the European Union, and the fragmentation of economic, social and industrial policies within Europe, hamper European countries in the process of technological and economic change. A major issue for the future, not only in Europe but also in North America and Asia, is therefore the design of efficient and legitimate institutions for a new, long wave of growth, similar to the regulation of the wage-labour nexus in the 1930s or, for that matter, the deregulation initiatives of the 1980s and 1990s. Robert Boyer's and Lars Jonung's contributions (Chapters 4 and 11) on their side points not only to the need for more durable regulatory mechanisms beyond those that were erected to curtail the impact of the financial crisis (and the social and political unrest that ensued), but also to the variation and experiments in institutional design during a crisis. Hence, we can expect the coming years and decades to be shaped by contested interpretations of the sources of economic growth and the adjacent institutional forms to articulate and embed these forces.

Will the crisis lead to a reconstruction of the political landscape? Will new movements appear and new ideological and institutional models with them? The crises of the 1930s paved the way for the postwar compact with the combination of Keynesian economic regulation and Fordist production organization. In a similar vein, the crisis of the 1970s fostered the neo-liberal turn which facilitated and embedded the rise of finance-led growth (Boyer 2000). Policy tendencies in the run-up to the crisis were decidedly in the direction of state policies conforming to, and propelling, continued financialization, and avoiding public measures distorting market exchanges. The question is whether new political alternatives and blocks are emerging in ways similar to those of the 1930s and 1970s (cf. Berman 2006). Johannes Lindvall's contribution (this volume) points to the cyclical developments of political blocs and political ideas (policy innovation) within and beyond economic crises. Historically, crises have been parts not only of structural economic change but also of structural political change, in the 'great transformations' that were discussed above. However, as Lindvall and Jessop note in their respective contributions, the political space appears more curtailed today, narrowing the search for new compromises and alliances in the shaping and reshaping of economic institutions. The sheer size and complexity of the financial market – together with the lax regulations (that were in themselves driven through by the financial actors) – have conjointly shrunk the space for viable institutional alternatives and, therefore, for genuine policy alternatives.

Despite this smaller political space, the crisis has opened up the political debate for a wider set of alternatives, which range from a retreat to an orthodoxy (where 'too big to fail' is deployed as a policy rationale and where markets will be left responsible to themselves again) to a revival of state activism more directly in the economy but also with more far-reaching public programmes for welfare and employment policies (Judt 2010). Some call for a return to welfare policies as market-correcting and indeed market-shaping interventions, focusing on human need rather than market dynamics (Wright 2010), while others point at the inherent imbalances of the financially dominated growth model without specifying a direction for societal development (Reich 2010; Stiglitz 2010; Akerlof and Shiller 2009). A whole range of studies have emerged of the human fallacies that led to the crisis, in particular how regulatory mechanisms were subverted by innovative and sometimes outright deceitful corporate behaviour (e.g. McLean and Nocera 2010; Tett 2009), and some of their descriptive insights may be translated into dynamic measures to regulate financial services (Boyer, Jonung, this volume, Chapters 4 and 11). Despite the lock-in effects of the explosive expansion of the financial sector, and the difficulties of creating durable regulatory measures, there is a tendency to search for new avenues for economic growth such as clean technologies and renewable energy. Public investments (and policy expectations) tend to go in that direction, often however blended with austerity policies to rescue ailing public finances. The Europe 2020 strategy, as a ten-year programme for 'smart and inclusive growth', encompassed both of these stances, as do the economic policies of the Obama administration in the US and possibly also some of the European Union member states. Such a piecemeal future may be the most ambitious crisis management model there is at the moment. It will not be unchallenged, either by those who baulk at even the most placid of regulations and interventions or by those who suffer from the social and economic consequences of the crisis.

STRUCTURE OF THE BOOK

Our work progresses along the following lines:

Chapters 1 to 4 by Schön, Backhouse, Hansen and Boyer trace the composition and anatomy of the 'growth bloc' of the post-Keynesian period, from its macroeconomic regulation and structure (including the structure of the global economy, techno-economic paradigms and their variegated deployment, and global trade and economic relations patterns) to microeconomic movements and relations. The chapters contribute to the understanding of the structural composition of the economy prior to the financial crisis as well as to the emerging and evolving patterns of growth and economic regulation beyond the crisis. They also deal with the evolution of institutional ensembles and their impact on growth patterns – including market regulation, in particular the regulation of microeconomic behaviour and incentives in the financial sector.

Chapters 5 to 7 by Svensson, Lundqvist and Lindvall deal with the social and political consequences of economic crises. A crisis of great depth and magnitude causes major disturbances in state functions and in social and political mobilization; these include transformed political patterns (electoral and party-based), as Lindvall highlights in his chapter, as well as transformations in policymaking and policy discourses, as dealt with in Svensson's chapter. Major economic crises also question established forms of interplay between social welfare and economic growth, as Lundqvist shows in her analysis of the transformation of family policy between two major economic crises in Sweden. These chapters together contribute to debates on the redeployment of economic and social policies in response to economic crises, as well as the reconfiguration of electoral and ideological landscapes (and their discursive forms) and of welfare state regimes within and beyond economic crises.

Chapters 8 to 12 by Lundvall, Sum, Gustafsson, Jonung and Jessop deal with the shape of the post-crisis society, economy and polity. Lundvall points to the importance of post-crisis visions and coalitions, including the mobilization of public and private resources behind 'new deals' that can simultaneously propel economic growth and address social and ecological concerns.

The financial crisis has triggered both new relations among leading economic powers as well as the formation of new power blocs, including the rise of the so-called BRIC countries. Sum in her chapter draws upon a cultural political perspective in scrutinizing the projections and visions enmeshed in the 'BRIC' concept and how it has been mobilized as a crisis measure to counter the impact of the North Atlantic financial crisis. The crisis of 2007–08 came at the height of an intense period of finance-dominated growth, and instantaneously provoked debates on the nature of the crisis as well as routes out of it – including the discursive construction of socio-economic relations, and the media's constitution of the crisis as an 'event' – as an outcome of human shortcomings, poor timing, deceptive behaviour or, even, systemic imperfections. The way out of the crisis can be seen as a battlefield between different linguistic constructions of the economy, and it has indeed fostered debates regarding how a more 'sustainable', 'robust' or 'resilient' model of socio-economic relations can be constructed, as Gustafsson points out in her chapter.

The broad issue behind Jonung's and Jessop's respective contributions (Chapters 11 and 12) is the relationship between short-term crisis management on the one hand and the possible emergence of a 'new' wave of economic growth embedded in a durable ensemble of socio-economic regulation on the other. Will new sources of growth and social identities emerge beyond the finance-led phase, and how may social mobilization, public policies and growth paths be aligned in that process? Jonung affords an in-depth analysis of the future of financial regulation and how new modes of regulation may be established to control the volatility of financial markets. Jessop's contribution scrutinizes the conditions for a productive interplay between economic growth and socio-economic regulation, including new forms of socio-economic imageries.

FINAL WORDS

To sum up, different ambitions have shaped this work. First, we have attempted to understand how the financial crisis emerged, what consequences it has had, how it has been understood, interpreted and acted upon. Second, we have sought to make a more general contribution to the understanding of crises as such, and the role they play in economy, polity and society, in shaking up existing growth models and institutional regimes and paving the way (or not) for new ones. Third, and perhaps most importantly, we have searched for novel combinations of state–society–economy relations, 'beyond the crisis', and ask if the financial crisis of 2007 and 2008 has led to the reconsideration of economic relations and their institutional embeddedness, the direction of which may be more open.

In doing so, we have realized that economic crises are multifaceted phenomena, in themselves, in their societal consequences, and in how they are met by, and form the basis of, institutional 'responses' of various kinds. We have done so drawing upon perspectives from economics and structural economics on incentives at the micro level and the dynamics of socio-technical development blocks on the macro level; from welfare studies of the articulation between economic growth models and social welfare regimes; from politics in our focus on governance issues; and from linguistics with regard to the discursive framings of economic models and relations.

The literature on economic crises, their historical roots and the factors that contributed to them is vast. What we can contribute in this respect is a wide and deep discussion of institutional responses, an issue that still remains rather weakly developed in the literature, which still focuses on various crisis interpretations. In this way, we hope to make a modest contribution both to the way out of the current crisis and to what lies beyond it.

REFERENCES

Akerlof, George A. and Robert J. Shiller (2009), *Animal Spirits: How Human Psychology Drives the Economy, and Why It Matters for Global Capitalism*, Princeton, NJ: Princeton University Press.

Albert, Michel (1998), *Capitalisme Contre Capitalisme*, Paris: Seuil.

Anderson, Perry (2009), *The New Old World*, London: Verso.

Backhouse, Roger E. (2010), *The Puzzle of Modern Economics: Science or Ideology?* Cambridge: Cambridge University Press.

Berman, Sheri (2006), *The Primacy of Politics: Social Democracy and the Making of Europe's Twentieth Century*, Cambridge: Cambridge University Press.

Blyth, Mark (2002), *The Great Transformation: Economic Ideas and Institutional Change in the Twentieth Century*, Cambridge: Cambridge University Press.

Borrás, Susana (2003), *The Innovation Policy of the EU: From Government to Governance*, Cheltenham: Edward Elgar.

Boyer, Robert (2000), 'Is a finance-led growth regime an alternative to fordism? A preliminary analysis', *Economy and Society*, **29** (1), 111–45.

Brummer, Alex (2008), *The Crunch: The Scandal of Northern Rock and the Looming Credit Crisis*, London: Random House.

Cohen, Stephen S. and J. Bradford DeLong (2010), *The End of Influence: What Happens When Other Countries Have the Money*, New York: Basic Books.

Crouch, Colin (2004), *Post-Democracy*, Cambridge: Polity.

Crouch, Colin (2011), *The Strange Non-Death of Neo-Liberalism*, Cambridge: Polity.
Crouch, Colin and Wolfgang Streeck (eds) (1997), *The Political Econmy of Modern Capitalism*, London: Sage.
Ferguson, Niall (2008), *The Ascent of Money: A Financial History of the World:* New York: Penguin.
Friedman, Thomas L. (2008), *Hot, Flat, and Crowded: Why We Need a Green Revolution – And How It Can Renew America*, New York: Farrar, Straus and Giroux.
Gamble, Andrew (1994), *The Free Economy and the Strong State: The Politics of Thatcherism*, Basingstoke: Macmillan.
Giddens, Anthony (1998), *The Third Way: The Renewal of Social Democracy*, Cambridge: Polity.
Glyn, Andrew (2007), *Capitalism Unleashed: Finance, Globalization, and Welfare*, Oxford: Oxford University Press.
Graham, Otis L. (1976), *Toward a Planned Society: From Roosevelt to Nixon*, New York: Oxford University Press.
Hall, Peter A. (1986), *Governing the Economy: The Politics of State Intervention in Britain and France*, Oxford: Oxford University Press.
Hardt, Michael and Antonio Negri (2000), *Empire*, Cambridge, MA: Harvard University Press.
Harvey, David (2010), *The Enigma of Capital and the Crisis of Capitalism*, London: Profile Books.
Hull Kristensen, Peer and Kari Lilja (eds) (2011), *Nordic Capitalisms and Globalization: New Forms of Economic Organization and Welfare Institutions*, Oxford: Oxford University Press.
Hutton, Will (2010), *Them and Us: Changing Britain – Why We Need a Fair Society*, London: Little, Brown.
Jessop, Bob (2002), *The Future of the Capitalist State*, Cambridge: Polity.
Judt, Tony (2010), *Ill Fares the Land*, New York: Penguin.
Krugman, Paul (2012), *End This Depression Now!*, New York: Norton.
Lindvall, Johannes (2010), *Mass Unemployment and the State*, Oxford: Oxford University Press.
Lowenstein, Roger (2001), *When Genius Failed: The Rise and Fall of Long-Term Capital Management*, London: Fourth Estate.
Lowenstein, Roger (2010), *The End of Wall Street*, New York: Penguin.
Lucas, Robert (2003). 'Macroeconomic priorities', *American Economic Review*, **93** (1), 1–14.
McDonough, Terrence, David M. Kotz and Michael Reich (eds) (2010), *Contemporary Capitalism and Its Crises: Social Structure of Accumulation Theory for the 21st Century*, Cambridge: Cambridge University Press.
McLean, Bethany and Joe Nocera (2010), *All the Devils Are Here: The Hidden History of the Financial Crisis*, New York: Portfolio.
Morel, Nathalie, Bruno Palier and Joakim Palme (2011), *Towards a Social Investment Welfare State? Ideas, Policies and Challenges*, Bristol: Policy Press.
Nocera, Joseph (1994), *A Piece of the Action: How the Middle Class Joined the Money Class*, New York: Touchstone.
Rattner, Steven (2010), *Overhaul: An Insider's Account of the Obama Administration's Emergency Rescue of the Auto Industry*, Boston, MA: Houghton Mifflin Harcourt.

Reich, Robert (2010), *Aftershock: The Next Economy and America's Future*, New York: Knopf.
Reinhart, Carmen R. and Kenneth S. Rogoff (2009), *This Time is Different: Eight Centuries of Financial Folly*, Princeton, NJ: Princeton University Press.
Rivlin, Gary (2010), *Broke, USA: How the Working Poor Became Big Business*, New York: HarperCollins.
Rodgers, Daniel T. (2010), *The Age of Fracture*, Cambridge, MA: Belknap.
Rodrik, Dani (2011), *The Globalization Paradox: Democracy and the Future of the World Economy*, New York: Norton.
Sachs, Jeffrey (2011), *The Price of Civilization: Economics and Ethics after the Fall*, London: Bodley Head.
Scharpf, Fritz W. (1987), *Crisis and Choice in European Social Democracy*, Ithaca, NY: Cornell University Press.
Scharpf, Fritz W. and Vivien A. Schmidt (eds) (2000), *Welfare and Work in the Open Economy*, vols 1–2, Oxford: Oxford University Press.
Shonfield, Andrew (1965), *Modern Capitalism*, London: Oxford University Press.
Skidelsky, Robert (2009), *Keynes: the Return of the Master*, New York: PublicAffairs.
Sorkin, Andrew Ross (2009), *Too Big to Fail*, New York: Viking.
Stiglitz, Joseph (2010), *Freefall: America, Free Markets, and the Sinking of the World Economy*, New York: Norton.
Streeck, Wolfgang (1992), *Social Institutions and Economic Performance*, London: Sage.
Tett, Gillian (2009), *Fool's Gold*, New York: Free Press.
Wolf, Martin (2008), *Fixing Global Finance*, Baltimore, MD: Johns Hopkins University Press.
Wright, Erik Olin (2010), *Envisioning Real Utopias*, London: Verso.

1. Crisis, structural change and new conditions for growth

Lennart Schön

INTRODUCTION

Since the financial meltdown in the US a few years ago, the steep business cycle decline has turned into a more critical situation. Structural imbalances have appeared, at both a global and a European level. Globally, rapidly rising peripheral economies have strengthened their position in relation to Europe and US; at the same time, within Europe, debt crises haunt a number of peripheral economies that have strong growth records over the last two decades.

Evidently, the crisis has developed from a financial phenomenon into a wider structural crisis, comparable to the crises of the early 1930s and the mid-1970s. At those earlier crises, institutional and structural changes of the economies followed at national and international levels, with new trajectories for economic growth. The present global economic and political situation opens up for such change. The crisis raises a number of challenges to the global economy of both an economic and a political nature and it might pave the way for new and more sustainable trends in economic growth from the 2010s onwards.

From an economic-historical perspective, the present crisis appears as no coincidence. Even if certain events are coincidental, the emergence of a structural crisis follows a pattern rooted in the modern world economy, with crises as important constituents in dynamic economic growth (Schön 1998, 2012a). There are indications that severe structural difficulties arise, in connection with financial crisis, over periods of roughly four decades. Prior to the 1930s, a worldwide crisis of similar magnitude in terms of trend breaks is held to have occurred in the early 1890s – with global shifts also in terms of economic growth. These crises appear as epochal shifts and turning points in long waves.

In this chapter, the present situation will be discussed in a framework of recurrent long waves in the global economy. The framework provides perspectives upon the crisis and upon paths to follow in the future.

Furthermore, indications of structural change will be discussed in relation to some conditions for further growth, with an analysis of the global economy based upon two different measures of economic growth over the last two decades.

BIG WAVES AND LONG WAVES

A historical perspective on the present situation is provided by the experience of two industrial revolutions followed by *big waves*[1] that swept the nineteenth and twentieth centuries, and with a third industrial revolution as a recent event of the late twentieth century.

- The First Industrial Revolution took off in the late eighteenth century with steam engines and the factory system as the major innovations. It was geographically centred in Britain and in the regions surrounding the Channel but spread during the nineteenth century over much of Europe and North America.
- The Second Industrial Revolution accelerated from the late nineteenth century with the electric motor, the internal-combustion engine, sophisticated machine industry and scientifically based industries. This revolution had a geographically widened centre with Germany and/or Continental Europe and the northeastern US, around the North Atlantic, as leading parts, and with diffusion globally throughout the twentieth century.
- The Third Industrial Revolution was a late-twentieth-century phenomenon with the breakthrough of microelectronics and with knowledge-intensive interaction between industry and services. Once again, the geographical strongholds widened considerably with Western US and Japan, and thus the Pacific Economy, joining the regions of the old North Atlantic Economy.

Furthermore, one can discern a pattern within each big wave with two structural epochs of about 40–50 years forming *long waves* or long cycles. The first long wave comprises the period of the Industrial Revolution and, consequently, this wave has its focus on the breakthrough of radical innovations in the production sectors. The second long wave is characterized by the wider infrastructural, institutional and social developments that have turned the radical innovations into general-purpose technologies (GPT),[2] which have been integrated into the backbone of society. Historically, the second waves have entailed the following major enlargements of the radical innovations:

- From the 1850s and 1860s upswings were directed to the wider constructions of railway networks, telegraphs and steamships, combined with institutional adaptations to enlarged global interaction in all markets.
- From the 1930s and 1940s, upswings started regionally that gained much wider momentum in the 1950s with the diffusion of internal-combustion engines and electrical motors into everyday life, and with institutional adaptations to the industrial mass-consumption society.
- Following the same logic and timing, one can envisage an upswing from the 2010s with the wider diffusion of networks and infrastructure based upon microelectronics and the thorough digitalization of all means of communication, with intensive social change and with institutional and juridical adaptations to these new conditions.

These second upswings have created greater scope for the diffusion of modernization and economic growth globally based upon reduced transaction costs institutionally and technologically. However, the wider diffusion has also meant that bottlenecks or new obstacles to growth have appeared which have to be addressed by technological and institutional innovations. The present threat of dramatic climate change in the wake of further economic growth illustrates that point.

Each long wave has been demarcated by international or global crises that have been both financial and structural in character. Such crises occurred in the late 1840s, early 1890s, early 1930s and mid-1970s. These crises have been the lower turning points in the long waves.[3]

So far, the events around 2010 combine the characteristics of prior financial and structural crises and have, furthermore, appeared according to the time pattern of the long waves:

Pattern of big waves and long waves

1790s – First Industrial revolution

    1850s – New infrastructure/institutions

1890s – Second Industrial Revolution

    1930s – New infrastructure/institutions

1970s – Third Industrial Revolution

    2010s – New infrastructure/institutions

CONDITIONS FOR FURTHER ECONOMIC GROWTH

Ever since the First Industrial Revolution, modern industrialization has spread in wider circles. Over each wave, new competitors have appeared that have challenged the old industrializers. The structural crises have been preceded by decades of increased global competition and aggravated imbalances, while the crises have been dramatic and critical events in global structural change. Old industrializers have been forced into more comprehensive structural changes, upgrading their production sectors in the direction of higher knowledge intensity. The need for such change is, however, felt not only in old industrial centres but in all economies. Emerging industrializing economies are not immune to the structural crises since they also have to adapt to a new situation, as well as to the threat of competitors rising from below.

While each economy has its own prerequisite for structural adaptation to a new situation, there are some general conditions for further economic growth globally.

1. Pressure on natural resources

During the past two decades, the widening of the global economy has been unprecedented in scope with the Chinese and Indian growth. The growth rates are perhaps not spectacular from a historical point of view but the numbers are. More than 2 billion people have become actively integrated into the global economy in the path of high annual growth rates. This means a fundamental shift in the relationship between factors of production. The increase in the supply of labour has been enormous while at the same time the pressure on natural resources is increasing rapidly.

There are still steps to be taken in the modernization process in both China and India as well as in a number of neighbouring Asian countries. Thus, it is reasonable to assume that pressure from demand will continue to increase, even accelerate, on goods intensive in natural resources such as construction materials, energy and food. With further growth in China and India, the contribution to total demand for such resources will increase every year over the next decade or two. This is particularly so, since any increased output in the area of raw-material-intensive production needs long-term investments, which during the construction phase tend to further increase demand for materials and energy over a couple of decades.[4]

We should also note that the present state of globalization has the opposite effect to the historical globalization of the nineteenth century in terms of factor proportions. In the late nineteenth century, the combination of steamships, railways and machine guns opened up vast plains in the Americas and Australia for European settlement and agriculture as well as rich mineral resources on all continents for European and US industries. Thus, globalization at that time shifted the frontier outwards in terms of natural resources. Technologies developed that were energy- and material-consuming and labour-saving, particularly in the US. On that basis, a new American lifestyle emerged in the twentieth century that consumed natural resources very lavishly – a lifestyle that presented new ideals to many global citizens when modernization spread in the second half of the century.

Accelerating economic growth in a much more populated world raises new challenges to technological change and to lifestyles in the twenty-first century. The situation is aggravated, beyond the economic sphere, by the threat of climate change from the increased global use of fossil fuels.

2. Technological and institutional change – a new wave from the Third Industrial Revolution

The Third Industrial Revolution was a late twentieth-century phenomenon that started with the breakthrough of microelectronics in the 1970s and developed into a global phenomenon with the revolution in information and communication technology (ICT) and with increased knowledge-intensive interaction between industry and services. Following earlier patterns, one can envisage an upswing from the 2010s with the wider diffusion of networks and infrastructure – with IT technology integrated with other means of communication, and with institutional and/or juridical adaptations to these new conditions.

Thus, while the radical innovations of the industrial revolutions created a strong transformation pressure in the production spheres, the following waves (as from the 1850s and 1930s) created a strong pressure on institutions and social organization. In the present situation of the early 2010s, we see wide consequences of IT for transaction costs – ranging from political storms around immaterial property rights and information disclosures through WikiLeaks to the new role of social media in the organization of popular movements in repressive states.

Rapidly decreasing costs of communication have a great impact also upon business organizations and innovative opportunities. When barriers to horizontal communication are lowered, more complex multidisciplinary organizations may evolve with less hierarchical structures. Conditions for such organizations with new knowledge-intensive services are particularly favourable in countries with non-authoritarian social traditions in combination with high levels of knowledge and competence. Such countries may adapt more easily to new circumstances and adopt more thoroughly the logic of the IT revolution.

In earlier big waves, economic growth has accelerated in the second phase of wider social and geographical diffusion. Modernization and economic growth have intensified globally. However, wider diffusion and accelerating economic growth will also mean bottlenecks or new obstacles to growth that have to be addressed technologically and institutionally. It is most likely that such bottlenecks will appear in relation both to natural resources and to climate conditions. Obstacles to growth also tend to stimulate innovative and entrepreneurial activity. Over the next decades one can for instance foresee a closer interaction between nanotechnology and biosciences in addressing bottlenecks in resource-intensive areas such as energy, food and minerals. Obstacles will also put further pressure for innovative change upon lifestyles, infrastructures, institutions and organizations at large.

3. Trends in relative prices

Relative prices play very significant roles in economic growth. Prices present guidelines for behaviour – in allocating resources between different needs, in production, consumption and in innovative activities. Thus, rising relative prices will, other things being equal, attract more resources to production and innovation in the area affected but reduce consumption. In the longer run, over some two or three decades, such reactions may inhibit price rises, depending upon the strength and viability of the demand reaction and the innovative response.

It is reasonable to assume that the Asian expansion will continue to put downward pressure on the relative price of labour in large segments of both industry and services – particularly in areas where the labour process is fairly standardized and suitable for large-scale operations and for catch-up processes. At the same time, the continued expansion will sustain the demand for energy and material, while relative price increases may be even further sustained by institutional measures taken to restrict climate change.

Another reasonable trend is that demand will shift towards new services with limited material content, as input both in production and in consumption. This will be particularly pronounced among medium- and high-income countries. So far, both US and Europe have been dominant in advancing new consumption patterns. That has been due to factors such as high income levels, a prominent role of consumption in economic growth and the degree of openness in these societies. With a shift in demand – and with a less elastic supply of factors – the relative price of less standardized, more customized or more complex services will increase over the next decade. Thus, the importance of such services in the formation of value added may increase.

The hypothetical relative price development over the next two decades may be represented thus:

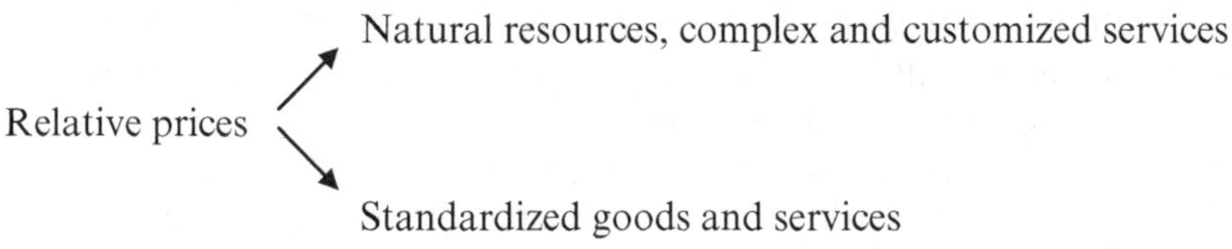

Shifts in prices affect income. These shifts may, hypothetically, be inversely related to changes in productivity and in that case the effect of the price change on income is minimal. However, relationships are not that direct. Rather, one could say that the pressure to increase productivity is strongest in areas of falling relative prices (due to increased competition), while the anticipated remuneration to innovation is highest in areas of rising prices.

It is best of course if demand shifts and innovative supply shifts are combined. Knowledge and innovations that combat bottlenecks and enhance the supply or reduce the demand of, for instance, energy, material or food may be richly remunerated over a period of some decades (until competition in such innovative areas increases again). Knowledge of energy-intensive processes both in traditional industries and in new areas such as biotech will be important in meeting the challenges.

VOLUME GROWTH AND PURCHASING POWER – TWO PERSPECTIVES ON GLOBAL TRENDS

Economic growth is more important than ever as a yardstick of national or regional performance, not least in public political debate. While spectacular growth figures in China over the last two decades create both admiration and fear in the Western world, differences between US and European growth are heavily scrutinized and are the basis for diverse economic policy recipes for growth. Thus, the widespread opinion regarding US acceleration and European sluggishness in growth during the 1990s was one starting point for formulating the Lisbon Agenda for the EU that was intended to meet the challenges posed by the new knowledge economy in the West.

Economic growth rates provide an aggregate measure that easily lends itself to international comparisons of performance. The measurement is based upon a set of fixed prices for all goods and services, in order to eliminate the effect of inflation or deflation upon the sum of value added produced in the economy as an unbiased volume of production. The fixed-price approach may seem a trivial procedure but in fact it is not, particularly when comparisons of growth rates are made between countries.

In international comparisons of economic growth rates and levels, two principles are usually combined. First, growth rates are calculated within each country with a set of fixed prices taken from each country. Thus, the different branches and sectors are weighted according to the price relations prevailing within the country. Second, the level of the time series of GDP is adjusted for every country to one benchmark according to a measure of global purchasing power parity (PPP) – i.e. a large set of 'world market prices' for all goods and services included in GDP is constructed for the benchmark year and each country's GDP is recalculated for that particular year. Thus, the levels of all series are adjusted to the PPP benchmark but not their slopes, i.e. their growth rates, which are determined by the domestic calculation.

National growth rates may deviate from changes over time in purchasing power parities, mainly for two reasons.[5] First, the national price structure is different from the constructed world price structure. This is particularly the case if large sectors of an economy are closed to world trade. In many economies at an early stage of industrialization there are 'traditional' sectors particularly in agriculture and services that usually produce at much lower prices than the world market prices. The opposite may be the case in some industrialized countries, where some non-traded services may be supplied at relatively high prices. If growth rates differ much between the closed and the open sectors, differences in relative prices affect the calculation of aggregate growth rates. A typical case is China. The modern sector in Eastern China has grown very fast and it operates at prices close to the world market, while traditional sectors in Central and Western China have grown more slowly and with low prices compared with the world market. A PPP calculation increases the size of the economy at a benchmark by inflating the size of the traditional sector, which at the same time would reduce the overall growth rate – if the GDP growth rate was adjusted for the greater weight of the slow-growing sector.

Second, price relations change over time. With fixed prices only the volume of goods and services is accounted for, but the purchasing power or the income of a country is affected by how the volume is priced over a period of time. Thus, the income effect will differ from the volume change if growth is directed mainly to areas where prices are either falling or rising. With the price trends over the last decade, the purchasing power effect will generally be positive for countries specialized in natural resources or in complex services, while specialization in standardized goods and services will have a negative effect on the purchasing power.

Relative price changes may be put into the dynamics of technological change and innovations that are essential to economic growth globally. Their relation to income growth is not straightforward, however. It is not certain that a concentration of resources to innovation areas, usually defined as high-tech, leads to a more favourable development in terms of income growth than allocation to complementary activities (such as a number of services), since relative prices may shift. That is clearly so following the logic of the development block, first presented by the Schumpeterian economist Erik Dahmén.[6] While a technological innovation at the centre provides goods or services at falling relative prices through a decisive supply shift, the increase in demand for complementary goods or services leads to rising relative prices, since these are usually supplied less elastically. Thus, volume growth and purchasing power growth in high-tech areas may deviate considerably.

Historically in economics, it was understood early on that the use of different price structures would result in different growth rates. That is, for instance, very often the case in industrialization processes characterized by rising quantities of advancing, innovative commodities at falling relative prices. Differences in computed growth rates due to structural changes are usually regarded as a problem by the statistician, but these effects were turned into an analytical method by Alexander Gerschenkron to identify spurts in industrialization, connected to increased productivity in modernizing branches.[7] The rise of quantities at lower prices within an economy was regarded as a positive sign of modernization. In an international context, however, rising volumes and falling prices may indicate that pressure from competition is increasing, while development with prices rising together with rising quantities may indicate a more favourable orientation to demand.

The potential difference between volume growth and income growth per capita due to shifts in relative prices is clearly realized if one compares sectoral productivity growth and income growth respectively between industrial regions and service-oriented regions. While productivity and volumes at fixed prices usually grow much faster in industrial regions, income may grow as fast or even faster in service-oriented regions. That is of course due to shifts in relative prices between manufactured goods and services.

In this chapter, two global PPP benchmarks, constructed in 1990 and 2005, will be used to gauge the overall effects of differences in internal price structures and growth orientation on segments of rising or falling prices. The method is to compare the traditional growth rates, based upon internal price structures, with the PPP-adjusted growth rates over the period in order to estimate to what extent volume growth has resulted in growth of purchasing power. The adjustment procedure is very straightforward. The adjusted growth rate between these two benchmarks is calculated according to the annual percentage change in per capita purchasing power from a global supply of goods and services at fixed world prices.[8]

A New Global Picture

Overall, the effect of the adjustment of growth rates to changes in purchasing power parity is highly systematic. It is positively related to the average income level and negatively related to the size of the economy. Thus, rich and small economies in particular have increased their purchasing power at a higher rate than their volume growth. The opposite is of course true for poor and large economies. There is also a systematic relationship to the structure of the economies. A large agricultural sector and export specialization in standardized manufactured goods are both negative to the PPP effect, while high export shares of fuel and of services are positive. Hence, the PPP effects seem to be systematically related to changes in relative prices on the world market and to the structures of the economies.

Furthermore, the adjustment changes the picture of global growth in a rather dramatic way. The effect is particularly significant and systematic within the globally leading zones of the US, Europe and Asia. In Africa and Latin America the effect of PPP adjustment is, on the other hand, less systematic and rather weak overall, which may indicate less structural changes, lower effects from recent modernization trends or more random effects in measurements.

In Table 1.1, annual growth rates for major regions are calculated 1990–94 to 2005–09, both in the traditional manner, with weighted aggregates of domestically calculated GDP, and with adjustment of growth rates in relation to changes in the purchasing power parities between 1990 and 2005.

The most dramatic change is obtained for the Middle East, where a rather modest volume growth is turned into a world-leading purchasing power growth, obviously driven by rising oil prices. The dynamic effects upon the region are considerable. Very ostentatious modernization in some small economies coexists with rapidly increasing social pressure upon traditional hierarchical structures in a large part of the region. The transforming power of income growth has combined with the social effects from a numerous young generation that has embraced the IT revolution.

The most significant change in a global perspective is however the downsizing of growth in the very hothouse of volume growth, Eastern and Southern Asia. Almost all countries in the region encountered a negative PPP-effect with a purchasing power increase that was considerably lower than the volume growth.[9] Only the advanced city-states of Hong Kong and Singapore and the economies of Japan and Taiwan experienced a positive effect. The background is clearly that the Asian mix of goods and services saw prices that were falling relatively. This is a general 'Gerschenkron effect' within manufacturing during industrialization and

Table 1.1 Annual growth rates in GDP per capita from 1990–94 to 2005–09 in major regions: traditional growth rates and PPP-adjusted growth rates

Region	Traditional growth rate	PPP-adjusted growth	Effect of PPP adjustment
Western Europe	1.6	2.4	+0.8
Central-Eastern Europe	3.4	4.8	+1.4
Former USSR	1.4	2.0	+0.6
USA	1.9	2.0	+0.1
OECD	1.6	2.2	+0.6
Middle East	2.1	4.9	+2.8
Asia South and East	3.7	2.8	–0.9
Asia SE excl. Japan	5.5	3.8	–1.7
Africa	1.7	1.1	–0.6
Latin America	1.7	1.6	–0.1

Notes:
Western Europe = Austria, Belgium, Cyprus, Denmark, Finland, France, Germany, Greece, Iceland, Ireland, Italy, Luxembourg, Malta, Netherlands, Norway, Portugal, Spain, Sweden, Switzerland, Turkey, UK.
Central-Eastern Europe = Albania, Bosnia-Herzegovina, Bulgaria, Croatia, Czech Republic, Hungary, Macedonia, Poland, Romania, Serbia-Montenegro, Slovak Republic, Slovenia.
Former USSR = Armenia, Belarus, Estonia, Georgia, Kazakhstan, Kyrgyz Republic, Latvia, Lithuania, Moldova, Russian Federation, Tajikistan, Ukraine.
Asia = Bangladesh, Cambodia, China, Hong Kong, India, Indonesia, Japan, Malaysia, Pakistan, Philippines, Singapore, South Korea, Sri Lanka, Taiwan, Thailand, Vietnam.
Africa = Algeria, Angola, Burkina Faso, Cameroon, Côte d'Ivoire, DR Congo, Egypt, Ethiopia, Ghana, Kenya, Madagascar, Malawi, Mali, Morocco, Mozambique, Niger, Nigeria, Senegal, South Africa, Tanzania, Tunisia, Uganda, Zambia.
Middle East = Bahrain, Iran, Iraq, Israel, Jordan, Kuwait, Oman, Qatar, Saudi Arabia, Syria, United Arab Emirates, Yemen.
Latin America = Argentina, Barbados, Bolivia, Brazil, Chile, Colombia, Costa Rica, Dominican Republic, Ecuador, Guatemala, Jamaica, Mexico, Peru, St Lucia, Trinidad and Tobago, Uruguay, Venezuela.
OECD = the 24 countries of OECD 1990.
All countries are weighted according to the size of the economy.

Source: The Conference Board (2012).

the effect was greatest in some large and newly industrializing countries such as India and Indonesia (in those two cases, volume growth was reduced by about 2.3 and 2.7 percentage points, respectively, when turned into purchasing power growth). In the Indian case, this may indicate a fall in the relative price of IT services, provided by relatively low-salaried labour. The decrease in adjusted growth rates is probably also the consequence of using world market prices that put more weight to slow-growing traditional domestic sectors, particularly agriculture, which still represents a large part of the Indian economy.

Also, the growth rate of China is substantially reduced (from 8.1 to 6.4 per cent), although the adjusted rate is still high in an international comparison. The Chinese adjustment effect is weaker than the Indian, which may indicate that growth in China is more broadly based with more structural change undertaken, but it may also be due to a large Chinese domestic production of raw materials, notably of coal, at rising prices that counteracts negative influences from falling prices of manufactured goods and from relatively slow growth in the up-weighted agricultural sector.

Even the US economy stands out as rather gloomy in purchasing power terms – the PPP-effect is only very weakly positive. This is remarkable, taking into account the high income level and the very positive general view of the American economy that was transmitted from the new economy of the 'roaring 1990s'.[10] The alleged new American vitality was, as mentioned, one of the starting points for the Lisbon agenda in the EU, and this view is called into question. The US is actually the advanced country with the smallest purchasing power gain relative to volume growth. Technically, the weak PPP-effect may be due either to a relatively slow-growing and low-paid domestic sector in the US that is up-weighted by international prices – such as a sector of low-paid services that has been important in American employment creation over the last decades – or, more positively, to a fast-growing modern sector being down-weighted by internationally falling prices, such as the large IT sector in the US. Actually, American growth figures of the 1990s were boosted by the use of so-called hedonic prices of IT equipment to a much larger extent than in Europe – growth was boosted by methods to calculate fixed prices that took into account the rapidly rising technical capacity of the IT equipment.[11] Such methods increased the production volumes in traditional growth rates in relation to the value added produced in a sector that encountered rapidly falling market prices.

The calculation of purchasing power effects is yet another indication of a weakening American economy well before the financial crisis and it is congruent with growing deficits in the American trade balance over the last decades.

In contrast, the effect of PPP adjustment is strong and positive all over Europe. Judging from these data, there was a continued European catch-up with the US – contrary to many beliefs in recent decades. Both Western and Eastern Europe increased their purchasing power significantly in relation to their volume growth rates. This indicates that the overall mix of products (goods and services) in European countries met with relatively rising prices. One may presume that there was an overall structural change directed to the increasing demand for more complex services as well as to an upgrading of manufacturing industries. The effect of structural change was particularly strong and positive in Central-Eastern Europe with a number of high-growth post-communist countries, but the effect was considerable and positive also in Western Europe.

High-growth countries such as Norway – favoured both by rich oil resources and a highly developed service sector – surpassed average Asian levels with an adjusted growth rate of 4.3 per cent annually. The financial centre of Luxembourg performed even better with growth rates enhanced from 2.9 to 5.3 per cent.

The Irish level was as high, increasing from 4.5 to 5.3 per cent annually, and Ireland and Luxembourg were both trailing close to China in terms of adjusted growth rates. This goes for some of the debt-stricken PIGS countries as well. Greece had very positive growth rates and had strong adjustment effects – growth rates rising from 2.8 to 4.5 per cent – and also Spain performed in a similar fashion, increasing growth rates from 2.3 to 3.6 per cent with PPP adjustment. On the other hand, the Portuguese growth rate was rather low and there was only a weak adjustment effect.

The performances of Ireland, Greece and Spain indicate that the debt crises, which have haunted the eurozone since 2009, were due neither to low growth rates nor to the absence of structural change but rather to the vicissitudes inherent in accumulated debts and soaring equity prices during an investment boom, which was interrupted by a financial crisis in the global economy – a recession that in turn has revealed weaknesses internally in the financial basis of public sectors and externally in competitiveness with other catching-up economies.[12]

Competition arose not only from Asia but also from neighbouring Central-Eastern Europe. A number of high-growth countries in PPP-adjusted rates – such as Poland 5.4 per cent, Hungary 5.2 per cent, Romania 5.1 per cent, Czech Republic 4.9 per cent, Croatia and Slovakia 4.6 per cent – made the region one of the growth centres of the world over the period. In all these Central-Eastern European cases, the adjustment effect was strong and positive, indicating a more knowledge-intensive structural change than in most industrializing Asian countries. In some ways, the region played a role comparable to that of China, albeit at a much lower level, with similar high growth rates also in manufacturing exports (Schön 2010). The export growth contributed to increasing the competition pressure on European markets up to the end of the decade.

Also further to the east, in the former USSR, the adjustment effect was clearly positive. Growth rates were, however, on a lower level. The post-communist crisis was more prolonged and the transformation to market economies took a longer time. The region was, of course, dominated by the Russian Federation, where natural resources played a large role in the positive adjustment effect.

ADAPTATION TO NEW CONDITIONS

At the surface, the present crisis has been dominated by financial matters but more fundamentally a set of challenges confronts all economies. The need for structural transformation in relation to the rapidly changing global economy is paramount – it affects economies at all levels of modernization. It is an adaptation to new conditions for competition and new demand patterns as well as to global shortages endangering further economic growth. This involves not only the economics of structural change but also the politics of infrastructural and institutional change.

The latter aspect is even more emphasized since the present crisis may become crucial for the broader social adaptation to the changes inherent in the Third Industrial Revolution – in that sense the crisis of the 2010s resembles the crisis of the 1930s where there was a focus on institutional adaptations to the wide social changes in the wake of the Second Industrial Revolution. In that era, the Swedish or the Nordic models developed into important contributions – indicating also that small economies may play important roles in designing institutional solutions. The institutional challenge today is however very different from that in the earlier period. In the postwar era, economic growth was to a great extent driven by capital investments in large-scale Fordistic organizations, which made the productivity of the individual very dependent upon the whole system. Today, human capital and individual competencies play a more significant role in determining productivity and, thus, wages. That poses a new challenge to politicians in reforming institutions, in order to combine economic and social goals.

US

The US was the leading economy in both the Second and the Third Industrial Revolutions. The present challenges facing the US are however to a large extent of a different character than advancing new radical innovations. Basically the challenges are more social in character with the adaptation of institutions to a number of new imbalances. In that sense, the situation has greater similarities with the crisis of the 1930s, which put a heavy transformation pressure on US politics – as did even the upswing from the 1850s, when controversies about the railway system and economic policy ended in civil war. Around 2010, one of the challenges is to come to grips with the imbalances that have emerged in relation to foreign markets and to natural resources owing to a too lavish consumption. While, on one hand, US political and economic hegemony has weakened in face of growing competition, the US demand for resources has, on the other hand, stayed at a high level both from consumers and from the global political apparatus. In particular, the American lifestyle developed during two centuries with an extremely rich supply of natural resources is at stake. Innovative change in the direction of economizing with natural resources, above all with energy, would show a new American leadership, involving rearmament of the social and material infrastructures as well. It is highly questionable whether such a constructive American response to global questions will appear within the next decade.

China

Chinese reactions to the present crisis are of utmost importance for the global economy in the longer run. In the upswing from the crisis, China will face the need of profound structural transformation. On one hand, international price development will probably turn negative for the Chinese specialization as 'the workshop of the world', with price increases in the primary and tertiary sectors and with a further relative price decrease in the secondary sector of manufacturing. That will be particularly the case if industrialization keeps its global momentum and spreads to new regions of low-cost labour. Furthermore, consumer demand for Chinese exports from the American and European markets may weaken due to policies to get rid of current imbalances, not least in the US. On the other hand, internal pressure for transformation will probably increase, particularly if the present global crisis is prolonged and if the two main driving forces over the last 15–20 years – investments and exports – are faltering. Demand will increase for social reforms and regional balance within China, which is a situation similar to the one that confronted industrial countries in the crisis of the 1930s.

The new five-year plan, 2011–15, addressed this situation and aims at a new social balance that would mean a fundamental transformation of the Chinese growth process. Such reforms will probably be necessary in order to achieve the overarching goal of keeping the nation intact. Reforms will also raise consumption and wages. Higher wages and social expenditures will strengthen internal growth forces and increase pressure towards structural change, but profits will fall within those companies that have been a mainstay in growth so far. Productivity will have to be raised further, particularly when confronted with competition from new low-cost countries or regions. The profit squeeze from falling prices and rising costs is already felt in hot regions in southern China, where firms have moved to adjacent low-cost countries in Southeast Asia. This is a transformation pressure towards structural upgrading that all industrial countries have to confront and react to. A number of much smaller Asian countries have done so in a rather orderly fashion and very successfully since the 1960s, while industrialization has been diffused to new countries.

Structural change is however a problematic issue in many ways. For one thing, such shifts take time and will generally lead to a period of slow growth and unemployment. For another, reforms which strengthen consumption and regions in western China will at the same time work against strong groups in eastern China that have become prosperous and established interests over the last decades. Implementing these changes poses a particular challenge to the political leadership in an economy that is both market-driven and planned.

Europe

Economic growth during much of the twentieth century was characterized by the technology of the Second Industrial Revolution that gained momentum from the late nineteenth century – industrial mass production of standardized complex products. For a long time, Europe was handicapped in relation to the US with small political units and fragmented markets that made it difficult to implement this technology in manufacturing. The handicap was overcome with market integration during the postwar period and the technological gap was closed by the 1970s. At that time, however, a new European handicap to the US emerged out of the Third Industrial Revolution. With the internet and globalization in the 1990s, a new potential of service integration appeared. Hence, one of the major political challenges that confronts Europe is in services, where markets to a large extent are fragmented nationally, despite decades of increased integration. Fragmentation is due both to the greater importance of cultural specific competencies in services than in manufacturing and to the national regulation of national social security systems, strengthened out of the crisis of the 1930s.

The internet has helped to lower cultural obstacles to integration, particularly with the rapidly increasing role of English as the lingua franca – a role that accelerated notably in the 1990s. Furthermore, pressures upon European service sector regulations are increasing as part of the present crisis – one possible (if not the only) result is a further deepening of political and social integration in Europe.

The IT revolution and globalization do not only favour large-scale market operations, however. The digital revolution has brought about a shift in the economies of scale. The cost of flexible adaptation to the preferences of the customer is reduced, while the importance of effective communication both within the organization and with customers increases. Overall, indications of structural change in Europe in relation to new market conditions, combined with traditions of customizing rather than standardization, may give Europe, or some European countries, an important role for leadership in the technological and institutional innovations of the 2010s.

CONCLUSION

The purchasing power parity adjustment of growth rates gives a very aggregate picture of structural changes over the last two decades, but the result points clearly in one direction – to a dynamic European economy coping quite well with the major new conditions for growth indicated by the relative price shifts. It is a different light from that cast by the 1990s idea of 'Eurosclerosis'. In such a light, the region is better situated in global competition than is indicated by traditional volume-based growth rates, which overall tend to inflate Asian rates.

The European position will be particularly important if there is also a political willingness to tackle some of the major problems confronting further global growth, related to limitations in natural resources and to climate change. As in the crisis of the 1930s, small and open economies in Europe may play a significant role in the institutional adaptation to new conditions.

Structural change towards a socially more balanced growth in China will have a very great impact upon the global economy – strengthening social infrastructures, increasing Chinese demand and decreasing global imbalances. It will not, however, meet the challenges from climate change or decrease pressure upon natural resources.

This should have a bearing upon the US position as the leading economy globally. In the 2010s, US leaders have to come to grips with the imbalances that have emerged in relation to foreign markets and to natural resources due to a too lavish consumption. While, on one hand, the US political and economic hegemony has weakened in the face of growing competition, the US demand for resources has, on the other, stayed at a high level both from consumers and from the global political apparatus. Innovative change in the direction of economizing with natural resources, above all with energy, would show a new American leadership. It is still an open question whether such an American response to global questions will materialize within the next decade.

NOTES

1. 'Big wave' comes originally from Gordon (1999) as an interpretation of US economic growth in the twentieth century springing from the innovations of the Second Industrial Revolution.
2. On the concept of GPT, see Breshnahan and Trajtenberg (1995). It is however important to notice that it is only in the second phase of diffusion that a radical innovation may turn into a GPT.
3. This pattern is developed in a long cyclical model – see e.g. Schön (1998, 2000, 2009, 2012a, 2012b).
4. This mechanism of long gestation periods of investments in the primary sector is fundamental in Rostow (1978) with respect to secular changes in the relative price of primary products.
5. A third reason, not discussed here, is errors in the measurements of PPP or growth. Differences in the PPP adjustment effect are however systematic in relation to the two logical factors presented here, which indicates that a randomly distributed error factor is of limited importance.
6. Cf. Dahmén (1988).
7. Gerschenkron (1962).
8. The procedure is to recalculate the 1990 GDP for every country at 2005 price levels but with 1990 global PPP structure according to this formula: (Country share of world GDP 1990 in 1990 PPP) × (world GDP 1990 in 2005 PPP) and then calculate the difference in growth rates between series with the adjusted and non-adjusted base year of 1990.
9. India, China and Japan make up about 75 per cent of the economy of Asia, South and East – with India and China making up 60 per cent (or 70 per cent of the region except Japan).
10. See Rhode and Tonniolo (2006).
11. See e.g. Faini in Rhode and Tonniolo (2006).
12. See the model in Schön (1998) with the combination of structural crises and debt crises at the end of long investment booms, particularly those ending in global structural crises.

REFERENCES

Bresnahan, T.F. and M. Trajtenberg (1995), 'General purpose technologies: engines of growth?', *Journal of Econometrics*, **65** (1), 83–108.

Conference Board, The (2012), *Total Economy Database Output, Labor and Labor Productivity: Country Details, 1950–2009*, January; available at: www.conference-board.org/data/economydatabase/.

Dahmén, E. (1988), 'Development blocks in industrial economics', *Scandinavian Economic History Review*, **36**, 3–14.

Faini, R. (2006), 'Europe: a continent in decline?', in P. Rhode and G. Tonniolo (eds), *The Global Economy in the 1990s: A Long-Run Perspective*, New York: Cambridge University Press, pp. 69–88.

Gerschenkron, A. (1962), *Economic Backwardness in Historical Perspective*, Cambridge, MA: Belknap.

Gordon, R.J. (1999), 'U.S. economic growth since 1870: one big wave?', *American Economic Review*, **89**, 123–8.

Rhode, P. and G. Tonniolo (eds) (2006), *The Global Economy in the 1990s: A Long-Run Perspective*, New York: Cambridge University Press.

Rostow, W.W. (1978), *The World Economy: History and Prospects*, London: Macmillan.

Schön, L. (1998), 'Industrial crises in a model of long cycles: Sweden in an international perspective', in T. Myllyntaus (ed.), *Economic Crises and Restructuring in History*, Stuttgart, Germany: Scripta Mercaturae.

Schön, L. (2000), 'Electricity, technological change and productivity in Swedish industry, 1890–1990', *European Review of Economic History*, **4** (2), 175–94.

Schön, L. (2009), *Technological Waves and Economic Growth – Sweden in an International Perspective 1850–2005*, CIRCLE working paper 2009/06.

Schön, L. (2010), *Vår världs ekonomiska historia: Den industriella tiden*, Stockholm: SNS.

Schön, L. (2012a), *An Economic History of Modern Sweden*, London: Routledge.

Schön, L. (2012b), 'Long-term innovation waves and the potential dissonance between Europe and Asia', in L. Oxelheim (ed.), *EU–Asia and the Re-Polarization of the Global Economic Arena*, New York: World Scientific Publications.

2. Responding to economic crisis: macroeconomic revolutions in the 1930s and 1970s

Roger E. Backhouse

1. INTRODUCTION

The twentieth century saw two major revolutions in macroeconomic theory, each of which can be associated with a worldwide economic crisis. The Great Depression of the 1930s gave rise to the Keynesian revolution, laying the foundations for the approach to economic theorizing and policymaking that dominated what a French journalist, Jean Fourastié, called '*les trentes glorieuses*' – the three decades of unparalleled prosperity, at least in North America and western Europe, following the Second World War. This 'age of Keynes' was followed by another revolution, for which there exists no widely agreed name. The most concise label is the Friedman–Lucas revolution, after Milton Friedman and Robert Lucas, whose analysis of policymaking was central to turning the Keynesian orthodoxy about demand management on its head. The Friedman–Lucas revolution did not cause Keynesianism to disappear, as had pre-Keynesian economics after the Keynesian revolution,[1] but the 'new Keynesians', who emerged as the most prominent challengers to the new orthodoxy, were on the defensive. Ongoing debates between the new Keynesians and their new classical or real-business-cycle counterparts laid the foundations for what Goodfriend and King (1997) called the 'new neoclassical synthesis', summed up in Michael Woodford's *Interest and Prices* (2003). It was this second revolution, sometimes called a 'counter-revolution', on account of its restoration of a classical orthodoxy, that was called into question by the financial crisis of 2008.[2]

The aim of this chapter is to compare these two revolutions. Conventional accounts focus on how economists became aware that the old theories were not working and so developed ones that were better able to explain the phenomena they were encountering: Keynesian economics provided an account of mass unemployment as it was experienced in the 1930s, and the new classical macroeconomics explained how inflation could coexist with rising unemployment (stagflation) in the 1970s. On the basis of these new theories, so it is argued, new policy positions were developed: deficit-financed fiscal policy to deal with mass unemployment and monetary targeting (later evolving into inflation targeting) to deal with the problem of high inflation.

In contrast, in this chapter it will be argued that the Keynesian and the Friedman–Lucas revolutions had such a profound effect on macroeconomic thinking not so much because of the ideas involved (though these were, of course important) but because the changes each revolution wrought in macroeconomics were aligned with much deeper social, political and intellectual changes. There are several strands to this argument. The first is that, though the changes involved were sufficiently profound to merit being described as revolutions, there were significant elements of continuity, with many of the key theoretical novelties involving ideas that had been developed well before the crisis that prompted the revolution. The second is that the relations between theory and policy were much more complicated than the conventional account suggests: there was no simple path from theory to policy. Changes in macroeconomic thinking were bound up with much broader and more profound changes in the role of the state in economic and, indeed, social life. Thus these revolutions were so profound not simply because the crisis that provoked them was so deep, or because the ideas were so novel, but because the intellectual climate and cultural milieu had changed radically.

2. FROM GREAT DEPRESSION TO WELFARE CAPITALISM

The story of the Keynesian revolution unquestionably centres on a single book, John Maynard Keynes's *The General Theory of Employment, Interest and Money*, published in February 1936. This book was presented by its author as a turning point in economic theory – he did not leave it to others to make the comparison with Einstein's theory of relativity, but did this himself, and it rapidly came to be seen as providing a theoretical explanation of how depressions could come about and hence of what could be done to cure them. As James Tobin, one of the leading American Keynesians in the 'golden age', put it, referring to the excitement of Keynesianism in the 1930s:

> [A]nybody alert to world problems was distressed by the economic and political problems of the day and the apparent inability of anybody to do anything

> about them. And here was a book that logically said what to do, what could be done. It wasn't hopeless. (Quoted in Blaug 1990, p. 65)

Or to quote Paul Samuelson, the main popularizer of Keynesian economics in the 1950s and 1960s,

> The success [of the *General Theory*] was due to the fact that the Great Depression, the world as it was, was calling for a new theory of economics, and Keynes was the first with the mostest . . . [T]he old theory had no handle at all to explain what was happening in London, in New York and in Main Street, Iowa in the years 1930 to 1936. There was a tremendous opening here, and it was Keynes who magnificently made a beginning in filling that opening. (Quoted in Blaug 1990, p. 56–7)

This all suggests, quite simply, that a major crisis, inconsistent with the theory prevailing before the crisis, called forth a major shift in economic theory that merited being called a revolution.

Textbook accounts of the Keynesian revolution often present a simple story of the relationship between theory and policy. Keynes provided the theoretical justification for the use of fiscal policy as a stabilization tool; this was used to design policies that were applied to lift the world out of the Great Depression, thereby vindicating the theory. However, popular as this account is, it is a myth, flawed on several counts.

The first complication is that the policy changes that brought the world out of the Great Depression came about largely for reasons that had little to do with Keynes (Hall 1989). Franklin Roosevelt fought his 1932 and 1936 campaigns on a platform of balancing the budget and the New Deal was not based on Keynesian ideas, but rather involved a series of pragmatic responses to unemployment that had nothing to do with Keynesianism (in 1933 Keynes was disappointed with Roosevelt's lack of interest in his ideas). The US government turned to deficit spending only when the 1937 recession caused some young economists in the Commerce Department to notice that this appeared to be linked to cuts in disposable income caused by, among other things, the ending of bonus payments to First World War veterans and the collection of the first social security taxes. In Sweden, the case for expansionary policies had been made by economists at the University of Stockholm, drawing inspiration from Wicksell, not Keynes. In Germany, deficits arose because political pressures under the Nazi regime made it impossible for taxation to rise in line with government spending. In Sweden, the change in policy involved a compromise between farmers and workers. What happened, in virtually all countries other than Canada, where young Keynesians were influential, was that demand management policies were introduced for reasons that had nothing to do with the *General Theory*, and that the label 'Keynesian' came to be attached only retrospectively (Bateman 2006). However, though this undermines the simple story about the Keynes's influence, it does not, in itself, undermine the notion that the Great Depression had a significant effect – that a major crisis led to major changes in economic theory and policy.

A more significant problem is that many of the changes, in both theory and policy, had roots that go back long before 1929. Many of the policies, such as social insurance, that came in the 1950s to be linked to the idea of the welfare state, with which Keynesianism came to be so strongly associated, had been developing, since the late nineteenth century, in an international network of thinkers concerned with what has been called 'social politics' – ameliorating the social effects of capitalist market economies (Rodgers 1998). While William Beveridge, author of the influential report (1942) widely seen as inspiring the creation of European welfare states after the Second World War, was very much part of this network, Keynes was not. Members of this network of social reformers centred on what would now be considered microeconomic issues, hence their focus on policies such as social insurance and planning. In so far as the great depression did lead to the rapid implementation of 'progressive' policies in the New Deal, it was because there was a backlog of worked-out schemes available, inspired by earlier developments in Western Europe (notably Germany, France and Britain), that had not been implemented because they could not get through the US political system. The shock of the great depression did not lead to new thinking so much as change the political climate so that these policies suddenly became acceptable.

Even more to the point, Keynes's own theory drew heavily on work undertaken in the 1920s (see Laidler 1999). The concepts of saving and investment, the basis for income-flow analysis, had been developed in the 1920s by Keynes and his colleague Dennis Robertson, as well as by Swedish students of Wicksell. The same is true of the ideas of liquidity preference and the propensity to consume, while the third key component of the *General Theory*, the marginal efficiency of capital, explicitly drew on the work of Irving Fisher. There was thus an important sense in which A.C. Pigou, Jacob Viner, Wassily Leontief and Joseph Schumpeter were right to say that Keynes's depiction of 'classical economics' (a term he used, somewhat confusingly, to refer to the entire literature from Say and Ricardo to Pigou that presumed that there could never be a shortage of aggregate demand) was no more than a caricature and that his ideas were far less revolutionary than he claimed. There was even a sense in which, as Bertil Ohlin (1937, pp. 235–7) pointed out, the *General Theory* was old-fashioned, for it was static, spurning the dynamic analysis that had been developed in Sweden. Thus when John Hicks (1937) summed up both Keynes and 'the classics' in what Alvin Hansen later labelled the IS-LM model, it pushed many issues linked to the problem of time, and which later turned out to be very important, out of economics (Backhouse and Laidler 2004). Keynes may have fomented a revolution, but he did not create macroeconomics *de novo*.

To understand the depth of the Keynesian revolution – why it was so profound – we have to look forward, for its impact cannot be understood apart from the Second World War (see Backhouse 2008, 2010a, 2010b; Backhouse and Bateman 2011). The Second World War demonstrated how economic planning could be used to manage the level of demand, and also how the generation of demand could restore full employment. It was the planned expansion of demand for military purposes that cured US unemployment and enabled a massive expansion of output at the same time as millions were drafted into the armed forces. It was also during the war that important steps, both conceptual and administrative, were taken, that were essential to the national income statistics on which Keynesian policymaking, both during and after the war, depended. But the war had a much deeper significance than this. In many countries, especially in western Europe, it encouraged the view that the state should intervene. Keynesian economics entered the public imagination as one plank of a welfare capitalism, in which state institutions purged capitalism of some of its worst defects. This is consistent with the view that a major crisis produced a major change in thinking – though that crisis became the combination of Great Depression followed by war – but it points to the importance of political and social changes that run much more deeply than simple economic changes. It also reinforces the view that these changes, traceable back to the nineteenth century, have roots that stretch back before the Great Depression.

But the Keynesian revolution owed still more to the Second World War. The war contributed to the rise of a more technical, mathematical economics. Economists became involved in the war effort, dealing not only with conventionally economic issues, but also with what is best termed operations research. They worked alongside scientists and mathematicians as general problem-solvers – as engineers, for whom mathematical and statistical skills were crucial – for whom there was no sharp distinction between economic problems (how best to allocate scarce shipping resources) and problems of military tactics and strategy (how to use weapons more effectively). They acquired a vision of economics as a technical, engineering discipline, that was different from the view typically held before the war. After the war, owing to the GI Bill and other measures, the massive expansion of higher education enabled these technical economists to enter academia, in a new intellectual climate, involving government support for research both directly, via the National Science Foundation, and via the military. Economists were, like their natural-science counterparts, part of the military-industrial-academic complex (which also extended into academia), to which Dwight Eisenhower drew attention.

The result of this change was that, in a way not true before 1940, economists saw themselves as modellers. Mathematical models became the accepted way of doing economics. When they turned to macroeconomics, Keynesian economics provided the framework for such modelling, whether by Keynesians (such as Paul Samuelson, James Tobin or Lawrence Klein) or by opponents of Keynesianism (such as Milton Friedman). 'Pre-Keynesian' macroeconomics suddenly seemed out of date, not so much because it was based on different assumptions, as because it did not involve the rigorous modelling of the type that had become the norm. The Keynesian revolution in economic theory involved looking back over the gulf created by the rise of mathematical modelling. There was no doubt that a revolution had taken place, and that Keynes's was the only name to which it could plausibly be attached, irrespective of his own attitude to mathematical economics; but it was a revolution that was so profound because it had become caught up with much broader political, social and intellectual changes that went far beyond economics.

3. FROM OIL CRISIS TO 'FREE-MARKET' CAPITALISM

The 1970s did not see an economic crisis on anything like the same scale as the Great Depression, and as a result capitalism was not called into question as it had been in the 1930s. However, it did nonetheless represent a major crisis, closely linked to changes in economic theory that, by the 1980s, were sufficiently profound to merit being described as a revolution. Though the roots of the crisis lie deeper, in fiscal and monetary expansions that began in the 1960s (the term 'oil crisis' is used as a convenient label, not as indicating the underlying causes of the turbulence of these years), it was the dramatic rise in the price of petroleum, and the OPEC embargo that followed the Arab–Israel war in 1973, that brought the crisis to a head. It was only after 1973 that the Keynesian forecasting models broke down, and that economists were presented with demands for advice on policy for which existing theories were seen as providing inadequate guidance. It would be difficult to claim that the receptiveness of economists to the new classical macroeconomics, as macroeconomics based on the twin assumptions of rational expectations and continuously clearing markets came to be called, was not linked to the new macroeconomic environment, in which changes in economic thinking were needed.

The revolution in macroeconomic theory that took place in the 1970s and 1980s had two strands. Friedman was a long-standing critic of Keynesianism and supporter of the quantity theory of money. However, his theorizing exhibited strong parallels with Keynes's (see Backhouse and Bateman, 2012). He had a Marshallian approach to economic theory, sceptical about elaborate, formal mathematical modelling, and he did not assume either that markets were continuously in equilibrium or that agents were completely rational. Utility maximization and perfect competition were useful, fruitful assumptions – good approximations (Friedman 1953). He worked within a theoretical framework according to which economies could be out of equilibrium, exhibiting complex dynamic behaviour that could not be modelled formally (Gordon 1974). In contrast, Lucas (1972, 1976) worked with formal models of rational agents operating within competitive, continuously clearing markets. During the 1970s and 1980s, it was Friedman's monetarism that dominated debates over macroeconomic policy, but it was Lucas's approach that had the more profound long-run effect on macroeconomic theorizing.[3]

As with the Keynesian revolution, very strong claims were made about the revolution that was taking place in macroeconomics, the classic exposition of it being that of Robert Lucas and Thomas Sargent (1978, p. 49–50):

> We dwell on these halcyon days of Keynesian economics because, without conscious effort, they are difficult to recall today . . . That these predictions [based on Keynesian economics] were wildly incorrect, and that the doctrine on which they were based is fundamentally flawed, are now simple matters of fact, involving no novelties in economic theory. The task which faces contemporary students of the business cycle is that of sorting through the wreckage, determining which features of that remarkable intellectual event called the Keynesian Revolution can be salvaged and put to good use, and which others must be discarded. Though it is far from clear what the outcome of this process will be, it is already evident that it will necessarily involve the reopening of basic issues in monetary economics which have been viewed since the thirties as 'closed,' and the re-evaluation of every aspect of the institutional framework within which monetary and fiscal policy is formulated in the advanced countries.

Lucas and Sargent did not adopt Keynes's rhetoric of instigating a revolution – to the contrary, they criticized Keynesians by arguing that 'no novelties in economic theory' were required – and they presented the future as still to be determined, but no one reading this passage can be left in any doubt that they saw what was taking place in economics as an upheaval that could legitimately be described as revolutionary.

Despite the differences between the two crises and their associated revolutions, there are numerous parallels that can be drawn. The roots of Lucas's theoretical approach go back long before 1973. Its immediate progenitor is the work of Edmund Phelps and others on labour markets when information is not perfect (Phelps et al. 1970). Before that lies a long and complex search for what came, in the 1970s, to be labelled microfoundations for macroeconomics (see Backhouse and Boianovsky 2013). It was also the case that, as with the Keynesian revolution, the changes associated with Lucas involved losses as well as gains: the consequences of heterogeneity among agents, without which it is impossible to have coordination failures, cognitive limitations of agents, and the time taken for markets to adjust were assumed away (some of these, of course, came back with the new Keynesian macroeconomics, though in a limited way). The Friedman–Lucas revolution was also, like the Keynesian, associated with the creation of caricatures of previously held ideas. After Friedman's presidential address (1968), his highly influential critique of demand management that arguably did more than any other paper to call demand management policy into question, the myth emerged that Keynesians, such as Samuelson and Solow (1960), had believed that demand management could be used to lower the rate of unemployment without any danger of runaway inflation, yet this was demonstrably not the case (Forder 2010a, 2010b). Similarly, it was claimed that Keynesian economists failed to anticipate that expanding the level of demand at the end of the 1960s would lead to rising inflation, when in fact this actually happened because policymakers failed to heed the advice coming from the Keynesians on Lyndon Johnson's Council of Economic Advisors that this would happen (Bernstein 2001).

In retrospect, the changes associated with the Friedman–Lucas revolution can seem more or less inevitable. Faced with inflation running at over 10 per cent per annum (and closer to 30 per cent in Britain), it was no doubt inevitable that economists would pay significantly more attention to the dynamics of inflation than they had in the Keynesian golden age when inflation had generally been much lower and far less variable. Given the trend towards more formal modelling, which had been present throughout the Keynesian era (see Backhouse 2010b) it was probably inevitable that expectations would have been modelled more formally, and the data would have pushed economists towards assuming more forward-looking behaviour on the part of economic agents. However, what was not inevitable was that economists would have turned to what came to be called new classical models. A good illustration of this is that when Edmond Malinvaud (1977) tackled the problem of stagflation, he chose to model markets as being out of equilibrium (in the sense that prices did not adjust to equalize supply and demand) because he took the view that the stagflation experienced during the previous four years demonstrated that markets could not be in equilibrium. His work later had an impact on an influential study of stagflation by Michael Bruno and Jeffrey Sachs (1985). The bulk of the profession took a different view, but this does not vitiate the point that different paths could have been taken.

So why did economists make the choices that they did? A major part of this question is why did models based on individual rationality have such appeal to economists, whether new classical or not (and it is important to stress that even critics of the new classical macroeconomics felt this appeal)? An important factor is that it is obvious that decisions are made by individuals, and that a macroeconomic theory that cannot explain why individuals make the decisions implied by the theory is missing something. It is also obvious that people respond, often intelligently, to the circumstances that they face, and there is something inherently wrong with any model that implies that they must be stupid. There is thus a strong sense in which, if we have not explained how reasonably intelligent individuals will behave in ways that produce the outcomes predicted by our models, our understanding is inadequate. However, this is not the whole story, because models of completely independent individuals fail to take into account either interactions between individuals (there is, for example, overwhelming evidence that preferences are interdependent and that someone's welfare depends on their position in the income distribution) or phenomena that may arise solely at the aggregate level as a result of aggregating heterogeneous individuals.[4]

These motivations clearly drove developments in macroeconomics in the 1970s. However, these are not sufficient to explain what happened, for they do not explain the very specific way in which individuals came to be modelled, by both new classical economists (broadly, assuming that markets were efficient and competitive) and their opponents (who were more open to the consequences of market imperfections, limited information and other problems). Economic agents were modelled as having unchanging preferences that were given from outside the model. The reason for this is a belief that, as economic agents are individuals, they must be modelled as having their own preferences. Clearly, people are individuals but this does not make it illegitimate to generalize about how groups of individuals may behave, even if we do not know precisely the relationship between the behaviour of individuals and that of the group. However, in macroeconomics, because it was believed (incorrectly) that theories about groups *must be* grounded on rigorous, formal theories about individual behaviour, it became normal to assume a 'representative agent' whose behaviour could be taken to sum up how the economy as a whole would behave. This assumption, though made in the interests of creating tractable models that could be easily solved, and in the name of individualism, involves assuming that everyone is the same – removing the individuality that motivates the assumption that individuals have given preferences. The assumption that all agents are identical is not a harmless simplification that can easily be removed, for representative-agent modelling simply is not consistent with having any significant differences between economic agents: the models work only if all agents are identical (Kirman 1993).

There is also a large jump from assuming that individuals are not stupid to the degree of rationality that it has become conventional to assume. It has become conventional to model agents as making optimal choices over their entire lifetimes, sometimes taking into account the situation their descendants will face. In the absence of knowledge about what information they will have as the basis for this intertemporal optimization, it is often assumed that they will know everything that could be known: that a model should assume that the agents whose behaviour is being modelled have access to the model's predictions, subject of course to random errors, since anything else will imply making systematic mistakes.

There were clearly problems with Keynesian models as they existed prior to 1973, for they frequently made assumptions that were based on individuals following rules of thumb or acting in ways that, in the absence of other explanations, did not seem sensible. Keynesian models might be based on observed regularities in the data but, as the Lucas critique (Lucas 1976) made clear, such regularities might break down in response to the policy changes they were being used to design. However, there were also problems with the new theories, for if Keynesian theories assumed insufficient rationality, new classical theories perhaps assumed too much rationality. For example, Robert Barro (1974) might be right to criticize Keynesians for paying insufficient attention to the possibility that consumers would adjust their spending to take account of anticipated future tax changes; yet that was hardly sufficient to justify going to the other extreme, assuming that every future tax liability was perfectly anticipated, as was needed for Ricardian equivalence to hold. Such theoretical choices could be justified empirically: by arguing that new classical models explained the data better than did alternative models. However, while there was some success, the evidence was far from decisive (given the state of econometric knowledge it seems inconceivable that it could have been otherwise), leaving reason to conclude that empirical evidence was not the only factor behind the success of the new theories.

A widely canvassed explanation for the success of new classical models is politics, or ideology: the claim that the new theories appealed because of their conservative conclusions. There is no doubt that the revolution in macroeconomics was connected with the rise to power of conservative politicians among whom Margaret Thatcher and Ronald Reagan are the most significant: that it was part of a move within society towards questioning government activities and creating a larger role for private enterprise. These changes have been described as the rise of 'neo-liberalism', often identified with the Mont Pelerin Society, established by Friedrich Hayek in 1947 and which became the centre of a network of free-market advocates (see Mirowski and Plehwe 2009; Backhouse 2005; Klein 2007). The Mont Pelerin Society had strong links with the University of Chicago, the centre of many of the developments that transformed economics in the 1970s (see Burgin 2012). However, though the connections are clearly there, causal relations are very difficult to establish. Politicians were certainly influenced by economic theories produced by academic economists, but the extent to which these ideas influenced them, as opposed to telling them what they wanted to hear, is inevitably difficult to establish clearly. Thatcher, after all, was strongly influenced by the political philosophy of Friedrich Hayek, and in particular his Constitution of Liberty (Hayek 1961) as well as by Friedman's ideas. On the other side, though many economists associated with the new classical macroeconomics held conservative views, in the sense of wanting to reduce the role of government in the economy, and though rational-choice models could easily be used to support such political views, the success of rational choice theories owed much to the fact that such modelling was attractive to many economists on purely intellectual grounds. It was not just the new classical economists but also many of their new Keynesian critics who based their models on the assumption of rational agents.

A more serious problem is that, while it is clear that the revolution in macroeconomics was clearly tied up with wider social and political developments, conservative thinking was both heterogeneous and evolving. The early Mont Pelerin Society sought to reach out to those on the left – social democracts – as well as conservatives (Jackson 2010). Moreover, many of those whose names are linked to the founding of this movement, such as Walter Lippmann, Friedrich Hayek and Wilhelm Röpke, took the view that the Great Depression showed that laissez-faire capitalism had failed, and that it was necessary to work out a reformed capitalism; it was only later that a policy of laissez-faire came to dominate its thinking (Burgin 2012). Narratives that run in terms of neo-liberalism can also overlook both the variety within conservatism and the way in which changes in attitudes transcend any left–right division. For example, so-called 'analytical Marxists' (for example, Roemer 1986) turned to rational-choice modelling.

What was happening was that notions of the 'social' were increasingly called into question. Clearly, part of this was commitment to freedom, as something that differentiated western societies from communist regimes. Given the political dimension of this point, it is reasonable to describe it as ideological, though it is important to note that it covers the cold war use of rational-choice theory at RAND and the position of Robert McNamara as well as those we would now consider conservatives (see Amadae 2003; Abella 2008). But this fracturing of notions of the social extended much more widely. In the 1960s, radical individualist ideas were expressed by people on the left – the culture of the hippies was in some respects highly individualistic, emphasizing personal rather than collective experience. And yet notions of society remained strong, found in the labour movement, with its rhetoric of class solidarity, and movements centred on the shared experiences of women, or minority racial groups. However, in the 1970s, this changed: it became harder for white, middle-class feminists to claim that they understood the experiences of black, working-class women, calling into question the idea that it was useful to talk of a common experience shared by all women. Similarly, notions of class and race were called into question. In ways that were not always predictable, the common reality of individual experience over social experience was being felt across all sectors of society.

This might seem a long way from discussion of a revolution in macroeconomics, but it is not. In Daniel Rodgers's account of what he calls *The Age of Fracture* (2011), he argues that economists got there first, and he begins by explaining how economists stopped thinking in terms of aggregates and started to think in terms of individuals. Individual rational choice became both a normative criterion and an assumption about how people actually behaved. Though it would seem absurd to argue that economists caused these changes on their own, they clearly played a significant part in them. The implications of this for the point being made here about the response of macroeconomics to economic crisis is that it suggests, very strongly, that a major reason why the new way of thinking took such deep root is that it resonated with broader intellectual trends.

Consider Rodgers's summary of these changes:

> What crossed between these widely flung fronts of thought and argument was not a single, dominant idea – postmodernism, new right, or neoliberal – but a contagion of metaphors. Intellectual models slipped across the normal divisions of intellectual life. Market ideas moved out of economics departments to become the standard currency of the social sciences. Certain game theory set-pieces – the free-rider problem, the prisoner's dilemma, the tragedy of the commons – became fixtures of common sense. Fluid, partial notions of identity, worked out in painful debates among African-American and women's movement intellectuals, slipped into universal usage. Protean, spill-over words, like

> 'choice' were called up to do more and more work in more and more diverse circumstances. In the process some words and phrases began to seem more natural than the rest – not similes or approximations but reality itself. (Rodgers 2011, pp. 10–11)

In a world where the social was losing its meaning, explanations that ran in terms of individual rational choice had a persuasiveness they would not otherwise have had: metaphors and approximations became reality itself.

To say this is not to deny that economists were motivated by the search for theoretical coherence and rigour, by the desire to achieve consistency between different branches of the subject, or by the search for models that were empirically successful. These are undoubtedly part of the story but they are not the whole story.

4. ECONOMIC, SOCIAL AND INTELLECTUAL CHANGE

The Keynesian and the Friedman–Lucas revolutions in macroeconomics were undoubtedly revolutions and both were undoubtedly very important because they were in large part responses to profound economic crises. It is also undeniable that the economists with whom these revolutions are associated were responding creatively to the economic problems that they faced. There are, however, two other factors that need to be balanced against this. The first is that both revolutions built on work that had been done many years earlier. Despite his claims, Keynes owed much to ideas developed in the 1920s, by himself and others. Friedman's monetary project dated back to the 1940s. The work on the economics of information on which Lucas drew had been going on throughout the 1960s, and arguably links to ideas about which Herbert Simon was thinking in the 1950s. Equally important, there had been extensive prior work on economic policies that might be implemented: Roosevelt's New Deal drew on decades of 'progressive' policy analysis, and the changes introduced in the 1970s and 1980s drew on work going back to the 1950s by think tanks, from the Institute of Economic Affairs to the Heritage Foundation, on free-market economic policies. One does not have to go as far as those, such as Klein (2007) or Mirowski and Plehwe (2009), who trace the rise of an organized neo-liberal movement back to Hayek's establishment of the Mont Pelerin Society in 1947, to concede that the ground was well prepared.

The second factor, perhaps the most important, is that the importance and hence the depth of these two revolutions stemmed from the fact that the ideas that underpinned them were part of much broader intellectual changes. The Keynesian revolution came at a time when notions of society were strong, Keynesian policies blending with ideas of welfare capitalism that had been emerging since the late nineteenth century. Perhaps even more important was the way in which Keynesianism became entangled with the changes associated with the Second World War, which had no links to the economic crisis. The Friedman–Lucas revolution, in contrast, came at the time when the presuppositions on which the view of society on which Keynesianism and the welfare state rested were being called into question. The rise of individualism and the fracturing of ideas of the social are developments that, while they may have been accelerated by responses to economic crisis, were much broader. Profound changes took place in the way society was organized that would have been widely considered morally objectionable a generation earlier: the range of decisions subject to economic calculation expanded greatly, and the distribution of income and, above all, wealth became much more unequal.

When the current economic crisis began, there was much talk of it producing a new approach to economics. If this has not come about, and in many ways there appears to have been remarkably little change, perhaps the reason is that the conditions that made the Keynesian and Friedman–Lucas revolutions so profound are simply not in place. For example, Tony Judt (2010) recently argued that we have lost the ability to imagine a better future, something that was certainly not true either of the progressives whose ideas inspired the New Deal, or the free-market economists who inspired Margaret Thatcher and Ronald Reagan. Profound changes to economic crisis require not just 'technical' improvements in our economics, but the willingness to believe that the future can be better than the present.

ACKNOWLEDGEMENT

I am grateful to Bradley Bateman for invaluable comments on this draft. Though responsibility for the contents is mine, it reflects ideas on which we have been working together over several years.

NOTES

1. This is an exaggeration but it is close enough for the argument being presented here. Pre-Keynesian elements were more influential than often thought (see Mehrling 1997), but the Keynesian victory was nonetheless far more decisive than the anti-Keynesian victory after the 1970s.
2. An early user of the phrase 'counter-revolution', referring specifically to Friedman

(1956) and monetarism, was Harry Johnson (1971). However, the approach being taken here means that it is more appropriate to focus on the revolutionary nature of both of these transitions in economics.
3. Their approaches have been described as Monetarism Mark I and Mark II. This terminology is not used here, for it begs the question of whether the type of macroeconomics inspired by Lucas is correctly described as monetarist.
4. Hoover (2002) offers a useful philosophical discussion of the relationship between macroeconomics and microeconomics. A forceful popular account of the dependence of welfare on inequality can be found in Wilkinson and Pickett (2010).

REFERENCES

Abella, A. (2008), *Soldiers of Reason: The RAND Corporation and the Rise of the American Empire*, Boston, MA: Houghton Mifflin Harcourt.
Amadae, S. (2003), *Rationalizing Capitalist Democracy: The Cold War Origins of Rational Choice Liberalism*, Chicago, IL: University of Chicago Press.
Backhouse, R.E. (2005), 'The rise of free-market economics: economists and the role of the state since 1970', in S.G. Medema and P. Boettke (eds), *The Role of Government in the History of Economic Thought* (Annual Supplement to *History of Political Economy* 37), Durham, NC: Duke University Press.
Backhouse, R.E. (2008), 'Economics in the United States since 1945', in S. Durlauf and L. Blume (eds), *The New Palgrave Dictionary of Economics*, 2nd edn, London: Macmillan, available at: www.dictionaryofeconomics.com.
Backhouse, R.E. (2010a), 'Economics', in R.E. Backhouse and P. Fontaine (eds), *The History of the Social Sciences Since 1945*, Cambridge: Cambridge University Press.
Backhouse, R.E. (2010b), *The Puzzle of Modern Economics: Science or Ideology?* Cambridge: Cambridge University Press.
Backhouse, R.E. and B.W. Bateman (2011), *Capitalist Revolutionary: John Maynard Keynes*, Cambridge, MA: Harvard University Press.
Backhouse, R.E. and B.W. Bateman (2012), '"The right kind of an economist": Friedman's view of Keynes', in T. Cate (ed.), *Keynes's General Theory Seventy-Five Years Later*, Cheltenham, UK, Northampton, MA, USA: Edward Elgar.
Backhouse, R.E. and M. Boianovsky (2013), *Transforming Modern Macroeconomics: Exploring Disequilibrium Microfoundations, 1956–2003*, Cambridge: Cambridge University Press.
Backhouse, R.E. and D. Laidler (2004), 'What was lost with IS-LM', in M. De Vroey and K.D. Hoover (eds), *The IS-LM Model: Its Rise, Fall, and Strange Persistence* (Annual Supplement to *History of Political Economy*, 36), Durham, NC: Duke University Press.
Barro, R.J. (1974), 'Are government bonds net wealth?', *Journal of Political Economy*, **82** (6), 1095–117.
Bateman, B.W. (2006), 'Keynes and Keynesianism', in R.E. Backhouse and B.W Bateman (eds), *The Cambridge Companion to Keynes*, Cambridge: Cambridge University Press.
Bernstein, M. (2001), *A Perilous Progress: Economists and Public Purpose in Twentieth Century America*, Princeton, NJ: Princeton University Press.
Beveridge, W. (1942), *Social Insurance and Allied Services*, London: HMSO.
Blaug, M. (1990), *John Maynard Keynes: Life, Ideas, Legacy*, London: Macmillan.

Bruno, M. and J.D. Sachs (1985), *The Economics of Worldwide Stagflation*, Oxford: Blackwell.

Burgin, A. (2012), *The Great Persuasion: Reinventing Free Markets since the Depression*, Cambridge, MA: Harvard University Press.

Forder, J. (2010a), 'The historical place of the "Friedman–Phelps" expectations critique', *European Journal of the History of Economic Thought*, **17** (3), 493–511.

Forder, J. (2010b), 'Friedman's Nobel lecture and the Phillips curve myth', *Journal of the History of Economic Thought*, **32** (3), 329–48.

Friedman, M. (1953), 'The methodology of positive economics', in *Essays in Positive Economics*, Chicago, IL: Chicago University Press.

Friedman, M. (ed.) (1956), *The Quantity Theory of Money: A Restatement*, Chicago, IL: University of Chicago Press.

Friedman, M. (1968), 'The role of monetary policy', *American Economic Review*, **58** (1), 1–17.

Goodfriend, M. and R.G. King (1997), 'The new neoclassical synthesis and the role of monetary policy', *NBER Macroeconomics Annual*, vol. 12, pp. 231–96, available at: www.nber.org/chapters/c11040.

Gordon, R.A. (ed.) (1974), *Milton Friedman's Monetary Framework: A Debate with His Critics*, Chicago, IL: University of Chicago Press.

Hall, P. (1989), *The Political Power of Economic Ideas: Keynesianism Across Nations*, Princeton, NJ: Princeton University Press.

Hayek, F.A. (1961), *The Constitution of Liberty*, London: Routledge.

Hicks, J.R. (1937), 'Mr Keynes and the "classics": a suggested interpretation', *Econometrica*, **5**, 147–59.

Hoover, K.D. (2002), *The Methodology of Empirical Macroeconomics*, Cambridge: Cambridge University Press.

Jackson, B. (2010), 'At the origins of neo-liberalism: the free economy and the strong state, 1930–1947', *Historical Journal*, **53** (1), 129–51.

Johnson, H.G. (1971), 'The Keynesian revolution and the monetarist counter-revolution', *American Economic Review*, **61** (2), 1–14.

Judt, T. (2010), *Ill Fares the Land: A Treatise on Our Present Discontents*, London: Allen Lane.

Keynes, J.M. (1973 [1936]), *The General Theory of Employment, Interest and Money*, The Collected Writings of John Maynard Keynes, vol. 7, London: Macmillan.

Kirman, A.P. (1993), 'Whom or what does the representative agent represent?', *Journal of Economic Perspectives*, **6** (2), 117–36.

Klein, N. (2007), *The Shock Doctrine*, London: Penguin.

Laidler, D.W. (1999), *Fabricating the Keynesian Revolution: Studies of the Inter-War Literature on Money, the Cycle, and Unemployment*, Cambridge: Cambridge University Press.

Lucas, R.E. (1972), 'Expectations and the neutrality of money', *Journal of Economic Theory*, **4** (2), 103–24.

Lucas, R.E. (1976), 'Econometric policy evaluation: a critique', *Carnegie-Rochester Conference Series on Public Policy*, **1** (1), 19–46.

Lucas, R.E. and T. Sargent (1978), 'After Keynesian macroeconomics', in *After the Phillips Curve: High Inflation and High Unemployment*, Federal Reserve Bank of Boston, USA, Conference Series, 19.

Malinvaud, E. (1977), *The Theory of Unemployment Reconsidered*, Oxford, UK: Blackwell.

Mehrling, P.G. (1997), *The Money Interest and the Public interest: American Monetary Thought, 1920–1970*, Cambridge, MA: Harvard University Press.

Mirowski, P. and D. Plehwe (2009), *The Road from Mont Pelerin*, Cambridge, MA: Harvard University Press.

Ohlin, B. (1937), 'Notes on the Stockholm theory of savings and investments, II', *Economic Journal*, **47** (186), 221–40.

Phelps, E.S. et al. (1970), *Microeconomic Foundations of Employment and Inflation Theory*, London: Macmillan.

Rodgers, Daniel T. (1998), *Transatlantic Crossings: Social Politics in a Progressive Age*, Cambridge, MA: Belknap.

Rodgers, Daniel T. (2011), *The Age of Fracture*, Cambridge, MA: Belknap.

Roemer, J. (1986), *Analytical Marxism*, Cambridge: Cambridge University Press.

Samuelson, P.A. and R.M. Solow (1960), 'Analytical Aspects of Anti-Inflation Policy', *American Economic Review*, **50** (2, Papers and Proceedings of the Seventy-Second Annual Meeting of the American Economic Association), 177–94.

Wilkinson, R. and K. Pickett (2010), *The Spirit Level: Why Equality Is Better for Everyone*, London: Penguin.

Woodford, M. (2003), *Interest and Prices: Foundations of a Theory of Monetary Policy*, Princeton, NJ: Princeton University Press.

3. The efficient-markets hypothesis after the crisis: a methodological analysis of the evidence

Fredrik Hansen

INTRODUCTION

Economists belong to two camps when analysing the latest economic crisis. They are among the participating researchers (from different disciplines) analysing the crisis and examining the possibilities of avoiding any future economic crises. At the same time they are also part of the group accused of creating the crisis (and/or even having made it worse) in one way or another. Let me emphasize that in this chapter we are going to focus on reactions among economists of the financial crisis of 2007–08 that roughly started with the bankruptcy of Lehman Brothers (and not the current difficulties in the eurozone regarding especially the financial position of Greece). In the debates that have occurred concerning the financial crisis, what is known as the efficient market hypothesis (EMH hereafter) has been of special interest. In short, this hypothesis states that current asset prices reflect available information. Prominent economists have participated on both sides in the debate. In the criticizing team we have, for example, Paul Krugman. In a well-known column in the *New York Times* in 2009 titled 'How did economists get it so wrong?' he launched a quite fierce critique of the EMH (and what is known as neoclassical macroeconomics). According to Krugman (2009):

> By 1970 or so, however, the study of financial markets seemed to have been taken over by Voltaire's Dr. Pangloss, who insisted that we live in the best of all possible worlds. Discussion of investor irrationality, of bubbles, of destructive speculation had virtually disappeared from academic discourse. The field was dominated by the 'efficient-market hypothesis,' promulgated by Eugene Fama of the University of Chicago, which claims that financial markets price assets precisely at their intrinsic worth given all publicly available information.

The critique doesn't stop there. Krugman further argues:

> In short, the belief in efficient financial markets blinded many if not most economists to the emergence of the biggest financial bubble in history. And efficient-market theory also played a significant role in inflating that bubble in the first place.

The solution however is according to Krugman delivered by behavioural finance (and Keynesian macroeconomics):

> There's already a fairly well developed example of the kind of economics I have in mind: the school of thought known as behavioral finance. Practitioners of this approach emphasize two things. First, many real-world investors bear little resemblance to the cool calculators of efficient-market theory: they're all too subject to herd behavior, to bouts of irrational exuberance and unwarranted panic. Second, even those who try to base their decisions on cool calculation often find that they can't, that problems of trust, credibility and limited collateral force them to run with the herd.

In the responding camp we have, for example, John Cochrane. He answered Krugman in an essay called 'How did Paul Krugman get it so wrong?'. According to Cochrane (2009):

> It's fun to say we didn't see the crisis coming, but the central empirical prediction of the efficient-markets hypothesis is precisely that nobody can tell where markets are going – neither benevolent government bureaucrats, nor crafty hedge-fund managers, nor ivory-tower academics. This is probably the best-tested proposition in all the social sciences. Krugman knows this, so all he can do is huff and puff about his dislike for a theory whose central prediction is that nobody can be a reliable soothsayer. And of course it makes no sense whatsoever to try to discredit efficient-markets finance because its followers didn't see the crash coming.

Similar arguments have been offered by Eugene Fama, the initiator of the EMH.

We have here a typical example of a polarized debate where the EMH is used as a baseball bat. On these occasions methodological analyses can offer necessary clarifications. The purpose of the following study is to examine the status of the EMH. In order to get a clear picture of the critique and defence, as well as reaching suggestions for the future, we will characterize the arguments presented.

To begin with we deal with what the EMH says by looking at some typical descriptions of the concept. Then we turn to the offered critique and defence of the EMH. By these two steps we will get a decent picture of the limitations and possibilities of the EMH. With the help of Hindriks's (2007) work on explanatory models we will then be able to present a view on the status of the EMH and reflect on its position in financial economics in the light of the current crisis.

The structure of this chapter is as follows. We start with descriptions of the EMH. Then we look at the critiques. Next is to analyse the status of the EMH by focusing on its limitations and possibilities. Finally, some concluding remarks are offered.

WHAT DOES THE EMH SAY?

Examining what the EMH really asserts and what it assumes deserves an essay of its own. As mentioned by, for example, Lo (2007), it is not a well-defined concept. But in order to get a clearer picture, we will now look at some descriptions and developments, starting with the initiator, Eugene Fama.[1]

Fama's Description

In a recent interview Fama (2011) mentions he coined the terms 'market efficiency' and 'efficient markets'. In the same article Fama also mentions (p. 3) that '[m]y main contribution to the theory of efficient markets is my 1970 review'. Being a most humble statement, any detailed conceptual reasoning is not offered in this article (Fama 2011) and it focuses mainly on reviewing different statistical results. The following short description (Fama 1970, p. 383) is however well known to financial economists: 'A market in which prices always "fully reflect" available information is called "efficient".' Interestingly, a few years earlier Fama (1965) discussed market efficiency in relation to the intrinsic values of financial securities. According to Fama (1965, p. 90) what he calls an 'efficient' market is 'a market where, given the available information, actual prices at every point in time represent very good estimates of intrinsic values'. In later work by Fama, intrinsic value is however not in focus or even mentioned.

Returning to Fama (1970), in this article also three forms of market efficiency (that financial markets should be tested for) are suggested: *weak form* (all historical price information is reflected in asset prices), *semi-strong form* (besides all past prices, all publicly available information also is reflected) and *strong form* (besides past prices and publicly available information, all private information also is reflected). In the strong form it is impossible to beat the market (that is, get an extraordinary return without taking extraordinary risk). The weak version is the least demanding and according to Fama it has also got the best empirical support. This can be viewed as an attempt to specify the vague expression of 'available information' used by Fama earlier.

The empirical testing of the EMH is problematic owing to what is known as the 'joint-hypothesis problem'. This is nicely covered in Fama's (1991) sequel review article.[2] Basically, you cannot empirically test market efficiency in isolation but instead need to do it jointly together with some kind of asset-pricing model. If you then get a negative result you cannot be sure what parts are faulty. Fama (p. 1575) even argues that 'market efficiency per se is not testable'. Regarding this issue, Pesaran (2006) mentions that, on the other hand, basically every part of empirical economics is subject to the joint-hypothesis problem (he also emphasizes that the EMH is a useful concept – something we will return to later).

As mentioned, Fama (1970; 1991) does not offer any reasoning about a stock's intrinsic value and to what extent prices and values are able to diverge. As indicated in Fama (1991), testing for the existence of bubbles also falls under the joint-hypothesis problem. However, Fama (1970, p. 416) mentions the EMH as being 'a good first (and second) approximation to reality' and in the sequel article he argues (1991, p. 1576) that the performed research 'on efficiency and asset-pricing models passes the acid test of scientific usefulness'. On the same page Fama also argues that

> judged on how it has improved our understanding of the behavior of securities returns, the past research on market efficiency is among the most successful in empirical economics, with good prospects to remain so in the future.

Other Reasoning and Descriptions of the EMH

Turning to other descriptions and reasoning about the EMH, Malkiel (2003, p. 60), one of the most persistent defenders of the EMH, describes it the following way: 'such markets do not allow investors to earn above-average returns without accepting above-average risks'. That is, you can beat the market in the sense of getting a higher return than the market return, but only by buying riskier financial assets. Malkiel also emphasizes that markets can still be efficient even despite the following occurrences: errors in valuations, some market participants not adhering fully to the rationality view of neoclassical economics, and (which we will return to later) the market displaying a greater volatility. Interestingly, Malkiel (p. 80) mentions the following passage in his conclusion:

> Undoubtedly, some market participants are demonstrably less than rational. As a result, pricing irregularities and even predictable patterns in stock returns can appear over time and even persist for short periods.

However, Malkiel also argues that it is not really possible to take advantage of these irregularities and get extraordinary returns.

Ball (2009) is an article with a focus on the current crisis and the EMH. Among other things, Ball makes two interesting points regarding what the EMH does not say. To begin with, the EMH does not say that the market should have predicted the crisis. According to Ball (p. 10), 'If we could predict a market crash, current market prices would be inefficient because they would not reflect the information embodied in the prediction.' Second, and related, is that the EMH does not say that the market should have known we were in a bubble. Ball (p. 10) argues, perhaps with a degree of irony: 'Asset price bubbles, or episodes in which prices rise and then fall by substantial amounts, are much easier to spot using hindsight than they are to predict.'

One of the initiators of the Black–Scholes option valuation formula, Fischer Black, has made some interesting statements regarding efficient financial markets. In an article from the early 1970s, Black (1971) argues that a characteristic of an efficient market is that the cost of trading is low, the trading is continuous (if the trader demands it, the trading order is executed immediately; this is close to the issue of liquidity in financial markets) and finally that the price movements are random. Interestingly, Black (p. 35) says the following about stability in the form of price continuity:

> It is worth emphasizing again that price continuity or 'stability' is not in itself a desirable characteristic of an efficient market. It is both undesirable and unprofitable for a specialist or market maker to 'resist' changes in the price of a stock.

Later, Black (1985) emphasizes the concept of 'noise' (this term is also used in Fama (1965) and in a similar way). He argues that noise exists in financial markets owing to uncertainty about the future and in the form of our expectations (which are not necessarily rational). We then have two basic types of traders: those trading on information and those trading on noise. Basically, Black introduces the concept of the quality of information to financial economics. Noise is also incorporated in the prices, meaning that (Black 1985, p. 532) '[t]he price of a stock reflects both the information that information traders trade on and the noise that noise traders trade on.' Basically, noise will result in potential profits from trade for those trading on information but at the same time it creates a larger amount of uncertainty in the market (because noise is also incorporated in the price). Black (p. 530) even predicts that: 'someday, these conclusions will be widely accepted. The influence of noise traders will become apparent.'

Black's concept of 'noise' is obviously vague. It does not really offer any guidance since the value of a stock is not observable. But still, it is an interesting approach close to the idea of intrinsic value and it enriches the reasoning about the EMH.

The Fundamentals of the EMH

At this moment it is interesting to mention some points about the following three fundamental aspects of EMH: its assumptions, the relation to what is known as 'rational expectations' and the use of the term 'efficient' in financial economics (as compared with economics in general).

According to Pesaran (2006), the EMH makes the following three assumptions:

1. *Investor rationality*, meaning that the investors instantly update their beliefs when new information is available.
2. *The arbitrage condition*, meaning that any risk-free return is not possible.
3. *Collective rationality*, meaning that any errors of investors are random (even cross-sectional-independent) and are cancelled out in the market.

In this article, Pesaran (2006) also shows that the EMH needs to be accompanied by the assumption of rational expectations made famous by Lucas (1978), in order to reach results of interest to financial economists (that is, asset-pricing-related results). In short, the assumption of rational expectations states that the individuals will make correct predictions about the future. When discussing the EMH, it is often the case also that rational expectations are addressed and that occasionally they are believed to be one and the same concept. This is incorrect. As we have mentioned, the EMH is assisted by the assumption of rational expectation in order to reach asset-pricing models of interest. They are obviously close but at the same time they have vital differences. In fact, if you equate the assumption of rational expectations with the EMH, you will get a version of what is known as complete markets. This is a demanding market alternative and not commonly assumed by financial economists. To further illustrate this alternative let us turn to how 'efficiency' is used in financial economics.

In financial economics the use of the term 'efficiency' differs from that which is normal in economics (i.e. in addressing the outcome of allocations)[3] – as previously discussed by James Tobin (1984). The meaning of efficiency in financial economics that is in line with the way Fama and others have explained the EMH, Tobin calls 'information arbitrage efficiency'. The focus here is on arbitrage, meaning that if the price has drifted away there is the possibility of achieving a relatively risk-free return (which will also correct the price). Second, there is also the kind of efficiency Tobin calls 'fundamental valuation efficiency', meaning that the valuations correctly reflect any future payments. Thus, any valuation will be proven correct in the future and this is related to the assumption of rational expectations and close to what is known as a complete market. This kind of efficiency is a more demanding one. The third kind of efficiency is 'full insurance efficiency', the term Tobin uses to convey the possibility of transferring goods and services to future generations. Of course this is dependent on the existence of appropriate options and similar contracts, as well as on there being a connection to the question of liquidity (which we are going to briefly discuss later). The fourth and last kind of efficiency is 'functional efficiency', or whether the financial sector is of advantage to the economy as a whole. Needless to say, this kind of efficiency has been debated in the current crisis.

WHAT IS THE CRITIQUE?

A common line of critique has been to focus on the incapacity of the EMH to cover situations when the intrinsic value of a stock differs from its price, and, related to this issue, the development of bubbles. As mentioned above, earlier (1965) Fama discussed intrinsic value in relation to price but his later work does not even mention it. According to the interview with Richard Thaler (Cassidy 2010a), Fama does not even like to talk about intrinsic value. Intrinsic value is however a non-observable, complex concept and cannot be expected to be a specific part of the 'available information' Fama talks about. Basically the difference between it and price will not be predictable, and from that point of view cannot really be employed critically against the EMH. It does on the other hand display a limitation of the EMH that needs to be addressed – and absolutely *not* met with silence as it is by financial economists today. The same defence also applies to the development of a bubble (often believed to be displaying differences between value and price and driven by speculation).

The interaction between the EMH and rational expectations is more difficult. In the case of the EMH accompanied by rational expectations, there cannot be any difference between value and price, a standpoint that is hard to sustain these days. On the other hand, this does not mean that we should stop using models of this kind and their combinations, but rather that we need to be better aware of their limitations, and state them clearly. As mentioned earlier, the assumption of rational expectations is supporting the EMH in order to reach asset-pricing models of interest. Ross (2010) argues that it is important to distinguish between the concept of rational expectations as a literal truth and as a useful idealization (something its critics seldom do). In this case I believe it is appropriate to view it as a useful idealization. In the well-known article by Lucas (1978), the author is also quite honest about applying 'useful idealizations', arguing that he is offering a 'theoretical explanation' and bridging economic and financial theories.

That according to Krugman we have a Panglossian attitude among financial economists is interesting. It is however not clear what a Panglossian ('best of all possible worlds') attitude means when you use it in describing economists and their way of doing theoretical research. Perhaps it is something like the following. Idealizations are chosen based on the outcome you want to address (an outcome is viewed as a too optimistic description of reality). The limits of the models are going to have serious consequences if certain circumstances in fact occur, but these are disregarded. The prevalence of such an attitude is of course a serious situation, but unfortunately it is quite common in economics. The EMH is distorted by it, and so I would guess is work by Krugman too if we took a closer look. It is not acceptable from a methodological point of view, since above all the limits of your models must be taken into account. Nor should the role of rhetoric and sociological factors be underestimated. Black (1985, p. 537) makes the following comment regarding acceptance of theories, which I would guess applies to much of today's economics: 'In the end, a theory is accepted not because it is confirmed by conventional empirical tests, but because researchers persuade one another that the theory is correct and relevant.'

Krugman also mentions behavioural finance being part of the solution. As indicated in Barberis and Thaler's (2003) survey, behavioural finance has got basically two themes (although they are not separated): the first concerns investor psychology and the second examines market inefficiencies and possibilities of beating the market. The first part is clearly influenced by cognitive psychology and especially the area of 'behavioural decision-making'. Basically these authors examine the different heuristics and biases that are present in our financial decision-making (and observing also that we don't adhere to the neoclassical view of rationality[4]). The second part concerns empirical studies of the performance of the stock market and asset-pricing models. One famous approach here is Shiller's (2003) work on 'excess volatility'. The 'excess' is in relation to the difference between the price and what we could expect from rational investors and thereby indicates an irrational market.[5] Often irrationality at the market level is motivated by referring to some kind of irrationality on the individual level (basically the economist 'creates' the market by summing up the individuals and their behaviour). But connecting the levels of individual and market is problematic and can only be decided empirically. In the Cassidy (2010b) interview of Fama, the latter argues the following about the connection between individual irrationality and asset pricing:

> I've always said they are very good at describing how individual behavior departs from rationality. That branch of it has been incredibly useful. It's the leap from there to what it implies about market pricing where the claims are not so well-documented in terms of empirical evidence . . . It's a leap. I'm not saying you couldn't do it, but I'm an empiricist. It's got to be shown.

In the same interview series, Thaler, one of the initiators of the field of behavioural finance, is quite modest in his views and indicates a complementary relation between behavioural and neoclassical finance (Cassidy (2010a)):

> Well, I always stress that there are two components to the theory. One, the market price is always right. Two, there is no free lunch: you can't beat the market without taking on more risk. The no-free-lunch component is still sturdy, and it was in no way shaken by recent events: in fact, it may have been strengthened. Some people thought that they could make a lot of money without taking more risk, and actually they couldn't. So either you can't beat the market, or beating the market is very difficult – everybody agrees with that. My own view is that you can [beat the market] but it is difficult.

Both Fama and Thaler express a belief in behavioural and neoclassical finance being complements (although not perfect complements) targeting different parts of the financial reality. Behavioural finance has got its strengths from addressing the financial decision-making of individuals. Neoclassical finance on the other hand is in general interested in the performance of the stock market (i.e. the aggregate level) and therefore focuses on asset-pricing models. The results of behavioural finance do not necessarily affect how neoclassical finance works on aggregate levels, and vice versa. For Fama, and I would guess also guess for Thaler, any dependence of this kind has to be decided empirically. Thaler does on the other hand believe that you can beat the market, and this goes against the views of neoclassical finance to some degree, but he also emphasizes its being difficult and involving taking on more risk (i.e. we are not talking about any 'free-lunch' possibilities).

Krugman (2009) typically argues in line with the view that showing irrationalities on the individual level will indirectly also result in irrationalities on the market level. But that is a premature conclusion to draw, as we have argued above. Any dependence has got to be decided empirically and, for example, Fehr and Tyran (2005) performed economic experiments where they had individual irrationality but market outcomes in line with predictions from neoclassical economics.

Krugman does however belong to a group of distinguished economists who refer to behavioural finance being part of the solution of the crisis, though he does not provide reasonable arguments for this statement. The need for more behavioural finance is also the theme of a recent popular book by Akerlof and Shiller (2009), although they use the Keynesian term 'animal spirits'. Much of their discussion of the financial crisis goes back to the work by Shiller already cited (Shiller 2003). Just like individual irrationality, the step from animal spirits to market outcome needs to be argued and to be supported by empirical results. Unfortunately no such arguments are really presented in this book and above all, as indicated by Lo (2012), no empirical support is offered. In a quite critical review, Ross (2010) argues for the alternative version of the crisis being a large-scale macroeconomic event with macroeconomic causes. Ross mentions the growth pattern of Asia, especially China, global savings imbalance and rapid changes in the composition of the global labour force as possible macroeconomic causes.

One of the stranger cases regarding the need for more behavioural finance based on the current crisis is the twist presented in 'The Turner Review' (Turner 2009), a report issued by the UK Financial Services Authority. In the chapter on 'fundamental theoretical issue', Turner (p. 40) argues that 'individual rationality does not ensure collective rationality'. This is in line what we have argued above; just because we have a certain property on the individual level it does not necessarily follow that it also applies on aggregate levels such as the market level. Thus, individual rationality does not necessarily lead to (some kind of) market rationality. However on the next page, when addressing the idea that 'individual behaviour is not entirely rational', Turner (p. 41) argues that from individual irrationality follow decisions 'which at the collective level are bound to produce herd effects and thus irrational momentum swings'. Hence, when talking about irrationality on the individual level we are at the same time bound to have a collective irrationality according to Turner. Thus, individual irrationality does necessarily lead to (some kind of) market inefficiency. Why irrationality but not rationality necessarily travels from the individual to the market Turner does not explain. As we have mentioned above, this is uncalled for. Whatever property we find at the individual level does not necessarily occur at the market level, and a wise strategy is always to examine empirically the step from individual to market. Turner's twist between rationality/irrationality regarding individual/market is remarkable and lacks justification.[6]

Perhaps a middle ground between adherents to the EMH and its critics is advisable. One alternative then is what is called 'Samuelson's dictum'. The well-known economist Paul Samuelson seems to have thought a lot on the efficient/inefficient issue, although he did not write that much about it. Some of his take on it is mentioned in Samuelson (2009), and Jung and Shiller (2005) refer to private communication with Samuelson. Basically Samuelson argues that markets are firm-specific efficient (or micro efficient) while at the same time market inefficient (or macro inefficient). That is, individual stocks display efficiency (available firm-related information is included in the price) while the market as a whole displays inefficiency. For example, taking arbitraging positions on a stock is quite simple (for example buying similar stocks), but it is more difficult if you want to take positions against the market as a whole. This is of course difficult to test but Jung and Shiller (2005) reach results supporting Samuelson's view. They emphasize the danger in trying to decide the efficiency of a market by extrapolating from individual stocks. We may hope that more studies will be performed examining Samuelson's dictum.

It is not really a critique of the EMH, but it is interesting to mention briefly the sociological approach to financial markets called social studies of finance (SSF). There have been various sociological approaches to financial economics, as indicated in Preda (2007), and among them MacKenzie (2006) has been very successful, initiating SSF and getting a lot of attention. Part of that success can be explained by MacKenzie being familiar with the developments in neoclassical financial economics, another part by his having interviewed around 60 professionals in finance (both academics and practitioners). Basically, SSF deals with the interaction between the research performed in the area of financial economics and the actual practice of trading and the weight that is put on financial-economic models (mainly, the use of formal financial models in trading). Financial economists focus almost entirely on developing asset-pricing models and don't examine how their models are used in actual trading. MacKenzie, on the other hand, focuses on the Black–Scholes option pricing formula initiated at the beginning of the 1970s and the trading of options on financial markets. Interestingly, after the financial crash of 1987, traders started to apply this formula with caution (and a certain degree of suspicion). With the 1987 financial crash it became apparent that the Black–Scholes formula doesn't incorporate the fat tails that are likely to occur in the financial statistics at turbulent times. As far as I can see, SSF is to be viewed as an interesting complement to behavioural and neoclassical finance. We still need neoclassical asset-pricing models and behavioural finance approaches to individual financial decision-making, but it is also important to know how traders use financial theory in their profession and in what way it can affect financial markets.

THE LIMITATIONS AND POSSIBILITIES OF THE EMH

The EMH is a vital part in today's theory on asset pricing, an area in financial economics that has seen exceptional progress in economic theory (and empirical economics) during the last 50 years. At the same time it is a limited concept. It does not cover vital parts such as bubbles and crises. On the other hand, if you look at the descriptions of the EMH it does not purport to do so either. The EMH of Fama needs to be enriched by fill-ins. In particular, Black's (1985) work on noise is interesting, as well as the earlier work by Fama (1965) on intrinsic value (although his view then in 1965 on the relation between efficient markets and intrinsic value mentioned above is probably impossible to use today). The relation to rational expectation must also be examined.

For the non-economist reader this acceptance of the position of the EMH perhaps reads strangely. Well, to begin with there is not really any alternative. As of today we must incorporate the EMH in our studies in one way or another if we want to address questions of asset pricing. But who knows what will happen in the future?

Interestingly, there is support for the view of the EMH expressed in economic methodology. One of the classical papers in economic methodology is Friedman (1953), widely quoted and analysed even today (see, for example, Mäki 2009). In this paper Friedman defends the neoclassical by emphasizing its predictive capacity and arguing that the reality of the assumptions does not matter (or even in some passages arguing that the more unrealistic the assumptions are, the better). Recently Hindriks (2007) developed a similar, but improved, approach, focusing instead on the explanatory power of a theory and arguing that sometimes this can be achieved by using unrealistic assumptions. But this is no urging of unrealistic assumptions in general. It is, rather, about choosing the right kinds of assumptions. When referring to the success of the Modigliani–Miller model (that the value of a firm is independent of its capital structure), Hindriks (2007, p. 356) argues: 'The explanatory power of the MM theory is due to the fact that its original model is highly unrealistic and that, as history has proven, the choice of abstractions and idealizations was particularly good.' This is connected to what Ross (2010) said about useful idealizations.

In my opinion the EMH has got a reasonably high explanatory power and part of this success is due to its not incorporating some of the areas we today believe are important (for example bubbles). That is, given the quite limited purpose of the hypothesis, useful idealizations have been obtained. But now in the aftermath of the recent financial crisis a wider purpose is required. Perhaps the EMH should be left as it is and we should focus on finding complements. We have already mentioned the alternatives of behavioural finance and social studies of finance. Areas needing to be addressed include financial bubbles, crisis behaviour, regulations and the role of liquidity. Regarding the last of these, Black (1971, p. 1985) emphasizes the importance of liquidity in a financial market. The idea is that a liquid market is also an efficient market. This is possible to determine empirically and, for example, Chordia et al. (2007) find some support for this idea, but much more study is required. Related also is the research on counterpart risk that is especially important for the functioning of the interbank market (see, for example, Allen et al. 2009). Today's widespread diversification procedure creates a multitude of counterparty relationships. But, as mentioned by Acemoglu (2009), we then also face the risk of domino effects following quite small shocks. This is a different kind of risk that must be taken into account and examined further.

CONCLUDING REMARKS

I agree with parts of the critique offered by Krugman, especially regarding the blind spot of financial economics concerning the intrinsic value of stock and the development of bubbles. At the same time Krugman's description of neoclassical financial theory is insufficient and the belief in behavioural finance is methodologically unmotivated. In a later article Krugman (2011, p. 308) criticizes mainly macroeconomics but interestingly says the following about the EMH (my emphasis):

> So why were so relatively few economists willing to call the bubble a bubble? I suspect that the efficient-market theory, *in a loose sense* – the belief that markets couldn't possibly be getting things that wrong – played a major role.

It is not clear what Krugman means by 'a loose sense' but his critical view on the EMH is obviously downplayed. I also agree with parts of the response by Cochrane but he, and many other financial economists, must start to clearly state the limitations of the EMH and related financial models as well as initiate research specifically concerning the behaviour of financial crises. Let us now conclude this chapter with two remarks.

The first remark concerns asking ourselves why some scholars demand so much of the EMH. One explanation is of course that they are not really aware of what the theory of the EMH asserts. Another answer, that perhaps applies to representatives of other disciplines as well as other subdisciplines of economics, is that earlier financial economists have given the appearance of supremacy to the EMH and its related models. Basically, financial economists are victims of a view of the EMH that they are responsible for creating themselves. Regarding creating frictions, there is also the way financial economists use the term 'efficient' (mainly to describe information and asset prices). This is probably not noteworthy for financial economists but to the uninitiated it is a remarkable interpretation of the term. Fellow economists might also react, since 'efficient' is traditionally used in a different way (i.e. when addressing the outcome of allocations). Therefore a higher degree of modesty among financial economists is recommended, as well as a constructive attitude both towards the limitations of their models and regarding the behaviour of financial markets during crises.

The second remark is in relation to the recent calls for regulations and their interaction with the EMH. For example, in 'The Turner Review' we criticized earlier, Turner (2009) argues that before the financial crisis the idea was that an efficient market did not need any regulation. But now we have witnessed the failure of the EMH, and regulations are called for. To me, the claim that the EMH is part of the cause of the financial crisis is to exaggerate. Perhaps a distorted version of it ('a loose sense'?) combined with, among other things, an aversion to regulations might explain parts of the financial crisis. There is not really any conflict between the EMH and regulations. Even with regulations, asset-pricing models are still needed and in order to develop them the EMH in some form will be important. The EMH focuses on information and asset prices and doesn't really say anything about financial infrastructure such as regulations. But aren't economists often found opposing regulations based on the risk of a non-efficient outcome? In general such a position is correct, but be aware that we are now talking about 'efficiency' in the traditional economic sense, i.e. using resources in such a way that the outcome becomes as good as it can get. Roughly stated, an inefficient regulation will then result in more bad than good. Decisions about the efficiency of regulations must obviously be aided by economic analyses.

Let me clarify that I am not an enemy of regulations. After the latest turmoil I feel that they are justified. But they must be sustainable regulations, meaning that they must apply equally in both good and bad times. The risk is that we put too much emphasis on the recent past (thus becoming victims of what behavioural economists call a bias of the availability heuristic) as well as seeking patterns that do not apply in the long run (thus becoming victims of a bias of the representativeness heuristic).

ACKNOWLEDGEMENTS

This paper has benefited from discussions with Fredrik Andersson, Mats Benner, Björn Hansson, Robert Östling and from comments from the participants in the 'After the Crisis' series of lectures at the Pufendorf Institute at Lund University, Sweden.

NOTES

1. For an account of the fascinating history of the work and ideas leading up to the EMH, mainly concerning the random-walk approach to asset prices, see Bernstein (2005).
2. Fama (1991, p. 1575) has his doubts about offering a sequel, arguing that '[s]equels are rarely as good as the originals'.
3. For a critique of financial economists using the term 'efficiency' at all, see Frankfurter and McGuon (1999).
4. The neoclassical view of rationality means basically that preferences are rational (that is complete, reflexive and transitive), there is access to perfect information and decisions are made by maximizing utility.
5. The terms 'rationality' and 'irrationality' in this chapter are employed in their neoclassical senses.
6. Another extreme case is a report by Montgomery (2011), issued by the Swedish Institute for European Policy. This is a reasonable introduction to crisis psychology but lacks vital discussions of the financial issues in the crisis and, above all, does not in any way deal with market levels in its reasoning.

REFERENCES

Acemoglu, D. (2009), 'The crisis of 2008: lessons for and from economics', *Critical Review*, **21** (2–3), 185–94.

Akerlof, George A. and Robert J. Shiller (2009), *Animal Spirits: How Human Psychology Drives the Economy and Why it Matters for Global Capitalism*, Princeton, NJ: University Press.

Allen, F., A. Babus and E. Carletti (2009), 'Financial Crisis: Theory and Evidence', *Annual Review of Financial Economics*, **1**, 97–116

Backhouse, Roger E. (2010), *The Puzzle of Modern Economics: Science or Ideology?* Cambridge: Cambridge University Press.

Ball, R. (2009), 'The global financial crisis and the efficient market hypothesis: what have we learned?' *Journal of Applied Corporate Finance*, **21** (4), 8–16.

Barberis, Nicholas C. and Richard H. Thaler (2003), 'A survey of behavioral finance', in G. Constantinides, M. Harris and R. Stulz (eds), *The Handbook of the Economics of Finance*, vol. 1B, Amsterdam, the Netherlands: North Holland Publishing, pp. 1051–121.

Bernstein, Peter L. (2005), *Capital Ideas: The Improbable Origins of Modern Wall Street*, New York: Wiley.

Black, Fischer (1971), 'Towards a fully automated stock exchange', *Financial Analysts Journal*, **27** (4), 28–35, 44.

Black, Fischer (1985), 'Noise', *Journal of Finance*, **41** (3), 529–43.

Cassidy, John (2010a), 'Interview with Richard Thaler', available at: www.newyorker.com/online/blogs/johncassidy/2010/01/interview-with-richard-thaler.html (accessed 22 February 2011).

Cassidy, John (2010b), 'Interview with Eugene Fama', available at: www.newyorker.com/online/blogs/johncassidy/2010/01/interview-with-eugene-fama.html (accessed 22 February 2011).

Chordia, T., R. Roll and A. Subrahmanyam (2007), 'Liquidity and market efficiency', *Journal of Financial Economics*, **87** (2), 249–68.

Cochrane, John H. (2009), 'How did Paul Krugman get it so wrong?', available at: http://faculty.chicagobooth.edu/john.cochrane/research/Papers/krugman_response.htm (accessed 20 November 2010).

Fama, E.F. (1965), 'The behavior of stock-market prices', *Journal of Business*, **38** (1), 34–105.

Fama, E.F. (1970), 'Efficient capital markets: a review on theory and empirical work', *Journal of Finance*, **25** (2), 383–417.

Fama, E.F. (1991), 'Efficient capital markets: II', *Journal of Finance*, **46** (5), 1575–617.

Fama, E.F. (2011), 'My life in finance', *Annual Review of Financial Economics*, **3**, 1–15.

Fehr, E. and J-R. Tyran (2005), 'Individual irrationality and aggregate outcomes', *Journal of Economic Perspectives*, **19** (4), 43–66.

Frankfurter, G.M. and E.G. McGuon (1999), 'Ideology and the theory of financial economics', *Journal of Economic Behavior & Organization*, **39**, 159–77.

Friedman, Milton (1953), 'The methodology of positive economics', in *Essays in Positive Economics*, Chicago, IL: Chicago University Press, pp. 3–43.

Hindriks, F. (2007), 'False models as explanatory engines', *Philosophy of the Social Sciences*, **38** (3), 334–60.

Jung, J. and Shiller, R.J. (2005), 'Samuelson's Dictum and the stock market', *Economic Inquiry*, **43** (2), 221–8.

Krugman, Paul (2009), 'How did economists get it so wrong?', available at: www.nytimes.com/2009/09/06/magazine/06Economic-t.html?pagewanted=all (accessed 20 November 2010).

Krugman, Paul (2011), 'The profession and the crisis', *Eastern Economic Journal*, **37**, 307–12.

Lo, Andrew W. (2007), 'Efficient market hypothesis', in L. Blume and S. Durlauf (eds), *The New Palgrave: A Dictionary of Economics*, 2nd edn, Basingstoke: Palgrave Macmillan.

Lo, Andrew W. (2012), 'Reading about the financial crisis: a 21-book review', *Journal of Economic Literature*, **50** (1), 151–78

Lucas, Robert E. (1978), 'Asset prices in an exchange economy', *Econometrica*, **46**, 6, 1429–45.

MacKenzie, Douglas (2006), *An Engine, Not a Camera: How Financial Models Shape Markets*, Cambridge, MA: MIT Press.

Mäki, Uskali (ed.) (2009), *The Methodology of Positive Economics: Reflections on the Milton Friedman Legacy*, Cambridge: Cambridge University Press.

Malkiel, B.G. (2003), 'The efficient market hypothesis and its critics', *Journal of Economic Perspectives*, **17** (1), 59–82.

Montgomery, H. (2011), 'The financial crisis – lessons for Europe from psychology', SIEPS Report 2011:1.

Pesaran, M.H. (2006), 'Market efficiency today', CFS working paper no. 2006/01.
Preda, A. (2007), 'The sociological approach to financial markets', *Journal of Economic Surveys*, **21** (3), 506–33.
Ross, D. (2010), 'Should the financial crisis inspire normative revision?', *Journal of Economic Methodology*, **17** (4), 399–418.
Samuelson, P.A. (2009), 'An enjoyable life puzzling over modern finance theory', *Annual Review of Financial Economics*, **1**, 19–35.
Shiller, R.J. (2003), 'From efficient markets theory to behavioral finance', *Journal of Economic Perspectives*, **17** (1), 83–104
Tobin, J. (1984), 'On the efficiency of the financial system', *Lloyds Bank Review*, 153, 1–15
Turner, J.A. (2009), 'The Turner Review: a regulatory response to the global banking crisis', London: Financial Services Authority, publication no. 003289, March.

4. Macroeconomics after the crisis: bringing finance back in

Robert Boyer

> I am far from denying that in our system equilibrium analysis has a useful function to perform. But when it comes to the point where it misleads some of our leading thinkers into believing that the situation which it describes has direct relevance to the solution of practical problems, it is high time that we remember that it does not deal with the social process at all and that it is no more than a useful preliminary to the study of the main problem.
>
> Friedrich von Hayek, 'The use of knowledge in society', *American Economic Review*, **35** (4), 519–30 (1945)

> In this paper I argue that the current core of macroeconomics – by which I mainly mean the so-called dynamic stochastic general equilibrium approach – has become so mesmerized with its own internal logic that it has begun to confuse the precision it has achieved about its own world with the precision that it has about the real one. This is dangerous for both methodological and policy reasons. On the methodology front, macroeconomic research has been in 'fine-tuning' mode within the local-maximum of the dynamic stochastic general equilibrium world, when we should be in 'broad-exploration' mode. We are too far from absolute truth to be so specialized and to make the kind of confident quantitative claims that often emerge from the core. On the policy front, this confused precision creates the illusion that a minor adjustment in the standard policy framework will prevent future crises, and by doing so it leaves us overly exposed to the new and unexpected.
>
> Ricardo J. Caballero, 'Macroeconomics after the crisis: time to deal with the pretense-of-knowledge syndrome', *Journal of Economic Perspectives*, **24** (4), 85–102 (October 2010).

1. INTRODUCTION

As time has passed since September 2008, the costs, the severity and the uncertainty about the way out of the present crisis have been clearly recognized by every analyst and observer. Reference to the Great Depression has become more and more frequent, since the macroeconomic patterns observed do not fit with the post-Second-World-War typical business cycles. This is a matter of concern not only for policymakers but also for financial economists as well as macroeconomists. According to the modelling of risk by the former, a financial crash of this amplitude was supposed to happen with only an infinitesimal probability. The macroeconomic basic model elaborated by central banks was used to analyse the impact of interest rate policy directly upon the real economy without any intermediation via the financial system. After a few years of benign neglect by economists, the pressure of policymakers as well as informed public opinion, the profession has now to recognize that 'Something may well have gone wrong.'

One official now dares to state:

> I believe that during the last financial crisis, macroeconomists (and I include myself among them) failed the country, and indeed the world. In September 2008, central bankers were in desperate need of a playbook that offered a systematic plan of attack to deal with fast-evolving circumstances. Macroeconomists should have been able to provide that playbook. They could not. Of course, from a longer view, macroeconomists let policymakers down much earlier, because they did not provide policymakers with rules for avoiding the circumstances that led to the global financial meltdown. (Kocherlakota, 2010)

This chapter proposes to substantiate this hypothesis and to show that the present poor performance of macro theory dates back to the foundation of this discipline as distinct from microeconomic analysis. This is an invitation to economists to be more reflexive in their daily practice. The fundamentally deductive, if not axiomatic, method inherited from general equilibrium theory has been adopted by real business cycle (RBC) and dynamic stochastic general equilibrium (DSGE) models, but with far less rigour. It has shown its limits in removing from theorizing quite crucial and robust mechanisms linking finance and the real economy. It is more and more difficult to maintain that a simple and single model can capture the multiplicity of the links exhibited within more and more complex financial instruments.

Another methodological choice relates to the degree of adequacy of the modelling: is the objective to build a generic workhorse valid for successive bubbles or is the ambition to enlighten the specificity of the subprime crisis? Finally among this entire continent of pluralism of possible representations of a given complex economy, this chapter argues in favour of an institutionally and historically grounded approach to macroeconomics and proposes a specific modelling of finance-led contemporary accumulation regimes. A short conclusion puts into perspective these various proposals that share a common inspiration: *macroeconomists have to take seriously finance and its contemporary transformations.*

2. FROM THE *GENERAL THEORY* TO DSGE MODELS: A BIRD'S-EYE VIEW OF HALF A CENTURY OF MACROECONOMIC THEORIZING

The *General Theory* proposed three breakthroughs: the need and possibility of analysing *economic aggregates*, the concept of *involuntary employment* as distinct from any labour market friction and the crucial role of *financial markets* in the emergence of the conventions that shape expectations of firms facing *radical uncertainty*. The reluctance of John Maynard Keynes about modelling has led to a canonical formalization of his too complex and diverse ideas by John Hicks: the IS-LM (investment-savings–liquidity-money) model has focused upon a new mechanism of transmission of monetary policy to economic activity but it has bypassed Keynes's rich and fundamental analysis of finance and especially of the stock market. When the relevance of this model is challenged by the surge of inflation and then stagflation, the monetarist backlash is only the first step in the rehabilitation of microeconomics as the only starting point for any macroanalysis (Figure 4.1).

The forward-looking strategy of agents is central for real business cycle (RBC) models but it is associated with a quite paradoxical conception of the Walrasian message: a representative agent knows the deterministic part of the national economy that is fully adjusting only via price variations. Then the long-term equilibrium for the relative prices is only transitorily affected by shocks concerning the money supply. The worm is already in the fruit: the representative-agent hypothesis is a 'coup de force' against one of the major findings of general equilibrium theory and money is again a pure veil. Therefore finance is inessential since it only adjusts preferences with technical possibilities without any proper role for intermediation. Basically, recessions, even the Great Depression, are the efficient reactions to an adverse and very large productivity shock. Furthermore, state interventions can only delay necessary adjustments and private agents fully understand the consequence of the inter-temporal budgetary constraint of the state: they will not spend more if their taxes are reduced today because they know that they will increase tomorrow. Farewell to Keynes: the economy is self-regulating, and thus 'Governments are the problem not the solution.'

The only counterattack by opponents to this statement was to bring back a hypothesis put forward by disequilibrium theory but which had been defeated by market fundamentalism: the inertia in wages due to overlapping negotiations and oligopolistic price formation may give some room for an impact of budgetary policy on real activity. This new synthesis embedded into various variants of dynamic stochastic general equilibrium (DSGE) models has been adopted by most central banks. This framework, very flexible since calibration has frequently replaced econometric estimation, has given them a sense of unprecedented scientific foundations for their action. Their neglect of the recurring bubbles that have been more and more intense is the direct consequence of this vision, according to which the central bank has a direct dialogue with firms and households in order to convince them that inflation, measured by a consumer price index, is under control – no matter if a shadow banking system is pushing the price of assets by an explosion of leverage effects and thus feeds an unsustainable economic boom. Actually, within canonical DSGE models, implicitly the financial markets are informationally efficient and they redistribute the risks all over the world to the agents more able to bear them.

If one agrees with this brief retrospective, the present epoch is undergoing *two interrelated crises*: the financialization of most modern economies, now in trouble, has not been accompanied by an equivalent alertness of macroeconomists about the impact of these structural changes. The public authorities have until now prevented the repetition of the Great Depression but they navigate on uncharted waters. A huge research agenda is now opening for macroeconomists. It is time to reconcile macromodelling with the teachings of the history of financial crises and this requires taking a symmetrical account of the real and financial components of contemporary economies.

3. MACROECONOMIC THEORY AND HISTORICAL TRANSFORMATIONS OF CAPITALISM

Building macroeconomic models that would take finance into account is not only a matter of new econometric techniques and data sets, however important they might be. Clearly, if financial entities keep private any information about their net position on various markets, regulatory agencies will be unable to detect any coming systemic crisis. But modelling is also an epistemological and methodological issue. The last decade has experienced the triumph and then intellectual collapse of the conventional way of doing macroeconomics. Other approaches are possible.

3.1 Charm and Misery of the Axiomatic Approach

The DSGE approach is not without merits. It starts from a very general neo-Walrasian vision, it has attracted a lot of researchers and generated cumulativeness in dealing with the impact of monetary policy, and, finally,

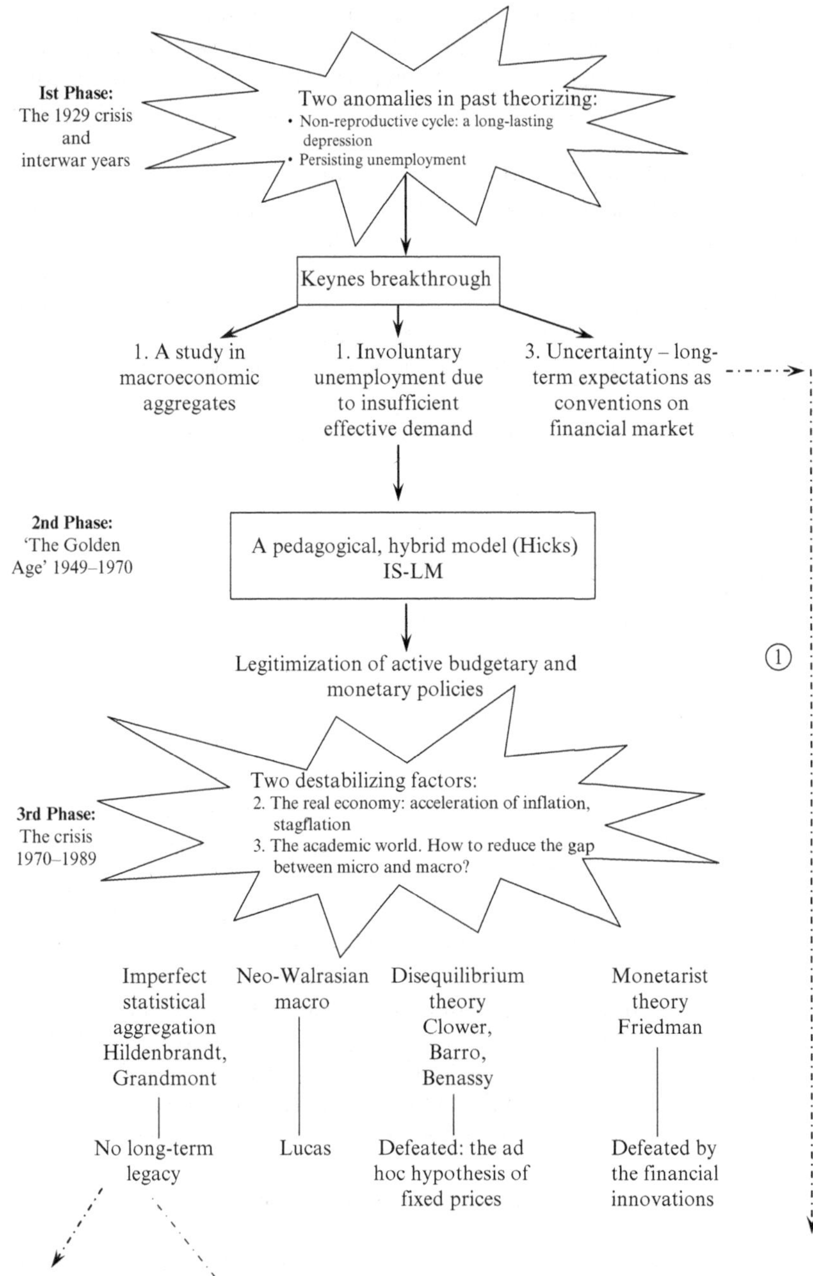

Figure 4.1 A bird's-eye view of half a century in macroeconomic theorizing

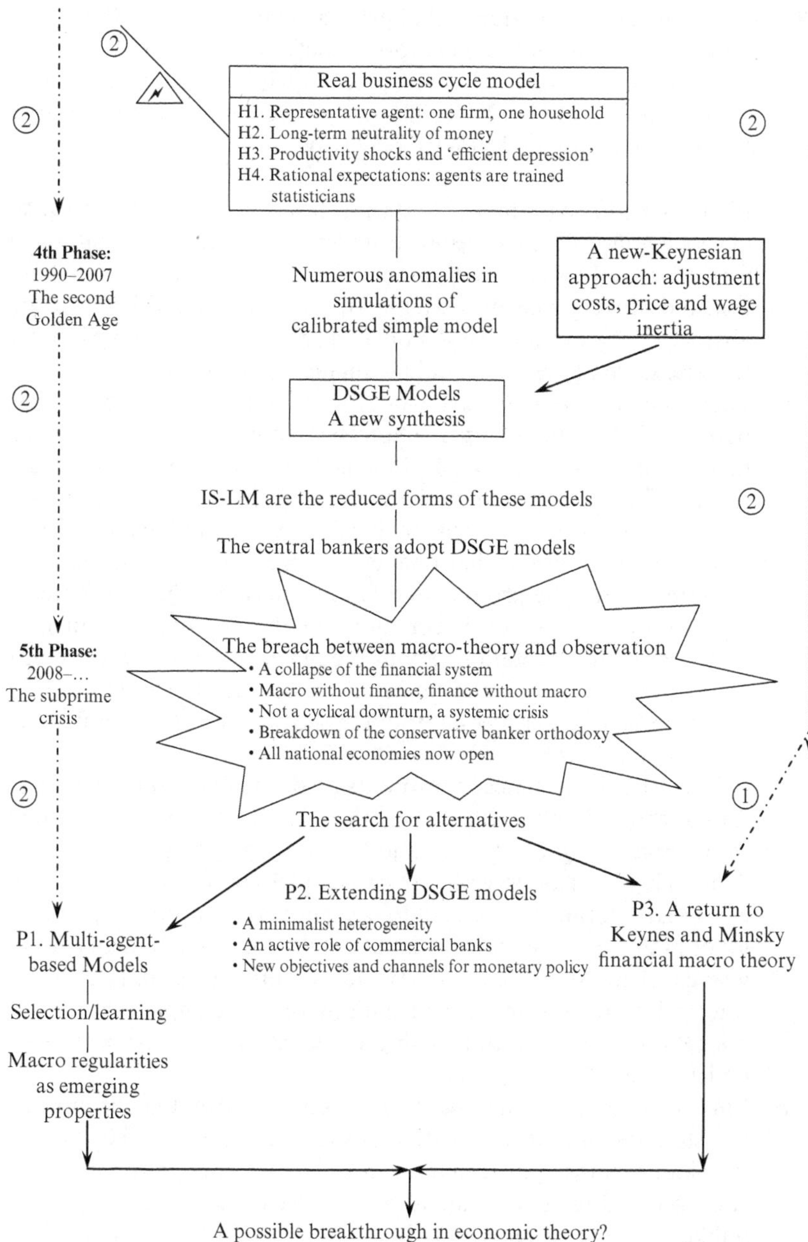

Figure 4.1 (continued)

the calibration and stimulation techniques have made possible the exploration of many variants of the same core model.

But the other side of the coin is most preoccupying indeed: these models were unable to anticipate the 2008 collapse and even to provide afterwards a satisfactory explanation of it (Wieland 2010).

- First, it is rather paradoxical to start from a *general equilibrium model* in which none of the stylized facts under review can be present, since it assumes full employment, money neutrality in the medium–long run, and convergence toward a long-term equilibrium. Therefore the absence of any cycle and still more of any speculative bubble is not a surprise since money is the unique financial instrument.
- Therefore, only *imperfections* can explain the existence of cycles and bubbles. Should these imperfections be removed, all the contemporary problems should vanish. But then, how to explain the recurrence of financial crises since the seventeenth century, even in epochs when nominal prices were highly flexible? More fundamentally, it is misleading to consider that financial markets suffer from the same imperfection as the product and labour markets. The existence of asymmetric information is common but the originality of finance is to deal with expectations about the intertemporal flow of return on a given asset. Risk and uncertainty prevent the formation of a single stable long-term equilibrium in the absence of a complete set of future markets.
- Frequently, the technical constraints associated with any analytical formalization imply a selection of the related hypotheses according to the *principle of tractability* and the ability to compute a reduced form. This is at odds with the choice of hypothesis according to empirical relevance. One could accuse mainstream macroeconomics of preferring aesthetics to empirical relevance (Krugman, 2009), whereas here the fidelity to Walrasian principles and technical tractability are the main explanations of the complete failure of the DSGE model in anticipating or diagnosing the present crisis (Wieland 2010).
- Finally, *calibration and simulation* are more frequent than econometric estimates and the falsification of successive models. The name of the game seems to prove that the model is rich enough to reproduce some stylized facts, with an ad hoc stochastic hypothesis, however unlikely are the parameters required to mimic historical series. This rebuttal of Karl Popper's celebrated falsification principle might well be crucial in explaining the progressive autonomization of the DSGE research programme with respect to real-world economies.

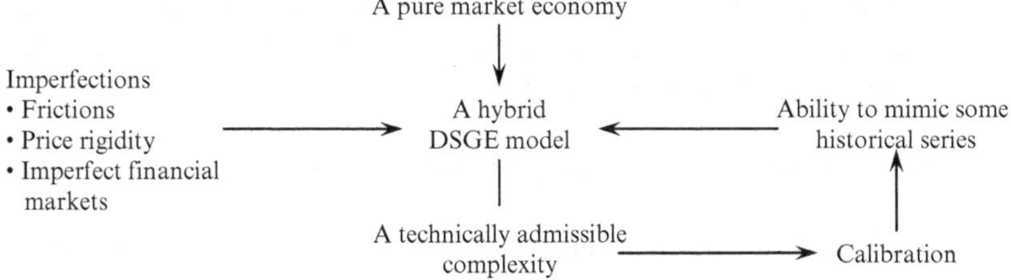

Figure 4.2 The deductive/axiomatic approach

Figure 4.2 summarizes the above discussion.

3.2 A Revival of the Classical/Keynes Methodology

There is thus room for an alternative conception of the role of theory and modelling (Colander 2009, 2010). Since economic interactions are multifaceted and more and more complex, along with the deepening of the division of labour and organizational and institutional innovations, economists might build *a multiplicity of models* supposed to be representative of the same economy. The *theoretical background*, the *specialization* in some techniques or subdisciplines, the *institutional position* of the economist, and finally their *ideological preferences* open up a large variety of macroeconomic models.

- The aim of the model might be typically academic and concern the tentative explanation of *one or several stylized facts*. Ideally, the same model should explain the largest possible number of them, but the parsimony principle is quite difficult to comply with in economics. A second source of modelling is related to *problem-solving*. For instance, how should the central bank adapt its monetary policy in response to a new wave of productive or financial innovations?
- The macroeconomist is entitled to select, from among the *many mechanisms* linking finance to the real economy, the ones he considers more important and robust. Given the fragility of econometric tests, the community of macroeconomists may propose a whole spectrum of models.
- Nevertheless, for a given line of macromodelling, the econometric tests should be taken seriously in Popper's sense. A model that fails after several thousand variants and estimates should be *rejected*. Some of its technical or economic hypotheses should be *changed* and a new cycle of modelling, testing and simulations should be

undertaken. The pursuit of such a rigorous strategy could deliver, in the medium–long run, a *better adequacy* between macromodels and observed macroeconomic patterns.

3.3 Institutionally and Historically Grounded Macroeconomics

But there is a third way between the culture of a single canonical model and the belief that 'everything goes', i.e. an endless list of equally valid and likely models. It is built upon the rebuttal of Milton Friedman's 'as if' hypothesis: no matter how unrealistic are the hypotheses, this does not matter provided they deliver interesting and likely results. In between these two extreme strategies, the founding hypotheses of macromodelling can be justified by the careful observation of the core institutions that shape individual and collective behaviours. This is the central message of the new institutional economics (North 1990; Aoki 2002). The rules of the game associated with the prevailing constitutional order, institutions and organizations define simultaneously constraints and incentives that shape economic behaviours. Macroeconomics is not an exception. The likelihood of the fit of the prediction of the theory with the observations is enhanced when the economist is deducing logical consequences out of an adequate abstraction of really existing institutions. For instance, when credit money is endogenously created by banks, if an oligopolistic competition prevails among them, if wages are determined by a series of overlapping negotiations and if a free mobility of international capital is moving the exchange rate, there can be no doubt that the financial and macroeconomic cycles will have a specific pattern.

This approach in macroeconomic modelling has been developed by regulation theory in order to understand the breaking down of macroeconomic regularities at the end of the 1960s (Boyer and Saillard 2001). Five core institutional forms are shaping short-run adjustment as well as the growth regime: the form of competition, the configuration of labour market institutions, the organization of the monetary and financial systems, the style of interventions of the state into the domestic economy and finally the mode of insertion of any national economy into the international relations (Figure 4.3). For each precise configuration of these institutional forms, prices, wages, interest rates and exchange rates exhibit definite regularities. A coherent mode of regulation may or may not exist but in any case the continuous slow transformations of these institutional forms generally lead, after two or three decades, to a major crisis during which the structural stability of the regulation mode is vanishing.

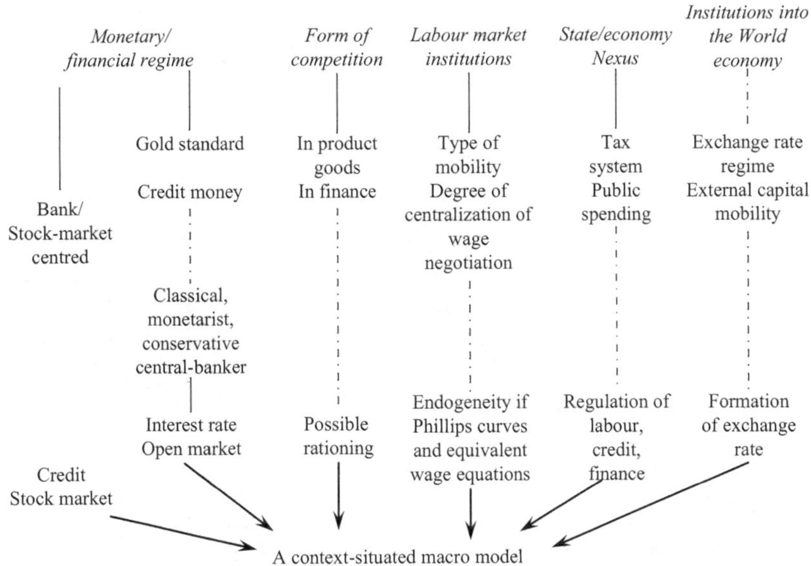

Figure 4.3 An institutionally grounded macromodelling: a given configuration of a capitalist economy

3.4 Towards an Institutional Macro Theory of Finance: a First Step

The recent advances in the field of this theory have pointed out that the coherence of a macro regime does not derive from chance and/or from a miraculous mix of *ex ante* independent institutional forms but from their co-evolution, from their complementarity or from the hierarchical domination of one of them. Since the mid-1980s, the dynamism of finance has progressively transformed the whole economic system, especially in countries such as the US and the UK that play a determinant role in international financial intermediation. Nowadays, there is an emerging consensus among macroeconomists about this dominance of finance. Let us mention some of the empirical evidence.

- Until the mid-1980s, credit was increasing nearly at the same rate for each entity: non-financial firms, households, investment banks. But with the rise of pension funds, financial liberalization and the multiplicity of financial innovations, the explosion of credit that took place afterwards has mainly been given to security brokers and dealers (Figure 4.4). Conventional wisdom tells us that households have been the centre of this structural change. Nevertheless, the

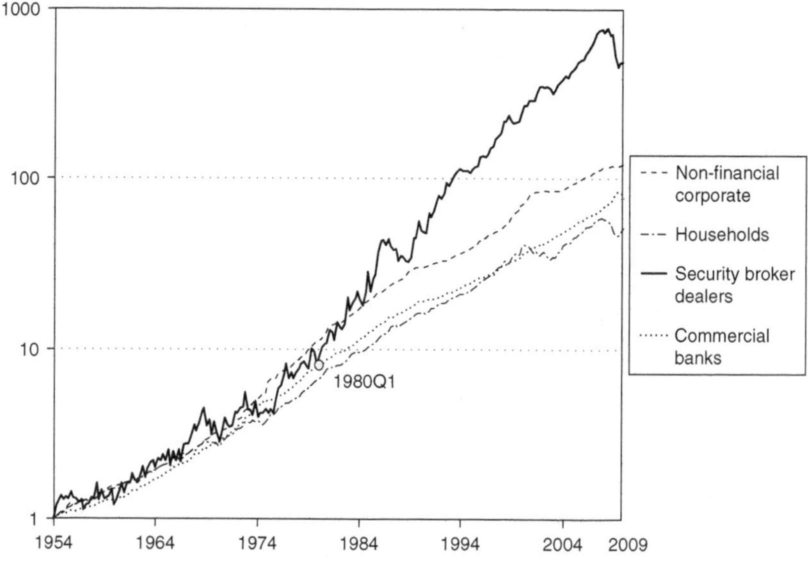

Source: Federal Reserve, Flow of Funds, 1954–2009.

Figure 4.4 Growth of assets of four sectors in the United States (March 1954 = 1) (log scale)

empirical evidence shows that in the US the access to credit has been a compensating mechanism for the slow growth of household wealth (Figure 4.5) and income. By contrast, the financiers themselves, the so-called shadow banking system, have been the main beneficiary of the credit boom: by a continuous rise of leverage effects they have been expanding their total assets at an unprecedented rate (Figure 4.6). The financial fragility affected neither the non-financial firms nor the majority of households but the financial system itself. Thus, any relevant model of the present crisis should deal explicitly with a quite detailed description of financial flows.

Three items of empirical evidence of an internally generated financial crisis (*Source:* Adrian and Shin, 2010)

- The related changes were not only quantitative – the continuous rise of the financial wealth/GDP ratio – since they were essentially qualitative. In the 1950s, the mortgage credit market was quite simple indeed: the deposits of some households were financing the mortgages of other households who were buying houses. Since the 1980s,

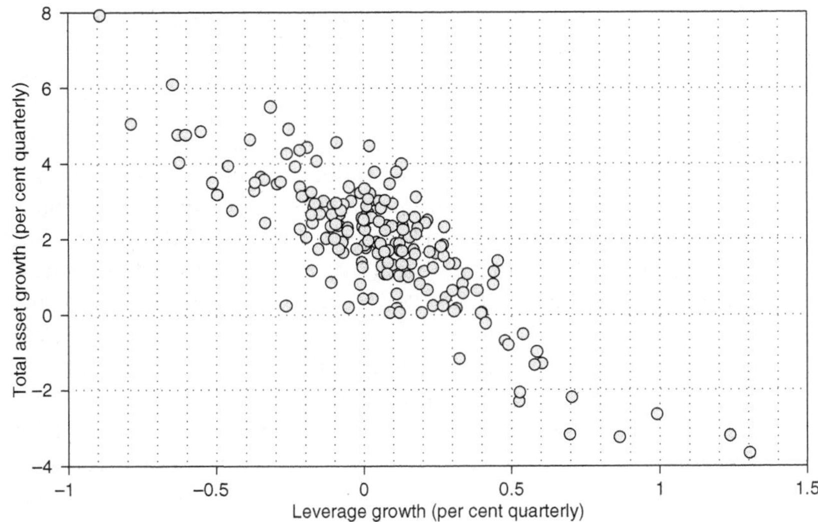

Source: US Flow of Funds, Federal Reserve, 1963–2007.

Figure 4.5 Household sector leverage and total assets

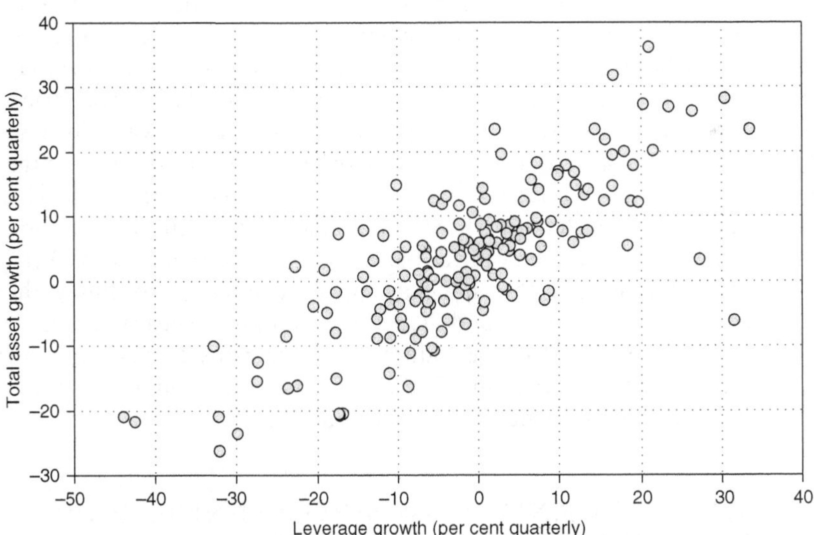

Source: US Flow of Funds, Federal Reserve, 1963–2007.

Figure 4.6 Broker dealer sector leverage and total assets

a myriad of financial intermediaries has permanently grown: this specialization has expressed an unprecedented division of labour with multiple interdependencies: the asset of one entity is the liability of another. A neo-Schumpeterian approach would stress that financial innovations have been much more dynamic than technological and organizational innovations in the productive system (Boyer 2008).

- If one adopts regulation theory method, these qualitative and quantitative transformations provide strong hints about the progressive domination of the financial system over absolutely all other institutional forms (Boyer 2000, 2010). The diffusion of shareholder value implies that the stock market is governing the investment and production strategies of firms. Consequently, labour management has to deliver a rather stable return on equity (RoE), with the welfare side, especially pension funds, relying more and more upon high rates of return. Last but not least, the central bank interacts continuously with the financial community and shapes their expectations. The evolution of the real economy is the consequence of these financial impulses and this is a novelty of the contemporary period. This is probably why many VAR models incorporating finance show that financial shocks have been crucial in the genesis of the present crisis (Lawrence et al. 2007; De Fiore and Tristani 2009).
- The understanding of the present crisis may of course build upon the general mechanisms put forward to analyse the previous crises. Nevertheless, the contemporary regime is so specific that one may have to design an ad hoc model in response to its idiosyncrasies. Productive investment is responding not only to variations in demand but also to the gap between the economic profit rate and the financial rate of return. Consumers take into account their financial and real-estate wealth when they decide about their consumption and investment. The central bank observes the financial markets, and consequently the monetary policy changes accordingly the short-term interest rate and the access to liquidity. The tax base itself becomes sensitive to the evolution of capital gains, however modest might be their taxation. Thus, a finance-led capitalism should display a genuine macroeconomic modelling.

4. SOME NEW AND PROMISING AVENUES FOR RESEARCH IN MACROECONOMICS

The research programme in the previous subsection is not the only one suggested by the present crisis. Let us mention briefly three others.

4.1 Formalizing the Resilience and Crisis of Financial Networks

The collapse of Lehman Brothers and AIG has shown that some financial entities were so big and so interconnected that their bankruptcy might be sufficient to provoke the meltdown of the entire American financial system, if not that of the world. This cannot be analysed in terms of nice supply and demand curves for financial assets. Instead, financial stability becomes a matter of network resilience and this general hypothesis is now recognized by experts in quantitative finance (Cont 2009) and by central bankers (Haldane 2009).

Some pioneering works already show the relevance of this approach (Gai and Kapadia 2010). Implicitly, models that adopt a representative-agent hypothesis for the banking system exclude a very important source of crisis: the collapse of one important bank even in the absence of any external macroeconomic shock. By contrast, really existing financial systems exhibit quite specific distributions in the size of banks and the number of their connections with other entities. The configuration of nodes, assets and liabilities may now become a discriminating factor in the dividing line between resilience and systemic fragility. Simulations of a simple system suggest that the influence of connectivity is strongly non-linear: very fragmented systems and, at the opposite, highly connected ones are the more resilient. On the contrary, moderately connected systems might be more sensitive to contagion and financial breakdown. What is the most convenient policy to counteract these tendencies? Again, simulations suggest that capital reserve ratios might be an efficient instrument.

Such formalization requires the transparency of financial transactions at a high level of disaggregation, and it is far from evident in the light-touch regulation regimes that were typical of pre-crisis institutional configurations. Had any public authority any precise information about the central role of AIG in credit default swaps (CDS) related to mortgage derivatives?

4.2 Adding Banks and the Real Economy into a Model Formalizing Stock Market Bubbles

The neo-Walrasian tradition continues to consider that any financial asset should quickly converge towards its fundamental value. Consequently, it is very difficult to generate stock market bubbles within a typical rational-choice model, and this is very detrimental to the understanding of the present crisis. Furthermore, within a historically and institutionally grounded macroeconomic analysis, the stock market was, and probably still is, the more fundamental market in contemporary finance-led capitalism. It is thus crucial to depart from conventional macroeconomics. Why not start from multi-agent-based models that endogenously generate speculative booms and their bursting? Experts in statistical physics (Sornette 2003; Bouchaud 2008) and some financial economists have proposed such models but they are only partial since they do not deal with the impact of macroeconomic evolutions upon stock markets and, conversely, the consequence of stock markets upon macroeconomic dynamics.

Thus, a possible modelling strategy would be the following. As a first step, develop the simplest possible formalization of the stock market with a distinction between productive firms, commercial banks and investment banks. Within a shareholder value economy, the credit strategy of commercial banks responds significantly to the signals of the stock market. Similarly, on the side of the demand of credit by productive firms, their quotation on the stock market is an important factor. Last but not least, the financial portfolio of households is sensitive to the evolution of the stock market, and individual decisions concerning consumption and housing react to perceived total wealth.

A priori, this integration of real economic activity into a large financial model could provide a quite complex but interesting approach to contemporary macroeconomic dynamics.

4.3 Learning and then Oblivion at the Micro and Institutional Level

Explaining the long-term *recurrence of financial crises* could be a last area for a quite different modelling. At the level of the banking system, detailed statistical investigations show that after a bankruptcy the expected probability of default is at first very high and overestimated. As time elapses this subjective probability continuously declines. After five or six years, individuals and organizations have totally forgotten this possibility of bankruptcy. Thus they take largely underestimated and growing risks by excess leverage. The brutal reversal of the situation is thus endogenous and a new cycle might begin, with new actors and new instruments. Nearly everybody is convinced that 'This time it is different.'

At the societal level, the same process of learning how to control finance is progressively forgotten. After two or three decades, authorities are convinced by powerful financiers that regulations are inefficient constraints. The deregulation is initially quite favourable since it removes the credit constraints, but the recurrence of more and more severe bubbles usually ends in a major structural crisis. It could be interesting to formalize the process of learning and lapse of memory by extending a model with overlapping generations of heterogeneous actors.

CONCLUSION

After this rather extensive but far from exhaustive survey, what are the perspectives for macroeconomic theorizing and modelling after the crisis? It might be useful to sum up some of the basic findings and proposals for future investigations.

The long-term history of financial crises, including the present one, displays both *stylized facts* and *specific features* that *cannot be derived* from the simulations generated by the numerous dynamic stochastic general equilibrium (DSGE) models, even the most innovative and recent ones. First, the financial cycles and bubbles are essentially *endogenous* and not at all the consequence of big and correlated productivity shocks. Second, a cluster of far-reaching innovations has extended the zone of *financial fragility*, especially in the US and the UK, two of the most advanced finance-led capitalisms. Third, the inefficiency of monetary policy when the viability of the banking system is uncertain points out the need for a detailed analysis of the *incentives and interactions* between various financial entities, including the shadow banking system. Fourth, a *confidence shock* about the resilience of the financial system may have specific and quite important impacts upon economic activity.

On top of these recurring patterns, the so-called subprime crisis has exhibited rather *specific new features*. It is now clear that the impulse of the September 2008 collapse took place inside the financial system itself: the excess of credit was devoted to the financing of the (speculative) activity of the shadow banking system. A complementary set of perverse incentives initiated and then propagated a quite unstable model based upon the principle 'originate and redistribute'. Not only was risk shifted far away from the informed agents, but each stage in the elaboration of derivatives was spoiling if not hiding the core information about the real solvency of initial credit-holders. The long chain between the initial mortgage credit and the final holder of the risk is evidence of an unprecedented deepening of the division of labour among commercial banks, money market funds, security firms, ABS originator companies, rating agencies, pension funds, insurance companies and so on. Logically, any relevant model should adopt a sufficiently detailed description of the financial system because it is not functioning at all as a simple appendix of the real economy.

The DSGE programme has been quite stimulated by all the anomalies and puzzles evidenced by the genesis and unfolding of the present crisis. Econometricians have extended the real-economy shocks to others affecting demand, the financial system and risk aversion: they have shown that they have exerted a significant impact on activity. The efficiency of monetary policy has been shown to depend crucially upon the degree of implementation of prudential regulation. This complementarity hypothesis challenges the previous conception of a totally autonomous monetary policy. It also stresses that one of the origins of the crisis is related to the surge of an uncontrolled and largely underscrutinized shadow banking system. Other researchers have taken into account the impact of a possible bankruptcy upon credit supply by commercial banks. It turns out that the related spread has a clear impact on economic activity on top of the normal transmission mechanisms via interest rates. Nevertheless, the neo-Walrasian theoretical inspiration of all these models is still limiting the amplitude of this *aggiornamento*: basically, the productivity shocks continue to be the primary mover of the real economy, and, ideally, finance should be a mere transmission mechanism. Furthermore, the convergence of asset prices towards their fundamental value continues to prevent the full understanding of financial market functioning, the recurrence of bubbles and their impact upon production and employment.

The bulk of the present chapter has thus been devoted to the presentation of various alternatives to the DSGE approach, via an extension of *evolutionary and institutionalist modelling*.

In retrospect, it is quite surprising that the Lucas critique of the IS-LM Keynesian model has rejuvenated the Walrasian tradition in macroeconomic theorizing, at the very moment when the researchers in general equilibrium theory (GET) recognized their inability to introduce rigorously the existence of money, the restrictive conditions warranting a dynamic process converging towards an equilibrium, and the incapacity of micro foundations to generate a well-behaved aggregate demand function. Still more paradoxically, the numerous pathologies generated by the absence of complete future-contingent markets should have prevented the naive extension of the Walrasian static model into a formalization of the intertemporal optimization of a representative agent. By contrast, a *first strategy* for reconstructing macroeconomics should begin with a precise *definition of economic and financial crises*: the freezing of financial transactions, the explosion of bankruptcies of financial and non-financial firms, the brutal and massive crash of the stock market. Such concepts should be carefully distinguished from the downward phase of a normal business cycle and the formalizing should be rich enough to allow such episodes to occur and favour dynamic models exhibiting non-ergodicity, i.e. the absence of convergence towards a pre-existing long-term equilibrium.

During the last two decades, the econometric research has made definite breakthroughs in the formalization of dynamic stochastic processes governing developed, as well as developing, economies. *A second strategy* is then to survey this enormous literature and to make explicit the more *robust mechanisms linking the financial system and the real economy*. Let us mention some of them: *procyclical risk-taking*, the importance of *credit rationing* for poor households and small to medium firms, the determinant role of *stock market* valuation within a finance-led regime and finally the dramatic impact of *radical uncertainty* when unprecedented shocks cannot be assessed by business employing the usual risk evaluation methods. Any relevant model should incorporate several or at least one of these features in order to possibly reproduce the pattern of *recurring financial bubbles*.

A third strategy builds upon the vast research programme concerned with *institutional economics* and its possible synergy with *evolutionary approaches*. One of the major advances of the former deals with the consequences of institutional hierarchy: a specific institutional form does permeate the organization of others and is influencing their transformations. Many analysts from quite distinct theoretical and ideological orientations do converge towards a common characterization of contemporary capitalism, especially in the US and the UK. Their economic regime would be finance-led, as opposed to the previous Fordist growth pattern in the US or export-led models in many Asian countries. According to this approach, the macroeconomic regularities cannot be explained without a full recognition of the domination of finance throughout the sphere of social and economic activity, at least in the US and UK. The CEOs look at the stock market and international finance when they decide production, investment, R&D, strategy and so on. Households take into account their real-estate and financial wealth when they make their decisions about consumption, saving and real-estate investment. In their credit decision, banks consider simultaneously their stock market valuation and the nature of the collateral provided by borrowers. Last but not least, the central banker, besides the inflation–employment dilemma, has now the task of trying to prevent financial instability and provide liquidity when a systemic financial crisis threatens the very existence of the payment system and the monetary economy. Such a research programme has two important consequences. First, each actor follows a fragmented and *institutional context-dependent rationality*, and macrodynamics might well be therefore the unintended consequence of the complex interactions of these quite diverse behaviours and embedded rationalities. Macromodelling should therefore be bottom-up, while taking into account the institutional architecture of the economy. Second, if the major institutional forms change, then the precise quantitative regularities observed at the macro level finally evolve along with these structural changes.

This chapter finally proposes a quite specific agenda for future research.

- In order to challenge the temptation encountered in most conventional economic theorizing to make finance a simple appendix of the real economy, it could be enlightening to start from the headquarters of contemporary economies, i.e. the *stock market and its bubbles*. Then there could be deduced the strategy of the commercial and investment banks, the demand for credit by firms and households. Finally, the objectives of the central bank and the degree of freedom of budgetary and tax policy are also financially constrained.
- A quasi-Copernician revolution would replace the idealization of supply and demand in potentially transparent financial markets by the modelling of financial actors via a typical *network analysis*. Then, given the concentration and/or distribution of assets and liabilities, the formalization of possible domino effects could attempt to diagnose the dividing line between *resilient* economic and financial systems and *unstable and crisis-prone* economies.
- Why have *bubbles recurrently emerged, matured and burst* over nearly three centuries? Should not fully rational actors learn from this history and change their behaviour in order to prevent the repetition of such dramatic episodes? A possible explanation is that financiers, non-financial firms, households and governments undergo a learning process when crises burst out and actually change their behaviours, organizations and institutions in the immediate aftermath of the crisis. Nevertheless, they progressively forget that they may go bankrupt, because they become confident that they have begun a new epoch, where past regularities are no more valid. They then take risks they are unaware of, until they generate another major crisis that calls for the return to a more realistic appraisal of risk. The contemporary actors usually forget the lessons learnt by their ancestors and a new long-term cycle may begin. A stimulating research agenda would be to discover the pattern followed by such a process by a close interaction between the macro level of bank management and the global one, where the rules of the game are elaborated, changed and reformed.

The Great Depression of the 1930s triggered a vigorous and multifaceted *aggiornamento* of economic theorizing. In spite of a stronger institutional path-dependency in academia, one may hope that this will also be the case for the 2010s.

REFERENCES

Adrian, Tobias and Hyun Song Shin (2010), 'The changing nature of financial intermediation and the financial crisis of 2007–2008', staff report no. 439, Federal Reserve Bank of New York, March–April, pp. 6–10, 11.

Amendola, Mario and Jean-Louis Gaffard (1988), *The Innovation Choice: An Economic Analysis of the Dynamics of Technology*, Oxford: Blackwell.

Aoki, Masahiko (2002), *Toward a Comparative Institutional Analysis*, Cambridge, MA: MIT Press.

Benassy, Jean-Pascal (1982), *The Economics of Market Disequilibrium*, Boston, MA: Academic Press.

Bernanke, Ben, Mark Gertler and Simon Gilchrist (1999), 'The financial accelerator in a quantitative business cycle framework', in J.B. Taylor and M. Woodford (eds), *Handbook of Macroeconomics*, Amsterdam, the Netherlands: Elsevier.

Bloom, Nicholas (2009), 'The impact of uncertainty shocks', *Econometrica*, **77** (3), 623–85.

Bouchaud, Jean-Philippe (2008), 'Economics needs a scientific revolution', *Physics. so-ph*, 29 October.

Boyer, Robert (2000), 'Is a finance-led growth regime a viable alternative to Fordism? A preliminary analysis', *Economy and Society*, **29** (1), 111–45.

Boyer, Robert (2008), *History Repeating for Economists: An Anticipated Financial Crisis*, Prisme no. 13, November, Cournot Centre for Economic Research, Paris, available at: www.centrecournot.org/prismepdf/Prisme_13_EN.pdf.

Boyer, Robert (2010), 'The rise of CEO pay and the contemporary social structure of accumulation in the United States', in Terrence McDonough, Michael Reich and David M. Kotz (eds), *Contemporary Capitalism and Its Crises: Social Structure of Accumulation Theory for the 21st Century*, New York: Cambridge University Press, pp. 215–38.

Boyer, Robert and Yves Saillard (2001), *Regulation Theory: The State of Art*, London: Routledge.

Brender, Anton (1982), *Socialisme et cybernétique*, Paris: Economica.

Caballero, Ricardo (2010), 'Macroeconomics after the crisis: time to deal with the pretense-of-knowledge syndrome', *Journal of Economic Perspectives*, **24** (4), 85–102

Challe, Edouard, Le Grand F. and Xavier Ragot (2010), Incomplete markets, liquidation risk, and the term structure of interest rates, Paris School of Economics (PSE) working paper.

Challe, Edouard and Xavier Ragot (2010), 'Precautionary saving in the business cycle', mimeograph Banque de France, July.

Challe, Edouard and Xavier Ragot (2011), 'Fiscal policy in a tractable liquidity-constrained economy', *Economic Journal*, March, **121** (551), 273–317.

Colander, David (2009), 'The Keynesian method, complexity, and the training of economists', Mimeograph prepared for the 1st Bi-Annual Symposium of the Thomas Guggenheim Program in the History of Economic Thought, 'Perspectives on Keynesian Economics', Ben Gurion University, Beersheba, Israel, 14–15 July.

Colander, David (2010), Testimony of David Colander, submitted to the Congress of the United States, House Science and Technology Committee, 20 July.

Cont, Rama (2009), 'Risques financiers: quelle modélisation mathématique?' *Pour la Science*, no. 375, January, 25.
De Fiore, Fiorella and Oreste Tristani (2009), 'Optimal monetary policy in a model of the credit channel', working paper series European Central Bank, no. 1043, April, Frankfurt am Main, Germany.
Fisher, Irwin (1933), 'The debt-deflation theory of great depressions', *Econometrica*, **1** (4), 337–57.
Gai Prasanna, and Sujit Kapadia (2010), 'Contagion in financial networks', Bank of England working paper no. 383, March.
Goodwin, R.M. (1967), 'A model of growth cycle', in C.H. Feinstein (ed.), *Socialism, Capitalism and Economic Growth*, Cambridge: Cambridge University Press.
Haldane, Andrew G. (2009), 'Rethinking the financial network', mimeograph, Bank of England, speech delivered at the Financial Student Association, Amsterdam, the Netherlands, April.
Hayek, Friedrich (1945), 'The use of knowledge in society', *American Economic Review*, **35** (4), 519–30.
Keynes, John Maynard (1930), *Treatise on Money*, London: Macmillan.
Keynes, John Maynard (1936), *The General Theory of Employment, Interest and Money*, London: Macmillan.
Knight, Frank Hynemann (1921), *Risk, Uncertainty and Profit*, New York: Harper & Row.
Kobayashi, Keiichiro and Masakazu Inaba (2002), 'Japan's lost decade and the complexity externality', RIETI Discussion Paper Series (02-E-004), Research Institute of International Trade and Industry, available at: www.rieti.go.jp/jp/publications/dp/02e004.pdf.
Kocherlakota, Narayana (2010), 'Modern macroeconomics models as tools for economic policy', May, available at: www.mineapolisfed.org/publications_papers/pub_display.cfm?id=4428.
Krugman, Paul (1979), A model of balance of payments crises', *Journal of Money, Credit, and Banking*, **11** (3), 311–25.
Krugman, Paul (1999), 'Balance sheets, the transfer problem and financial crises', in Peter Isard, Assaf Razin and Andrew K. Rose (eds), *International Finance and Financial Crises: Essays in Honor of Robert P. Flood, Jr.*, Washington, DC: International Monetary Fund.
Krugman, Paul (2001), 'Crises: the next generation?', Razin Conference, Tel Aviv University, Israel, 25–26 March, available at: http://econ.tau.ac.il/research/sapir/Krugman.pdf.
Krugman, Paul (2009), 'How did economists get it so wrong?', *New York Times*, 2 September.
Lawrence, Christiano, Roberto Motto and Massimo Rostagno (2007), 'Financial factors in business cycles', mimeograph, European Central Bank, 23 November.
Markopolos, Harry (2005), 'The world's largest hedge fund is a fraud', in Amir Weitman (ed.) (2009), *L'Affaire Madoff*, Paris: Plon.
Marx, Karl (1867), *Le Capital*, réédition, Paris: Folio Essais.
Minsky, Hyman P. (1974), 'The modeling of financial instability: an introduction', *Modeling and Simulation*, proceedings of the fifth Annual Pittsburg Conference.
Minsky, Hyman P. (1975), *John Maynard Keynes*, New York: Columbia University Press.

Minsky, Hyman (1982a), *Can 'It' Happen Again? Essays on Instability and Finance*, New York: Sharpe.

Minsky, Hyman (1982b), 'The financial instability hypothesis: capitalism processes and the behavior of the economy', in Charles Kindleberger and Jean-Pierre Laffargue (eds), *Financial Crises: Theory, History, and Policy*, Cambridge: Cambridge University Press.

Minsky, Hyman (1985), 'Structure financière, endettement et crédit', in Alain Barrère (ed.), *Keynes aujourd'hui, theorie et politique*, Paris: Economica.

Nomaler, Önder, Alessandro Nuvolari and Bart Verspagen (2010), 'Schumpeter and Keynes: the way forward for the macroeconomic debate', mimeograph plenary paper for the International Schumpeter Society Conference 2010 on Innovation, Organisation, Sustainability and Crises, Aalborg, 21–24 June.

North, Douglas C. (1990), *Institutions, Institutional Change and Economic Performance*, Cambridge and New York: Cambridge University Press.

Orlean, André (1989), 'Mimetic contagion and speculative bubbles', *Theory and Decision*, **27** (1–2), 63–92.

Schumpeter, Joseph (1911), *Théorie de l'évolution économique: recherche sur le profit, le crédit, l'intérêt et le cycle de la conjoncture*, Paris: Dalloz.

Shiller, Robert (2000), *Irrational Exuberance*, Princeton, NJ: Princeton University Press.

Sornette, Didier (2003), *Why Stock Markets Crash: Critical Events in Complex Financial Systems*, Princeton, NJ: Princeton University Press.

Stiglitz, Joseph E. and Bruce Greenwald (2003), *Towards a New Paradigm in Monetary Economics*, Cambridge: Cambridge University Press.

Taylor, Lance and Stephen O'Connell (1985), 'A Minsky Crisis', *Quarterly Journal of Economics*, **100** (Suppl.), 871–85.

Wieland, Volker (2010), 'Model comparison and robustness: a proposal for policy analysis after the financial crisis', working paper, Goethe University, Frankfurt, 28 November.

Weil, Philippe (1989), 'Increasing returns and animal spirits', *American Economic Review*, **79** (4), 889–94.

Wicksell, Knut (1898), *Interest and Price*, London: Royal Economic Society.

5. Discursive strategies in economic texts

Jan Svensson

The international financial crisis that burst out with the fall of Lehman Brothers in September 2008 was of course first and foremost a real-life crisis for individuals, groups of people, enterprises, institutions and nation states. Many people lost their jobs and had to leave their homes. Enterprises had to close down. Banks were given huge subsidies in order to keep the economic system going, and some nation states were brought to the edge of bankruptcy. These are facts that have to be acknowledged by everyone. But the financial crisis was also a discursive construction, brought about by countless texts by authors who from different perspectives and with a myriad of different aims proposed descriptions, explanations and consequences in order to position themselves and their interests in the most favourable way. What we meet in the texts – no matter what texts we choose to analyse – are reflections of these social constructions. Thus it is reasonable to engage not only in social, historic or economic analyses of the crisis, but also in analyses of the texts related to the crisis – that is, to do discourse analysis. This chapter is an example of that, with focus on the discursive patterns in texts from the Swedish public sphere.

One group of texts that could be of interest are media news texts – that is, texts spread by newspapers and radio and television companies as well as by different internet sites. However, these texts are to some extent rather predictable; the logic of the news media forces the text producers to exaggerate and look for the most dramatic angle. There is not much room for afterthought. In an analysis of the German public debate on the financial crisis, as it is reflected in *Die Zeit*, Fuchs and Graf (2010) show that some of the most common themes are drama and perplexity. They also notice the total lack of 'a vision of more fundamental political changes, an impetus to think outside the box' (Fuchs and Graf 2010, p. 30).

A possible question to pose is what happens when one changes the focus from the dramatized media coverage to less conspicuous accounts. There is an economic discourse going on independent of the recurring crises and independent of the media coverage. Perhaps one could even talk about an order of discourse (see Fairclough 1992) concerning economic matters. To what extent is this order of discourse affected by the events of the crisis? What happens to the textual strategies used? Do the authors change their strategies, or do they connect with established patterns of expression?

Thus, instead of concentrating on the media coverage, I have chosen to look at texts of different kinds that are mainly produced not in order to attract attention but instead keep a distance both from the subject matter and from the audience and where at least a certain amount of reflection could be expected. There are of course a very large number of texts that fit this description, but I have concentrated on texts that are produced by actors who do not primarily perform in the media, but who have professional reasons to articulate their respective notions in public. In this study, texts produced by the following four general categories of people have been considered:

1. Governmental officials, who have to formulate texts that are in accordance with the political aims of the government.
2. Economic analysts in public institutions, who likewise must be meta-reflexive but who must make considerations according to their tasks and the interests of their employers.
3. Researchers and scholars, for example economists, who have good professional reasons to relate meta-reflexively to the crisis, but who, whether they want it or not, will be affected by the theoretical frame in which they work.
4. Representatives of the dominating political parties, who have to formulate texts that are in accordance with the political aims of their party organizations.

A comprehensive study of texts by authors from these four categories would have required a vast corpus and extensive research efforts, neither of which has been available in this case. Instead I have gathered a small sample of texts in order to show what might possibly be found in a large-scale study. From texts by authors falling within category 1, I have chosen the governmental bills on the Swedish state budget for the years 2007–10, henceforth the *Financial Plan*. From among those emanating from category 2, I have chosen the reports from the board of Sveriges Riksbank (the Bank of Sweden), concerning financial stability in 2008–09, henceforth the *Stability Report*. The texts from these two categories are chosen so that it is possible to say something about changes over time. From the works by authors within category 3, I have chosen two texts from an issue of the Swedish journal *Ekonomisk Debatt* that was devoted to the crisis and its consequences. The authors are the prominent economists Torben

M. Andersen and Magnus Flodén, henceforth TMA and MF respectively. From writings originated by persons in category 4, I have chosen two speeches given in the Swedish parliament in October 2008 by the two most important party representatives, namely the Prime Minister Fredrik Reinfeldt and the then chair of the Social Democratic Party, Mona Sahlin, henceforth FR and MS respectively. The texts from categories 3 and 4 do not allow any conclusions about textual development, but serve to show how the crisis is handled in a specific situation.

Texts do not appear in a vacuum. A text (any text), whether spoken or written, private or public, can be said to stand in relation to a number of other entities: to the addresser, to the addressee, to other texts, and to that part of reality that the text is about. Discourse analysis in its various disguises has been developed in order to describe, understand and perhaps explain these different relations. Questions that can be raised are: What part of reality is in focus? What is included and what is left outside? What is considered important and what remains in the background? What textual and linguistic strategies are used in order to describe participants and processes, concepts and events? Which are the voices that are heard in the texts? To what extent are the texts homogeneous or heterogeneous? Methods of handling questions like these have been developed under the discourse-analytical umbrella, for example in works by Fairclough (1992, 2010) and Wodak (2009), but appropriate methods are also part and parcel of the mainstream language-based text analysis, for example the methods developed within the large-scale research project 'Svensk sakprosa' (see Svensson 2000).

An analysis dealing with questions like these can be said to remain on a descriptive level. In order to increase the insights of the analysis one also has to pose the why-question (or a couple of why-questions). And then there immediately arises a need of theoretical assumptions, not only linguistic but even social, historical and economic. The ultimate ambition could be said to be to explain the dialectic relationship that exists between texts and society. In the last section of the chapter, I return to these questions and discuss how far one can get with the help of language-based discourse analysis.

THE INVESTIGATED CORPUS – DISCURSIVE STRATEGIES

In this section I will try to create a picture by a close reading of each independent text (or group of texts). The aim is to unfold the discursive and intertextual dependencies in order to reach a deeper understanding of the discursive strategies. The respective readings are partly governed by the characteristics of each of the texts, but for all of the texts I have tried to say something about the content, the intertextual relations, and the blending of voices.

The *Financial Plan*

The texts used in the first group are the introductory parts of the governmental bills, that is the *Financial Plan*, presented to the parliament in October 2007, 2008, 2009 and 2010. When the first was written, the financial crisis was only in its beginning; most people didn't recognize it as a crisis at all. In October 2008 the crisis was in full swing, and in 2009 and 2010 the consequences were obvious to all, both professionals and laymen.

It is reasonable to say that the governmental budget bill is a genre in its own right, for three reasons: It fulfils very specific purposes. It is produced regularly and addressed to a well-defined audience (formally the parliament, but also to the public by media mediation). It also has a fixed name, '*budgetpropositionen*' (the budget bill). However, these rather steady social and functional criteria do not correlate with a fixed linguistic form or recurrent textual strategies. From a textual or discursive point of view, the budget bill could rather be considered a heterogeneous text type, with an interesting intertextual – or rather interdiscursive – variety, a variety that can at least partially be explained by the changing political and financial situations.

In some parts, the bills show great similarities to political texts produced by party organizations as manifestos or election campaign material. This is already obvious in the introductory paragraph from 2007, which describes the actual politico-economic situation:

> *Svensk ekonomi utvecklas starkt. Fler och fler får jobb, samtidigt som sjukskrivningar, öppen arbetslöshet och arbetsmarknadsåtgärder minskar. Därmed sjunker nu även det totala antalet personer i utanförskap påtagligt. Den politik som tidigare mest handlat om att öka eller omfördela utanförskapet bland över en miljon invånare i arbetsför ålder, har bytts mot en politik som minskar det totala utanförskapet.*
> (The Swedish economy is developing strongly. More and more people are in employment, at the same time as the numbers are falling of those who are on invalidity benefit, are registered unemployed or are in special work schemes. Thus, the total number of individuals excluded by society has also been reduced. Policies which formerly were mostly aimed at increasing or redistributing the marginalization among more than a million citizens fit for work have been replaced by policies that reduce the total marginalization.)

The passage is written in the present tense (or perfect tense when necessary), and the modality is unambiguously assertive. Passages written in this style can be found in all the texts under investigation. In other parts, however, the style is more like the style in historical accounts (Martin and Rose 2008, p. 105), as in the following passage from 2008:

> *Att återupprätta arbetslinjen och bekämpa människors utanförskap från arbetsmarknaden var Allians för Sveriges viktigaste löfte till väljarna i valet 2006. Alliansen vann svenska folkets stöd för att göra det mer lönsamt att arbeta . . . Därmed lades en grund för att fler människor skulle ges möjlighet till eget arbete och egen lön, men också skapa förutsättningar för att utveckla den svenska välfärden.*
> (To restore the will to work and fight marginalization from the labour market was the most important promise to the voters by the Alliance for Sweden in the 2006 elections. The Alliance gained the support of the Swedish people to make it more profitable to work . . . Thus a foundation was laid to enable more people to live off their own work and their own salary, but also to shape conditions for developing the Swedish welfare state.)

It is also possible to find more explanatory passages:

> *De mörka moln som hängt över världsekonomin har tätnat under sommaren och hösten till följd av tilltagande oro på de internationella finansmarknaderna. Finanskrisen, som inleddes 2007, har visat sig vara djupare och mer utbredd än vad som tidigare befarats. Ökad osäkerhet bland finansiella institut har drivit upp räntor samtidigt som t.ex. börskurser och andra tillgångspriser fallit markant. Utvecklingen har haft en dämpande inverkan på hushåll och företag och försämrat tillväxtutsikterna i omvärlden.*
> (The dark clouds that have been hovering over the world economy have thickened during the summer and the autumn owing to increasing instability on the international financial markets. The financial crisis that began in 2007 has shown itself to be deeper and more widespread than was formerly feared. Increased uncertainty among the financial institutions has forced interest rates upwards at the same time as, e.g. share prices and other asset prices have fallen sharply. The development has had a deadening effect on households and companies and made the prospects of growth in the world deteriorate.)

The content of this paragraph is expected (only a few weeks after the outbreak of the financial crisis) but the way of formulating the content is not as self-evident and linguistically it is definitively interesting. As one part of the investigation, I have studied the use of different semantic verbal categories, namely *actions*, *events*, *states* and *mental processes*, an analysis sometimes referred to as transitivity analysis (see Fairclough 1992, p. 177). The passage above contains not one single animate subject; the central/critical processes are described either metaphorically ('*molnen har tätnat*' (the clouds have thickened)) or as events with no responsible actor ('*osäkerheten har drivt upp räntor*' (uncertainty has forced interest rates upwards); '*kurser har fallit*' (share prices have fallen)) (see the next section below). Looking at the *Financial Plan* text for each year, we can see a small but interesting change. In the texts from 2007/08, *actions*, *events* and *relational processes* are rather evenly distributed. In 2008/09 *events* dominate heavily. The texts from 2009/10 are like 2007/08, and finally in the texts from 2010/11 *states* are in a clear majority. The text is reduced to descriptions of how (well) things are going.

The heterogeneity of the text type is also shown in the blending of voices. The major parts of the single texts are more or less homogeneous. The liberal–conservative government speaks with confidence and optimism about economic matters. In a comment on the beginning financial crisis, however, the complicating perspective cannot be fully ignored. What is happening is that you get a rather advanced intertextual play, which may also be described as textual polyphony. There is a vast literature on the subject of polyphony (see for example Therkelsen et al. 2007), but I have used a hands-on version proposed by Hellberg (2012), who with the help of grammatical criteria distinguishes between two different voices, the voice of 'Ego' and the voice of 'Other'. These two voices may be heard even in seemingly monologic texts. In the following example from the *Financial Plan*, there is a tension between the voice of 'Ego' and the voice of 'Other'.

> *Den senaste tidens turbulens på de finansiella marknaderna och bolånekrisen i Förenta staterna gör tillväxtutsikterna något mer svårbedömda och ökar osäkerheten i prognoserna något. I dagsläget bedöms den finansiella krisen få en relativt begränsad effekt på ekonomin.* Den finansiella oron kan emellertid komma att utvecklas på ett mindre gynnsamt sätt. (My emphasis.)
> (*The recent turmoil on the financial markets and the sub-prime crisis in the US make the growth prospects somewhat harder to judge and increase the instability in the forecasts to a certain extent. Today, the financial crisis is estimated to have a relatively limited effect on the economy.* The financial instability may, however, develop in a less favourable way.)

Here you can clearly hear the voice of 'Other' confronting the voice of 'Ego'. Metaphorically one can read this as a text produced by the Prime Minister, boasting about what has been done so far and reassuring the audience of a positive future. Then suddenly the minister of finance pops up behind the Prime Minister's back and utters a tiny warning. This happens now and then with formulations like the following:

> *Osäkerheten om utvecklingen i vår omvärld är stor.*
> (Uncertainty about developments in the world is immense.)

> *Ett osäkert framtida reformutrymme . . . bör dessutom inte intecknas för snabbt.*
> (Certain scope for future reforms . . . should furthermore not be cashed in too soon.)

> *Det finns därför skäl att vara vaksam . . .*
> (There is therefore good reason to be vigilant.)

What is rather surprising is that the financial crisis doesn't have a heavier impact on the texts. The only obvious traces can be found in the bill from 2009, with two traits worth mentioning.

The first is that the text has an alarming – perhaps even apocalyptic – tone. The seriousness of the situation is explicit already in the first sentence: '*Världen befinner sig i den djupaste och mest utbredda lågkonjunkturen sedan 1930-talskrisen.*' (The world is experiencing the deepest and most widespread depression since the crisis of the 1930s.) In a later section the wording underlines the problematic situation: '*BNP har rasat dramatiskt*' (GNP has decreased dramatically); '*regeringen har vidtagit exceptionella åtgärder*' (the government has taken exceptional measures); '*räntorna har sänkts till historiskt låga nivåer*' (interest rates have been reduced to historically low levels). Formulations like these stand out in rather heavy contrast to the self-confident, optimistic formulations of 2007 and the rather cautious and technical formulations of 2008. The second trait is a slight increase in frequency of the modality expressed ('*kan Sverige komma starkt ur krisen*' (Sweden may be strengthened by the crisis); '*hoten ska mötas med kraftfull politik*' (the threats will be met by strong political measures); '*problemen får inte hanteras . . .*' (the problems must not be handled . . .)) plus a higher frequency of different kinds of hedging ('*bedöms vara*' (is considered to be . . .); '*väntas bli*' (is expected to be) and so on).

To summarize, one could say a few different things. The *Financial Plan* could be seen as a genre in its own right; it serves certain well-defined functions and plays a role in reoccurring social processes. However, the text exhibits a certain amount of variability when it comes to the linguistic form and textual strategies, both within each text and between the texts. In the first case we may see a struggle between different voices, due to the delicate balance needed when you have to be optimistic and cautious at the same time. In the second case we may to a certain extent explain the variation by looking at the politico-economic situation; we may see reflections of both the financial crisis and the national elections.

The *Stability Report*

Just like the *Financial Plan*, the *Stability Report* can be considered a genre in its own right. In this case it is even more justified, as it is not only the communicative and social functions that are the same from text to text, but the linguistic form is homogeneous as well.

The dominant linguistic trait is the one that was mentioned above – that is, the very sparse use of expressions for actions and the frequent use of event-expressions and states, which lend the texts an abstract and unspecific character. It is reasonable to assume that those who have written the report agree on the fact that what is happening in the world in general as well as in economics is decided on by human beings, at least to some extent. Somebody pays or stops paying, somebody borrows and somebody sells. In the text one can see nothing of this. All the linguistic entities that from a textual and/or grammatical point of view function as participants are abstract or non-specific entities, and they take part in processes that seem to run automatically. The picture is further strengthened by the frequent use of nominalizations (that is, the use of nouns instead of corresponding verbs) and passives. The opening of the first report from 2009 provides an illustrative example.

> *Den globala finansiella krisen intensifierades kraftigt hösten 2008 i samband med att den amerikanska investmentbanken Lehman Brothers ansökte om konkursskydd. Funktionen på flertalet marknader stördes allvarligt till följd av ett bristande förtroende mellan finansiella institut. Handeln med vissa värdepapper upphörde helt att fungera. Detta medförde i sin tur att finansiella institut för att klara sin finansiering lånade allt större volymer till allt kortare löptider på interbankmarknaden, som fungerade allt sämre. Även de svenska finansiella marknaderna drabbades hårt och vissa delmarknader upphörde att fungera.*
> (The global financial crisis intensified seriously during the autumn of 2008, when the American investment bank Lehman Brothers asked for protection against bankruptcy. The functioning of most markets was seriously disturbed owing to weakened confidence between financial institutions. The trade in some securities ceased to function altogether. This in turn meant that financial institutions, in order to manage their financing, had to borrow increasing volumes at shorter terms on the interbank market, which functioned increasingly worse. Swedish finance markets were also hard-hit and some parts of the market ceased to function.)

This way of writing is almost prototypical for the types of abstract and non-specific texts that are described in textbooks on critical discourse analysis in order to show what makes texts diffuse and hard to understand. I do not see it as my task to evaluate the degree of readability of the texts under analysis, but it is obvious that the texts with the characteristics described put heavy pressure on the reader; for those who do not belong to the in-group, the texts are probably hard to grasp. On the other hand one could say that the *Stability Reports* in a very effective way summarize a complicated course of events. Most likely, the readers of the reports have prior knowledge and frames of reference that make the reading meaningful.

When one compares the different texts with each other, some changes over time become apparent. In 08:01 there are about as many *states* as *events*. In 08:02 and 09:01 *events* are about two-thirds of all instances, and in 09:02 *states* are once again in the majority. These changes are obviously reflexes of changes in the financial world that the texts are related to (see the *Financial Plan* above).

The abstract perspective does not mean that the texts lack precision or are void of distinct points of view. In the second report from 2008, published at the peak of the crisis, the authors are very explicit about what they think should be done in order to diminish future problems:

> *För det första krävs en ökad öppenhet om vilka banker och finansiella institut som har problem . . . För det andra finns ett behov hos vissa finansiella aktörer att se över sin kapitalsituation och anpassa denna till rådande förhållanden . . .*
> (Firstly, there is a requirement of increased openness as to which banks and financial institutions have problems . . . Secondly, there is a need for some financial actors to check their amounts of capital and adjust this to the given circumstances . . .)

This extract also shows another typical trait, namely homogeneous voicing. It is reasonable to believe that there were a lot of discussions going on during the preparation of the text, but none of this is seen in the text itself. There is only one tongue speaking. Together with the abstract representation of the contents, this is a way to create authority.

The best way to characterize the style of the *Stability Report* as a genre is to focus on the trait of matter of course. The board has seen the light, as it were; they have made relevant observations, they have brooded over them, and then they present their conclusions without letting any disturbing details or second opinions blur the picture.

Texts Written by Scholars

To the scholars working in economics, the financial crisis created multiple challenges. Just like any other group in society they might have been worried for private or professional reasons, and just like everybody else – and perhaps even more so – they had to try to understand what was happening. Furthermore – and this is my main point of view here – they had to defend themselves against accusations of not being able to foresee the crisis with the help of the scientific methods available.

In order to highlight these rhetorical problems, I have picked two articles from the 2010 issue of *Ekonomisk Debatt*, namely the articles by Martin Flodén and Torsten A. Andersen. Both are highly respected scholars in their fields, macroeconomics and fiscal policy/the labour market respectively, and both are members of the *Finanspolitiska rådet* (the Swedish Fiscal Policy Council), a position which raises expectations of advisory and prognostic abilities. Thus, both authors were challenged by the same rhetorical dilemma: how was it possible to explain the shortcomings of the macroeconomic scholars without dismissing the whole field of research? In the following I will try to show what discursive strategies they chose.

The article by Andersen is in two main parts, the first dealing with macro theory, the second with stabilizing policies. In his conclusion Andersen explicitly states that there is no need to change the research paradigm. The article can be read as a defence of that position.

The line of defence is established already in the first sentence of the part on macro theory, where Andersen states that great prognostic mistakes are embarrassing, but that the mistakes do not necessarily have to be the result of inferior or deficient methods. The fundamental ingredients in the macroeconomic research must be defended, and thus the shortcomings must be sought elsewhere. One sub-strategy is to point to the demands that are raised by the fact that macroprognoses must be a scientific enterprise. Had the researchers used ad hoc methods they could have been better off, but such methods do not allow for replications and thus cannot be used:

> *Vi kan bara förlita oss till systematiska prognosmetoder som kan och bör granskas noggrant.*
> (We can only rely on systematic methods of prognosis, which can and should be thoroughly checked.)

Another sub-strategy is that the prognoses weren't that bad at all; the problem was that the warnings were not taken seriously by those in power.

> *sådana rekommendationer följdes inte av de makthavande.*
> (such recommendations were not followed by those in power.)

It was also difficult to make news media report on complicated messages:

> *Det kan ingående debatt eras huruvida dessa rapporteringsproblem är ett fel från yrkeskårens sida eller resultatet av påtryckningar från media om tydliga, okomplicerade, kortfattade åsikter som kan uttryckas i en mening.*
> (It may be thoroughly debated whether these problems of reporting are a shortcoming among the professionals or the result of pressures from the media for clear, uncomplicated, short opinions, which may be expressed in a single sentence.)

The prognostic methods are construed for 'normal' situations. It is also hard to deal with expectations on the market as they cannot be observed. The prognostic methods are also construed for intranational analyses and not suited for global and international perspectives. From a non-economist's perspective this is startling. The startling thing is not the fact that the scientific methods are imperfect, although one could expect the methods to handle both expectations and international issues; the startling thing is the mismatch between the self-confidence shown in times of 'business as usual' and the downscaling of the ambitions when a challenge comes from a problematic reality. Andersen actually points to this situation himself:

> *Av något skäl verkar överdriven självsäkerhet utvecklas inom yrkesgruppen och ironiskt nog verkar det vara ett tidigt tecken på en annalkande stor kris.*
> (For some reason, exaggerated self-consciousness seems to have been developed within the profession and ironically this seems to be an early sign of an approaching big crisis.)

In the part of his article that deals with stabilizing policies, Andersen points out the lack of research on fiscal policies and an exaggerated interest on monetary policies. The part can be read as a critique of current trends in economic research. The critique of some parts of the research community is followed up in the part on modern macroeconomics, with the main point that it has been more important to solve self-defined riddles than to contribute to common research-goals.

The main discursive strategy in Andersen's paper is thus not to acknowledge some shortcomings of macroeconomic research but to characterize these shortcomings as accidental, due either to actors outside the field or to individual mistakes.

The article by Martin Flodén deals with three different aspects of the crisis and macroeconomic research. First he focuses on the question of rationality and market efficiency, second on the technical aspects of the analytical methods, and third on certain shortcomings of research practices. My analysis is concentrated on the first part of the article and the conclusion.

From a discursive point of view, Flodén's article is interesting in that it demonstrates a rather clear-cut example of textual polyphony that we also saw above in the *Financial Plan* – that is, a successive interplay between the author's voice (Ego) and voices with divergent opinions (Other), who criticize the macroeconomic research from various angles.

The interplay between Ego and Other is clearly seen already in the beginning of the section. The first voice that we hear is the voice of Other: '*att vi i alltför hög utsträckning har utgått från att marknaderna är effektiva*' (that we have taken it too much for granted that the markets are effective). Ego immediately objects to that: '*Jag menar att den senare delen av påståendet är felaktigt*' (In my opinion the latter part of the statement is false), and in the next sentence Ego strengthens his opinion: '*Vid närmare eftertanke är påståendet närmast absurt*' (On a closer look, the statement is virtually absurd). Nevertheless, the voice of Other is not silenced. In the first sentence of the following paragraph, Other says: '*Påståendet är ändå inte helt ogrundat*' (However, the statement is not totally unfounded), and the motivation for Other's statement is that the macroeconomic models actually work, provided that expectations are rational and markets effective. Then Ego is called in again to say that this is a natural point of departure, partly for the sake of simplification, partly to understand what actually makes a market effective. This wrestling between Ego and Other ends with Ego finding himself with his shoulders on the mat:

> *Denna fokusering på rationalitet och effektiva marknader har nog tidvis drivits för långt inom forskningen och kanske har den även fått vissa forskare att felaktigt se modellerna som en beskrivning av verkligheten.*
> (This heavy focus on rationality and effective markets has probably from time to time been pushed too far within research and probably it has forced some scholars to treat the models erroneously as a description of reality.)

After having admitted what 15 lines above was considered absurd, the rest of the text serves the purpose of explaining the failures of the macroeconomic model. One problem that Flodén points out is that the economic trends ('*konjunkturförloppen*') are different from time to time. Another problem is that if one accepts irrational behaviour as a part of the model, the analysis gets too complicated. In this he follows the same line as Andersen.

> *Med dessa antaganden blir analysen ofta komplicerad, vilket förmodligen förklarar varför de praktiska insikterna och tillämpningarna från denna litteratur varit begränsade.*
> (With these premises, the analysis often gets complicated, which probably explains why the practical insights and applications from the literature have been limited.)

Finally Flodén uses the same discursive strategy as Andersen, in that the responsibility is thrown upon the politicians who have to decide on the political measures.

> *Även de politiker och ekonomer som ska utforma politiken och regleringarna är människor som har begränsad förståelse för hur ekonomin fungerar.*
> (Also the politicians and economists who should decide on the policies and the regulations are individuals with limited understanding of the function of the economy.)

To conclude this section one could say that the discursive and rhetorical problem that the two authors have had to face is not an easy one. Of course, the macroeconomic researchers cannot be made responsible for the financial crisis, but they have rightly or wrongly been criticized for not being able to foresee it. It is probably the case that many economic analysts would never have dreamed of saying that their models would be able to predict future ups and downs in the international economy, but it is also true that there isn't any strong inclination to assert the opposite. From the viewpoint of the sociology of research, it is advantageous to represent a field of research that can justify its existence with arguments of utility. It helps to raise both research funds and one's self-confidence. It is thus not surprising that the authors do their best to defend the structure that they are part of and explain the shortcomings as the results of accidental deficiencies.

Texts Written by Representatives of Political Parties

In order to gain some insight into the textual strategies of responsible and active politicians, I have analysed two texts from a plenary debate in the Swedish parliament held on 15 October 2008, that is, about a month after the fall of Lehman Brothers and the outbreak of the crisis. The speeches were delivered by Mona Sahlin and Fredrik Reinfeldt. The media focus on the politico-economic situation was still intense, and it would therefore have been natural that the party leaders paid attention to the effects and consequences of the crisis for Swedish society and its members. It is therefore somewhat surprising when one reads Sahlin's text and sees that she does not say very much about the crisis as such. She does mention it, but mostly to get a springboard to more traditional political issues.

> *Finanskrisen är allvarlig. . . . Men det vore bra om regeringen kunde se också detta: Skymd av finanskrisen pågår en annan kris . . . nämligen krisen för jobben.* (The financial crisis is serious . . . But it would be a good thing if the government could also see this: in the shadow of the financial crisis there is another crisis . . . namely the job crisis.)

By this textual strategic trick she is back on the track where she can use the standard political rhetoric: unemployment is a great problem. The policies of the bourgeois government have made things worse, and the changes in the welfare systems leave many people in despair. The political alternative, according to Sahlin, is – of course – traditional social-democratic policies with state contributions in education and investments in public enterprises. And she explicitly mentions the fiscal consequences of her own suggestions:

> *Och ja, vi tar ut högre skatter än regeringen. Också de förmögna ska få vara med och bidra till välfärden.*
> (And yes, we count on higher taxes than the government does. Also, the wealthy should do their bit and contribute to welfare.)

Thus, the skeleton of the speech is rather predictable. The argument would not have been much different had there been no financial crisis. The same could be said of the minor details of the speech, the flesh on the bones so to speak. The vocabulary promotes traditional social-democratic virtues: '*sammanhållning*' (unity), '*solidaritet*' (solidarity), '*kunskap*' (knowledge), '*trygghet*' (security) and '*rättvisa*' (justice). The policies of the liberal–conservative government are characterized with expressions like '*ofinansierade skattesänkningar*' (unfinanced tax-cuts), '*rusta ned utbildningen*' (dismantle education), '*förstöra trygghetsförsäkringarna*' (destroy security insurance). The descriptions of the state of affairs, which is an important part of every text (see above), are also chosen to back up the general lines of the argumentation:

> *Herr talman! En halv miljon människor har tvingats ut från A-kassan. De går nu in i jobbkrisen utan ett ekonomiskt skyddsnät. Andra får försöka klara sig på en A-kassa som bara ger halva inkomsten om de blir arbetslösa.*
> (Mr Chairman! Half a million people have lost their unemployment benefit. They now enter the job crisis without an economic security net. Others must try to make it on an unemployment benefit that gives only half the income if they lose their jobs.)

The voice we hear in the text is unambiguously the voice of Mona Sahlin in her capacity as chair of the Social Democratic Party. There is no need for her to establish any neutral or objective facade, and she doesn't involve herself in any discursive passages where she weighs different alternatives against each other. She thus takes up the expected style of political speech, where opinions are put forward without much hesitation.

Fredrik Reinfeldt has a textual strategy that resembles Sahlin's in that he takes the financial crisis as his point of departure and later on changes the focus to the advantages of his own policies – and the drawbacks of the policies of the opposition. However, Reinfeldt dwells a little longer on the theme of the financial crisis, and he does so not only to get a bridge to other political issues, but also to discuss the handling of the crisis. In doing so, he has a clear ambition – consciously or not – to position himself as a responsible international statesman. An important word is '*samling*' (gathering).

> *det krävs samling i Sverige, Europa och världen . . . Vi tar vårt ansvar, men vi gör det samlat och tillsammans med andra.*

> (there is a great need for gathering in Sweden, Europe and the world . . . We take our responsibility but we do it in unity and together with others.)

When it comes to the use of different voices, Reinfeldt has a strategy slightly different from Sahlin's. The voice of the worried citizen is heard posing questions on the present situation, and then Reinfeldt can give a reassuring answer:

> *Då säger någon: Ja, men är det så här i Sverige? Ja, det är säkerhetsbältet som gäller för den händelse det knackar även på den svenska dörren.*
> (Then somebody says: Yes, but is it like this in Sweden? Yes, the safety belt is necessary in case there's a knock also on the Swedish door.)
>
> *Frågan är: Finns det resurser? Finns det stöd till omställning nu när prövningen sker? Nu samlas de goda krafter som vi har, och vi har erfarenheter av förut. Låt oss vara ett aktivt stöd . . .*
> (The question is: are there any resources? Is there any support for change now when we are being tested? Now all the good forces that we know and have experience of are being gathered. Let us be an active support.)

The words and expressions that may be loaded with value are partly the same as Sahlin's, but one can also see some differences:

> *Vi har en politik för jobb . . .* (We have a policy for jobs)
> *Vi har en politik för välfärd . . .* (We have a policy for welfare)
> *Det är också vi som har politiken för rättvisa . . .* (And it is we who have a policy for justice)

Formulations like these are part of the stock of liberal/conservative expressions (see Lorentzon 2006) and could have been used in any political situation, independent of any economic crisis.

Thus one may say that in the given situation, a month after the outbreak of the worst crisis since the 1930s, the crisis is an inevitable point of reference for both Sahlin and Reinfeldt. However, neither of them seizes the opportunity to discuss the causes and consequences in principle. Instead, both of them – with slightly different strategies – are more interested in stating their own positions and formulating their respective political alternatives in the domestic political situation.

CONCLUSION

In the introduction to the chapter I raised a bundle of questions, some relating to the rather abstract notion of 'order of discourse', others relating to the linguistic and textual strategies used. I also addressed the overarching question of why the texts look the way they do. In this concluding part I will try to relate to the different sets of questions. In doing so, I will make use of Fairclough's well-known tri-partition, with the textual level embedded in the discursive practice, which in turn is embedded in the socio-cultural practice (see Fairclough 1992, p. 73).

The content of the texts, that is, whatever part of reality is put forward, is of course dependent on the different tasks that the texts have to fulfil. It is therefore not surprising that the variation is great, but what is surprising is that the financial crisis attracts so little attention. It is mentioned in each of the six texts, but it is never very prominent. The authors have other agendas, which rules out penetrating discussions of the crisis as such. Instead, other, more text-specific issues are foregrounded. This result is of course partly due to the choice of texts, but nevertheless the tepid engagement in the crisis and its causes is unexpected in the light of the heavy media coverage (see below on the discursive practice).

One interesting aspect of the relation to reality is the way the authors refer to the events in the economic-political sphere and to those involved in the processes. The two text types that have the strongest reason to give accurate accounts of the events, i.e. the *Financial Plan* and the *Stability Report*, do so in a very abstract and unspecific way. To a large extent, the developments are described as events without any visible actors. We all know that what is going on is caused by conscious actions performed by responsible human beings, either individually or as organizations, but these human beings are more or less invisible in the texts.

The investigation has also focused on the blending of voices and the degree of textual homogeneity. In some of the texts, especially the *Stability Report* and the speech by Mona Sahlin, one does not hear more than one voice, in the former case because of the obvious ambition to be authoritative, in the second case because of the personal point of view combined with the wish to state an opinion on the issues at stake. In some of the other texts, however, the blending of voices is rather salient, but for partly different reasons. In the *Financial Plan* there are two competing voices owing to different interests that have to be handled at one and the same time. One is the wish to paint a bright and positive picture in order to show the efficiency of the government, the other is the simultaneous need to prepare the readers (the citizens) for possible future drawbacks due to the financial crisis. In the texts in *Ekonomisk Debatt*, especially in Flodén's text, there is a tension between the wish to defend the work of academic colleagues and the force of reality that shows the shortcomings of the same work. In Reinfeldt's speech, finally, there is a third kind of blending. He opens up for potential questions from voters, which gives him the opportunity to express suitable answers.

Thus the differences in voice blending create differences in the degree of homogeneity, but the texts also vary with respect to genre adherence. Once again the most clear-cut example is the *Stability Report*, which exhibits a very high degree of uniformity. The single texts look like blueprints of each other, and each text has the same character throughout. In the *Financial Plan*, on the contrary, there is an interesting discursive play between the respective styles of party programmes, of historical accounts, of academic seminars and of technical economic analyses. This heterogeneity is partly due to the changing politico-historic conditions, but it might also be explained by the competing interests, handled within each one of the texts.

The above-mentioned textual traits point in several directions, and it is not easy to give a coherent description of the situation. But if one relates the different findings to the discursive practice (the intermediate level in Fairclough's model), it may be possible to give an explanation for many – if not all – of the linguistic and textual traits. There is no such thing as 'the texts of the financial crisis', but there are texts of different genres and with different functions that each in their own way relate to the crisis. All these texts could be described as texts of the public sphere. Such texts may of course differ greatly from each other, but what is common to most of them is that they deal with serious matters, that they are informative and that they are more or less independent of the immediate context. Many of the similarities may thus be explained by the fact that all the texts are instances of the vast discursive practice that is provided by the public sphere. But the texts are also part of the order of economic discourse, a concept that overlaps with but does not identify with the public sphere. For some of the texts in my corpus, the *Financial Plan* and the *Stability Report*, it is possible to say something about the degree of variability over time. It is possible to detect some variation, at least in the different versions of the *Financial Plan*, but this variation is related to factors other than the financial crisis as such. As a general conclusion, one could say that the order of economic discourse is not influenced to any degree; what is important is the discursive practice, that is, the conditions under which the production, the distribution and the consumption of the texts take place.

Finally I will say a few words on the overarching why-question, relating to the societal level. Of the three parts of the tri-partition, the outermost part (the socio-cultural level) is the most elusive, at least in a situation where it is not possible to carry out large-scale socio-political investigations. It is not at all obvious how to relate textual traits to the overarching cultural and political situation. However, even a sketchy description of the socio-cultural practice could contribute to the understanding of the texts under investigation. Sweden, like the rest of Europe and the US, is integrated in a neo-liberal, capitalistic system that meets with recurrent crises. When a new crisis occurs, like the one in 2008, it could be an opportunity, even for serious commentators, to question the economic system, but that does not happen. The concept of market capitalism could be considered more or less hegemonic, and the analyses and descriptions aim at solving the problems within the frames of the system. Not even in the text by the Social Democrat Mona Sahlin do we see any traces of a critique of the system.

In the various discourse-analytical traditions there is a common thought that text and context interact in a dialectic fashion. It is of course hard to prove that any single text or group of texts dealt with in this investigation had any influence on the course of events or on the system as such. However, the fact that all the texts in the corpus (and the majority of all texts written on the subject) treat the socio-cultural practice as the natural order contributes to the strengthening of the system and the maintenance of the status quo.

REFERENCES

Fairclough, Norman (1992), *Discourse as Social Change*, Oxford: Polity.

Fairclough, Norman (2010), *Critical Discourse Analysis: The Critical Study of Language*, London: Longman.

Fuchs, Doris and Antonia Graf (2010), 'The financial crisis in discourse: banks, financial markets, and political responses', paper prepared for the SGIR International Relations Conference, Stockholm, 9–11 September.

Hellberg, Staffan (2012), 'First language paradigms in conflict: hidden dialogue in Swedish curricula', *Journal of Curriculum Studies*, **44** (1), 1–22.

Lorentzon, Thorwald (2006), *Mellan frihet och jämlikhet: jämförande studier av lexikala förändringar i Moderaternas och Vänsterpartiets valmanifest 1948–2002*, Göteborgsstudier i nordisk språkvetenskap, no. 6.

Martin, J.R. and D. Rose (2008), *Genre Relations: Mapping Culture*, London: Equinox.

Svensson, Jan (2000), 'Non-literary prose in Sweden: reflections on a multi-disciplinary approach', in Wenche Vagle and Kay Wikberg (eds), *New Directions in Nordic Text Linguistics and Discourse Analysis: Methodological Issues*, Oslo: Novus, pp. 32–44.

Therkelsen, Rita, Nina Møller Andersen and Hening Nølke (eds) (2007), *Sproglig polyfoni: tekster om Bachtin og ScaPoLine*, Århus, Denmark: Århus Universitetsforlag.

Wodak, Ruth (2009), *The Discourse of Politics in Action: Politics as Usual*, Basingstoke: Palgrave.

6. Regulating the family in times of economic crisis: Sweden in the 1930s and the 1990s

Åsa Lundqvist

INTRODUCTION

The relationship between the family and the state has a longstanding but shifting history. Throughout the twentieth century, various political initiatives have been brought forward to increase the well-being of the family across Europe. These initiatives vary in forms and outcomes, and the driving forces behind them are complex and differ over time and regions. They might be addressed as an outcome of war, conjugal instability or ideological shifts in policy history, or as a result of the social and political radicalization of the 1960s. Despite the variations, family and gender relations constitute – historically and today – an important field of intervention among policymakers across Europe (Hantrais 2004). As such the political regulation of the family is a forceful instrument in the attempt to change existing social structures.

In this chapter, the impact of economic crises on family policy is addressed. The setting is Sweden and the empirical focus is on the two great crises in Sweden during the last century, that of the 1930s and that of the 1990s. The question asked is how the impact of economic crisis affects the political regulation of the family in Sweden, especially its emphasis on reducing social and economic inequalities between families. The analysis takes as its point of departure the early development of family (or population) policies in the 1930s, a time when modern family policy was founded. One of the main characteristics of early family policy regulation might be the political initiatives to reform family relations by promoting state interventions and highlighting women's dual roles as mothers and paid labourers. These initiatives eventually led to the development of the 'dual earner/dual carer family model' in which men and women are equally encouraged to take part in working life as well as in care of the children.

Interestingly enough, many of the fundamental features of early family policy regulation, incepted at the height of the crisis in the 1930s, survived (compare Lindvall's analysis on political preferences and government formation in this volume) even the deepest and most profound economic crises in six decades, when Sweden went through a pattern similar to what many European countries are currently undergoing, with a concurrent breakdown of the financial system, a sovereign debt crisis and a rapid fall in employment.

This notwithstanding, temporal changes did result in changing conditions for families with children: the economic crisis in the 1990s triggered cuts in public finances including family-policy allowances and benefits, resulting in increasing poverty among families with children, in particular for groups that were most severely hit by the fall in employment. However, I will argue that it did not fundamentally alter the structure of Swedish family policy. By the end of the decade, the situation for many families recovered. Nevertheless, some patterns still prevail: lone mothers and migrant families have remained poor and have not fully recovered from the crisis, indicating a discursive shift in the political ambition of regulating the family.

The main text of the chapter is divided into four sections. The evolution of the political regulation of the family will be presented in the first of these. It is above all a description of dominating policy ambitions and ideologies concerning gender and family relations, which aim to present the introduction and institutionalization of a 'dual-earner/dual-carer family model'. This section is followed by an analysis of how family policy has been shaped in the wake of economic crisis: by taking the point of departure in two severe economic crises – the 1930s and the 1990s – I intend to explore how dominating views of the family have emerged and persisted. The chapter concludes with a discussion of the findings.

THE POLITICAL REGULATION OF THE FAMILY IN SWEDEN

The Nordic welfare states have a long tradition of family-policy intervention, not least in Sweden. Ever since the 1930s, the political regulation of the family has been seen as an important part of the modernization of Swedish society: social and economic development should be based on the renewal of labour market relations, new models for the management of economic swings, reduced social inequalities – and on reforms of family and gender relations. Moreover, and in order to prevent social meltdowns due to economic crises, social equality was to be combined with full employment, rapid growth increases, and macroeconomic stringency with low inflation. The foundation was a combination of a Keynesian stabilization policy to manage economic fluctuations without cost-push inflation with a selective policy for labour mobility, reducing bottlenecks in the labour market (Benner 1997; Rothstein 1992, 1996; Åmark 2005).

In this model, family and gender equality policy served as a means to adjust conditions between women and men in the labour market as well as in the home. Equal opportunities between women and men thus became part of the Swedish Model at an early stage. Moreover, transformed family relations and gender roles also became building blocks in the above-mentioned political programme for productivity and economic growth. Such a model has been described as a specifically Nordic – or, sometimes, social-democratic – welfare regime in comparative studies of welfare policies (Daly 2000; Ellingsæter and Leira 2006; Esping-Andersen 1990, 2009; Leira 2002; Sainsbury 1999). In the postwar period, until the late 1980s, family policy thus contributed to macroeconomic stability by generalizing consumption patterns and by empowering family members.

Throughout the twentieth century the family-policy field maintained its initial goals from the 1930s, that is, to level out unequal economic conditions between families with children and households without children. Modern family-policy making was thus initially designed to create economic stability among families with children in economic upswings, but also as a tool to prevent poverty and decreasing birth rates in times of crisis (Lundqvist 2007).

The ambition to reduce social inequalities between families with children and families without children was complemented with a gender equality policy goal which in turn grew strong in the 1960s. By emphasizing the importance of gender equality within the family, policy measures were taken to make it easier for mothers to get gainful employment and for fathers to stay at home with the children (for example the introduction of parental leave insurance in 1974). After the national insurance systems were in place, publicly funded daycare thus began to expand in the 1970s, and: 'traditional boundaries between the state and family were redrawn. The responsibility of the state and local government for welfare and social care services increased, while for the family it declined' (Leira 2006, p. 30).

Ever since, the goal of full employment, together with the social insurance programmes and publicly funded childcare, have represented powerful tools in the political drive to enable women and men to combine gainful employment with caring responsibilities. This specific family-policy model has been acknowledged and debated by scholars for a long time, showing that the effect of these policies has resulted in a 'weak male breadwinner model' and the establishment of a 'dual-earner/dual-carer family model' (Daly 2000; Lewis 1992; Leira 2002).

Family and gender equality policies have thus stressed gender neutrality and individual rights for its citizens. However, during the economic crisis of the 1990s, the 'dual-earner/dual-carer family model' came under pressure. Mass unemployment and the dismantling of welfare services and provisions undermined the stability of the 'dual-earner/dual-carer family model', as reflected in worsened living conditions for families with children. Three groups stand out as particularly vulnerable during the period: lone-parent families, young adults and citizens born outside Sweden. Among the group of young adults, higher education became the salvation for their situation, especially among middle-class youth. Among lone mothers and non-European migrants, however, unemployment rose by 56 per cent and 39 per cent respectively between 1992 and 1997 (Ds 2002:32, p. 82). For these two groups, unemployment and increasing inequalities regarding, for example, access to employment continued when the rest of the population recovered from the crisis by the end of the decade (Socialförsäkringsrapport 2009:4).

In the new millennium, the economy for many families with two incomes improved rapidly, and the disposable income increased for two-parent families with children. Employment rates increased, the cutbacks in the welfare system were to a certain degree reversed and several family-policy reforms were introduced, such as a maximum fee for childcare enabling families with children to improve their living standard. The 'dual-earner/dual-carer family model' was emphasized by politicians as this model was once again seen as the most effective way of achieving economic growth as well as gender-equal family relations (Lundqvist 2011). It is clear, however, that development during the new millennium has resulted in differences in income levels, causing increasing cleavages between rich and poor families. In 2008, 'the richest fifth of all households with children had 3.6 times as high disposable income as the poorest fifth. By the end of the 1990s, the share was 2.8' (Salonen 2011, p. 11).

In sum, ever since the 1960s, Swedish family policy has emphasized and enhanced a 'dual-earner/dual-carer family model'. Its historical roots can however be traced to the development following the crisis management in the 1930s, a time when the political regulation of the family became part of an overarching goal to level out economic inequalities between families with children and families without children. By taking the economic crisis in the 1930s as a point of departure, the following section aims to explore the context in which the 'dual-earner/dual-carer family model' was born.

CRISIS MANAGEMENT IN THE 1930s: TOWARDS STABILITY THROUGH EXPANSION

Sweden in the 1920s was marked by severe political conflicts as well as recurrent economic fluctuations. Political relations were tense, and Social Democrats and bourgeois parties could not agree on central political issues such as unemployment insurance, pensions and maternity support (Lundqvist 2001).

A short boom after the First World War, caused by demands for Swedish goods on the war-stricken continent, was soon followed by speculation and an inflationary crisis, triggering a rapid hike in unemployment that primarily affected rural areas and small industrial villages (Lundberg 1983). Economic policies were inflexible and shaped by the dogmas of the gold standard, which kept unemployment permanently at high levels, never going below 10 per cent in the 1920s and at times much higher.

The crash of 1929 made an already vulnerable situation even worse. The limited recovery of the late 1920s (brought about by infrastructural investments which benefited the raw-materials-based industries) came to an abrupt halt after the crash (Schön 2000).

Sweden left the gold standard in 1931, as a consequence of the stock market crash of 1929 and the ensuing economic crisis. This led to a de facto depreciation of the krona. At the same time, unemployment was reaching increasingly high levels – 27 per cent of trade union members in 1931 and large numbers of poorly paid labourers in agriculture. When industry begun expanding on the basis of the currency depreciation, it benefited from the large number of unemployed or underemployed workers, and industry could invest without being reliant on the financial market. Such investments primarily took place in the electro-technical and transportation industries, which surged on the basis of investments in infrastructure, electrification and the growing demand for automobiles (Schön 2000, pp. 348–58).

This notwithstanding, Sweden was stuck in a deep economic downturn in the early 1930s, even though it was not as deep as in other countries. The main thrust of the crisis was borne by workers in cities and industrial towns, and by farmers, which triggered the crisis agreement between the Agrarian Party and the Social Democrats in 1933 (the 'Horse Trading'). Two parties devised the crisis policy, in which Sweden pioneered a limited programme for loan-funded relief work for the unemployed (Odhner 1992). Other elements of the crisis deal included a pledge to underbalance budgets in economic depressions to fund relief work, and tariffs on agricultural products and milk subsidies to protect and support smaller farms (Bergström 1992).

The main priority was labour market policies and measures to combat unemployment. This also included programmes for housing construction to reduce the shortage of dwellings and with the indirect aim of supporting employment in the construction industry, which had been hard hit by the depression. In parallel, the new government and the minister of finance Ernst Wigforss (influenced by the economists of the Stockholm School which preceded the Keynesian revolution) devised counter-cyclical economic policies to sustain consumption and investments irrespective of economic fluctuations (Benner 1997; Schön 2000).

The transformation of economic policies was not isolated from other policy areas. With the growing awareness of the social consequences of unemployment there followed a broadly based discussion of the 'social question' in political and intellectual circles. Long-term social and economic development could not be based only on labour market reforms, which needed to be complemented by powerful social policy interventions (Lundqvist 2007). This in turn necessitated broad-based surveys of social conditions in Sweden, covering issues such as the spread of poverty and which groups were the most affected by unemployment, the living conditions of the urban working class, the sharp increase in infant mortality, and housing conditions in the country. A particular focus was on the conditions for families, how they lived and how they had been affected by the crisis.

The Family in the 1930s

The global economic depression and the massive hike in unemployment had transformed economic and social policies (Bergström 1992; Olsson 1992). A particularly alarming issue was the impact of the economic downturn on families with children, with the tandem consequence of unemployment and declining fertility. Social policy expertise was enrolled to survey the conditions of families: the consequences of the new division of labour for women, men and children; sexuality and intimate relations in transition; the interplay between marriage patterns and fertility; and the evolution of motherhood – these were among the issues that were scrutinized (Lundqvist 2007). Such knowledge was mobilized to underpin bold social and family-policy reforms.

Starting out from theories of the social consequences of industrialization – stressing the impact of the division of labour in modern industry on family organization and the declining importance of the family as an economic unit – policies to enhance the social conditions of families were devised (Sommestad 2001). The basic assumption of these studies was that industrialization led to a crisis in the family: when men left the familial sphere for salaried employment in industry, women were left with the full responsibility for childcare and household duties, creating a sharp split within modern families between men as economic providers and women as care providers. The analyses indicated that industrialization contributed to a situation where women suffered: marriage meant that women were relegated to the tasks of childbirth and unpaid household work, which made them more reluctant to marry and have children. Women, like men, analysts argued, wanted to participate on the labour market but this proved virtually impossible to combine with child-rearing (Lundqvist 2007). Hence, it was argued by social scientists and politicians alike, industrial society had become a society of cleavages, not only between classes but also between women and men as the meaning and character of the family had changed.

What was then to be done to enhance and stabilize Sweden with its poor families and declining fertility? The first step towards a more coherent family policy were taken in the mid-1930s when public loans for housing construction geared to families with many children were introduced ('*barnrikehusen*'), together with a programme for income support for large families (Olsson 1992). In parallel, debates were intensified on the conditions for families with children, not least in connection with Alva Myrdal and Gunnar Myrdal's book *Crisis in the Population Question* (1934). The debate concerned what actions could be taken to enhance living conditions for many of the country's families with children to raise fertility levels (Hirdman 1989; Ohlander 1992; Hatje 1974).

The efforts culminated in 1935 with the appointment of the Population Commission, which had as its remit the consequences of the economic crisis, mounting unemployment and the intensive debate about families and fertility. The commission analysed a string of reasons for and consequences of declining fertility levels. It also presented several proposals to reverse the tendencies, primarily in the area of labour legislation and in public support for pregnant women and mothers (Ohlander 1992). These reforms were preceded by an intensive debate on the future orientation of social and family policy. Which groups should be included? Which were to be excluded? How would social policy be devised to combat unemployment and declining fertility, and to steer Sweden away from the looming economic crisis?

Two themes came to dominate the debate. The first focused on women as mothers, the second on women as paid labourers. The themes were interrelated: was it possible to reconcile the demands of motherhood and paid labour, and was this desirable? Another issue was the conditions for pregnant women and mothers, and whether their conditions should be improved via general support, means-tested programmes and in-kind support. It was in particular during the latter debates that the social-policy conflicts became obvious.

The issue of support for pregnant women and mothers remained unresolved until 1931, when the Swedish parliament established mandatory maternity insurance. It was a bureaucratic and cumbersome insurance, in which sickness insurance funds and women who were members of these received public support via so-called maternity aid. Support covered costs in relation to delivery and a cash scheme. Women not covered by the insurance received aid via a public means-tested support scheme. The system came under increasing criticism, a critique that was taken up by the Population Commission. The Commission's proposals were adopted by the social-democratic government, which in 1937 proposed several changes in the maternity insurance. To begin with, maternity support ('*moderskapspenning*') would be publicly funded and given to women with newborn babies *in need* (which in calculation embraced almost all women). Furthermore, women in *pressing need* of support would receive so-called maternity aid ('*mödrahjälp*'), delivered in the form most suitable for the individual, either in kind or in cash (Governmental Bill no. 38, 1937).

The proposal triggered intense debate. There was no controversy about the need for an overhaul of the system, or about the need to support pregnant women and mothers. Controversies were stirred by the ideological confrontations on issues such as the transition from a policy of means-tested aid to mandatory and population-based insurance, and on the likelihood that the social-democratic government would establish a universal maternity insurance. This would then challenge the bourgeois parties and their orientation towards means-tested and targeted programmes. Out of these controversies arose a political will to pave the way out of the economic crisis – and to modernize Swedish society.

Interestingly, the proposals met criticism both from within social democracy and from the bourgeois parties. The critique from Social Democrats pointed to the relatively weak and modest changes and instead advocated a more comprehensive universal system. The bourgeois critique, on the other hand, argued vehemently against a 'socialization' of the costs for families and children. Instead, only the truly needy should be targeted by public support.

The minister for social affairs, Gustav Möller, rejected the radical demands from his fellow Social Democrats while at the same time claiming that the bourgeois critique was irrational. The path to be taken was that of a compromise between different political interests:

> When one takes action like this, one needs to be careful not to do it in such a way as to provoke a successful reaction against the social-policy decisions of

> parliament. Large parts of the Swedish population have difficulties in understanding that people of considerable economic means should receive support from the state even if this is as a kind of child premium, that is, with motives of population policy (First Chamber protocol no. 29, 1937, p. 10).

The government proposals were accepted in parliament, and a three-pronged strategy for family support was enacted: (1) means-tested maternity insurance; (2) maternity support for members of a sickness insurance fund; (3) means-tested maternity aid (Lundqvist 2007).

Another area related to the population issue and to the growing family-policy ambitions concerned the role of women in the labour market. A controversial issue was the right of employers to dismiss women who either became pregnant or got married. The impact of industrialization on female work had been debated since the late 1800s, and the question matured into a political issue in the 1930s (Frangeur 1998; Karlsson 2001). A large part of this change was the ambition to improve the conditions for working women irrespective of their marital status (responding to the right of employers to dismiss pregnant and married women). The Social Democrat government now turned its attention to this area of the labour market. Two government commissions had worked on measures to enhance women's position: the Population Commission suggested a ban on dismissals of pregnant and married women while another committee (on women's work) rejected the idea of a ban on female dismissals and instead proposed a voluntary system (SOU 1938:13; SOU 1938:47). The government followed the advice of the Population Commission and added the right of paid leave in connection with childbirth and reforms in the sickness insurance to 'guarantee fair and human treatment of those women on the labour market who want to marry or become pregnant' (Governmental Bill no. 114 1939, p. 22).

Different ideological positions were therefore pitted against one another in these debates. The conservatives argued that it was profoundly problematic to limit the freedom of employers to hire and dismiss workers – arguing that pregnant and married women were ill-suited for paid labour. Social democrats and liberals opposed the conservatives' standpoint, stressing women's right to paid labour. They based their opinion on arguments of justice but also of population and fertility – who would have children if they risked dismissal?

With the government's positions accepted in parliament, employers could no longer dismiss women freely. Together with the widened social policy ambitions for maternity support and maternity aid, this opened up the field for an even more ambitious transformation of labour relations in Sweden.

Public support for pregnant women and mothers was still rudimentary, and it took several decades before it was fully developed and integrated into the battery of welfare state instruments. The foundation had been laid however and would eventually lead to the ambition to enact a 'dual-earner/dual-carer family model', in which both women and men were encouraged to do paid labour and where the state provided public childcare. The crisis policies of the 1930s therefore radicalized the debate on women's roles in society and highlighted their dual roles as mothers and paid labourers, while it laid the basis for the family-policy regime which remained in place all the way until the economic crisis of the early 1990s.

CRISIS MANAGEMENT IN THE 1990s: FROM ANTI-INFLATION POLICY TO 'THE ACCOUNTANT'S STRATEGY'

Living conditions among the Swedish population underwent a number of major changes in the 1990s. The most noticeable change was the increase in the proportion of the population that encountered various kinds of disadvantage or illness. Along with higher unemployment and reduced employment, conditions of employment altered in many respects. Negative psychosocial working conditions and short-term employment became more common. Progressively larger groups suffered financial difficulties and low incomes (Ds 2002:32 pp. 9–10).

The goals of family policy, as founded in the wake of the economic crisis in the 1930s, developed but were also preserved until the financial breakdown in Sweden in the 1990s. If earlier phases of family policy (and social policy in general) were shaped by seemingly endless increases in economic growth, creating a manoeuvring space for ambitious reforms, the development from the early 1980s onwards changed the conditions for the political regulation of the family: the era of the big reforms and the ever-expanding state seemed to be over.

When the Social Democrats came to power in 1982 after six years of centre-left government, they launched a programme emphasizing that low inflation – rather than full employment per se – was the key to maintaining employment levels as well as welfare levels. The programme referred to itself as a 'third way' between monetarism and Keynesianism (Benner 1997). The first step towards an 'anti-inflation' policy was taken in connection with the 'big bang' currency devaluation of 16 per cent in 1983, with the outspoken aim of shifting to a hard-currency policy. The profit regulation of the Rehn–Meidner model, it was argued, was no longer viable. Instead, profit *as such* had to be the target of labour movement programmes. The novelty of the 'third way' was its explicit orientation to corporate profitability and the expectation that other elements in economic and labour market regulation would adhere to this target (Rothstein 1996).

In the wake of the political reorientation, three important decisions were taken which changed the landscape for Swedish policymaking. First, a major tax reform was implemented by the end of the 1980s (Government Bill 1989/90:110). Second, a restructuring of existing housing policy was effected (Lindbom 2001), and third, far-reaching deregulation of the financial sector was accomplished (Jonung 1997).

The aim of the tax reform was to reduce taxes on labour and savings while at the same time increasing taxation on consumption and borrowing. Moreover, a system where income from wage labour and income on capital were treated equally was intended to limit tax evasion (Ds 2002:32, p. 160). The tax reform was meant to be neutral in distribution terms, in the sense that reduced marginal tax rates were supposed to be compensated by raising child and housing allowances. According to Björklund et al. (1995) 'the tax reform meant that income from different income maintenance systems came to comprise an increasingly large part of disposable income, especially for families with children' (Ds 2002:32, p. 160). Moreover, the reform of housing policy – a highly subsidized area during the postwar period – made housing a source of government revenue rather than expenditure (Lindbom 2001).

In 1985, the credit market was deregulated, which further contributed to the development in the 1990s. The decision to deregulate credit markets contributed to a sharp rise in property prices. When housing prices fell in the early 1990s, Swedish banks and financial institutions made massive credit losses. The government intervened to save the financial actors, which further contributed to the deterioration of public finances (Ds 2002:34, p. 161). In an attempt to stabilize the economy, the Swedish krona was pegged to the ECU in 1991. In parallel, earlier pledges to expand paid holidays to six weeks and a prolongation of parental insurance were retracted. Replacement levels in health insurance were lowered as a harbinger of further cuts in welfare expenditure during the decade (Palme 2000).

In 1991, a centre–right government took power, comprising four parties – the Liberal Party, the Centre Party, the Christian Democratic Party and the Moderate Party. Its main rhetoric was 'a new start for Sweden' where deregulation, privatization and structural reform as well as a revolution in the 'freedom to choose' (as opposed to the alleged rigidity of welfare service provision hitherto) were emphasized (Benner 1997). However, when it came to economic policymaking, the government was not in a situation to make any radical moves. It continued its predecessor's hard-currency policy, which resulted in massive currency speculations at the beginning of 1992 while at the same time inflation began to fall markedly (owing partly to the effects of the tax reform and because wage increases had been kept down) and led to the Swedish krona being floated in late 1992 (leading to a de facto 20 per cent devaluation). When the hard-currency policy failed – and unemployment exploded – the government instead aimed to reduce the public deficit and lower inflation (Jonung 1997).

As a result, the government suggested that compensation rates and also sickness, parental and unemployment insurance should be reduced to 80 per cent (from 90 per cent). The decision led to a parliamentary crisis and an agreement with the Social Democrats on a common policy based on saving took place (Benner 1997). In addition to the reduction in the insurances, one unpaid waiting day was introduced and the qualification requirements were made more stringent. Unemployment benefit levels changed several times: from 90 per cent of income in 1990 to 80 per cent in 1993 and to 75 per cent in 1996. A year later the 80 per cent level was restored (Ds 2002:32, p. 138).

In these times of economic turmoil, the government took extraordinary decisions: to combat inflation a policy which aimed only to reduce government expenditure, or 'budget restructuring', as it was called, was developed. The restructuring of the budget was seen as the only cure to give stability in the economy (Ds 2002:43, p. 178).

The crisis had however hit Swedish society. Mass unemployment was a fact: in 1990, open unemployment was 1.6 per cent and only three years later, in 1993, 8.3 per cent were unemployed (Ds 2002:32). Together with the cutbacks in the social welfare system, mass unemployment contributed to the most profound crisis for the welfare state since the 1930s.

In 1994, a Social Democrat government came to power. The new government adopted a 'Consolidation Programme' (implemented between 1994 and 1998) based on the conviction that reduced budget deficits would lead to lower interest rates that, in turn, would stimulate economic growth and employment. Moreover, the government adopted a 'Convergence Programme' in 1995 which corresponded to the convergence criteria established by the EU and the coming of the Monetary Union (EMU) (the deficit in the public sector was not to exceed 3 per cent of GNP and the public gross debt was not to exceed 60 per cent of GNP). The strategy was later described by its chief architect and later Prime Minister, Göran Persson, as an 'accountant's strategy' (Benner and Vad 2000).

According to the Welfare Commission in Sweden, the Consolidation Programme created improvements in public finances, and in 1998 the budget was once again in balance. This induced the government to restore some of the levels in the transfer systems and also to improve the measures to create new jobs.

The 1990s was thus a decade marked by massive swings in the economy as well as in the social welfare system. The changes made in the transfer systems mainly concerned family policy (Ds 2000:32). This development will be analysed in the next subsection.

Family Policy Development in the 1990s

Financial family policy during the 1990s consisted of tax-financed benefits and insurances which in turn consisted of a wide and complicated net of social policy measures. These measures can be divided into three categories:

1. Insurance (including above all parental insurance, temporary parental benefit, pregnancy insurance and child pension – the last being a specific insurance programme within the field of economic family policy that provides a certain amount of money to children who have lost one or both parents)
2. General allowances (including child allowance and allowances for adoption)
3. Means-tested allowances (including housing allowances and alimony).

Developments in the 1990s changed some of these conditions. Public support of families with children was reduced, but with variation during the decade – a small increase in the early period turned into a sharp decline in the middle of the decade, with a modest hike towards the end. The main pillars of the system remained in place, though: child allowances remained universal and not means-tested (and with a bonus for families with more than three children), parental insurance was still based on the income-replacement model, and families with limited means received housing support. In addition, alimony was paid out to parents with limited means and parents with disabled children received special support (Palme 2000). Childcare both expanded and contracted: in 1995, the municipalities became obliged to arrange childcare for all children between one and twelve with parents who worked or studied, without delay. The number of children receiving childcare was also expanding by over 40 per cent between 1990 and 1999. These factors indicate an expansion during the crisis. However, at the same time the number of children in the child groups in daycare increased by 20 per cent at pre-schools and 65 per cent in after-school care activities, while at the same time staffing levels varied considerably (Bergqvist and Nyberg 2001).

Major changes in regulation and in replacement levels were also enacted in the 1990s (with the exception of children's pensions and the cash-for-care support scheme) and worsened conditions for families with children.

Parental insurance (established in 1974 in its current gender-neutral form) was affected by changes in the health insurance system. The level of compensation was 90 per cent between 1974 and 1995. The percentage was lowered, however, just as in the case of unemployment insurance, to 80 per cent in 1995, and to 75 per cent in 1996. It was restored to 80 per cent in 1998, owing to the recovery of the economy (Nyberg 2007).

Child allowances (introduced in 1948) remained universal. As mentioned, child allowances were used to compensate for the income reductions caused by the new tax systems. However, cuts in response to the economic crisis of the early 1990s contributed to a real decrease in compensation levels while the bonus for large families was first reduced and then later scrapped in 1996. However, compensation levels were raised just a few years later and the bonus for large families was reintroduced (Palme 2000).

Alimony for children ('*underhållsstöd*') who live with one of their parents was introduced in 1997. The alimony replaced an older form of benefit ('*bidragsförskott*'), which had been introduced in the 1930s to support lone-parent families. It was also reformed in the 1990s, primarily in the setting of compensation levels and in the conditions for payouts. In parallel, housing support was trimmed, reducing the redistributive impact that was intended in the new tax system.

The conditions for women and men on the labour market were affected by the retrenchments of the family policy systems. Women's labour market participation increased from 59.4 per cent in 1970 to 75.2 per cent in 1980, and the trend continued until 1990 when the figure had reached 82.3 per cent. However, the trend was broken with the crisis of the 1990s, and in 1998 it had reached 73.9 per cent. At the same time, differences in labour market participation between women and men, which had narrowed in the preceding decades, again increased. Both genders were affected by mounting unemployment, but while men's unemployment stabilized around 1994, female unemployment continued to increase until 1997. This can be explained by the gender-segregated labour market, where male-dominated sectors were hit before those dominated by women (Stanfors 2007, pp. 82ff.)

The principles of gender equality that had arisen from the crisis policies of the 1930s – where debate, legislation and political reforms targeted women's roles and conditions in the labour market – came under pressure in the 1990s. Women were particularly hit by the labour market crisis and the rising unemployment. The political scientist Diane Sainsbury has argued that the cuts in the welfare system also affected gender relations in a negative way:

> Reducing replacement levels for care-related benefits, available to both women and men, may undermine the incentives for men to take responsibility for care. This risks locking women into the traditional role of care provider. (Sainsbury 2000, p. 103; author's translation)

The welfare systems were, however, reset after the crisis ebbed out and female labour market participation returned to pre-crisis levels. Two groups were left behind, however: lone parents and citizens born outside Europe. Economic growth in the late 1990s did not improve the social and economic conditions of these groups. Instead, the marginalization of these groups on the labour market continued, making their standard of living considerably worse than that of other groups in society.

Generally, citizens born outside Sweden also have lower income than Swedish-born citizens. For citizens over 20 years old, the net income was 203 100 kronor per year for Swedish-born citizens and 154 700 kronor for citizens born outside Sweden. There are however large differences depending on the origin of foreign-born citizens: persons born in a Western country earned 191 800 in 2007, while those born in a non-Western country earned only 111 500 kronor the same year (SCB inkomststatistik 2008).

Moreover, there are fewer Swedish-born citizens who live under the poverty line (an income below 60 per cent of the median income). More than 11 per cent of the population live in relative poverty (2007). Nine per cent of Swedish-born citizens live in relative poverty, and the corresponding figure for foreign-born citizens is 23.9 per cent. There are again large differences depending on what country a person was born in, but there are also big differences depending on how long a person has lived in Sweden (Hammarstedt 2008).

Poverty is also higher among lone-parent families than two-parent families. The income gap between two-parent families and lone-parent families widened in the 1990s, mainly owing to rising unemployment, and small improvements in income. Almost one-third of all lone parents received social assistance during that decade (Ds 2002:32, p. 68). There are, however, differences within this group: lone mothers tend to be poorer than lone fathers. Prognoses indicate that there will be even more lone mothers living under the poverty line: from about 20 000 lone mothers in 2003 the group will increase to 57 000 lone-mother households in 2010. Another factor is tied to existing wage gaps between men and women: men's higher wages and the fact that most children live with their mothers contribute to increasing poverty among lone mothers. Unemployment is yet another factor that affects poverty among lone-parent families. The unemployment rate among lone parents was 10 per cent in 2010, and within this group, lone mothers with children under 7 years of age have the highest unemployment incidence (Statistical Yearbook of Sweden 2011).

In sum, the economic crisis of the 1990s affected all women and men. Unemployment and cutbacks in the welfare system resulted in increasing poverty and gender inequalities in the labour market. For many families with children, the situation improved by the end of the 1990s. But not for everyone: for lone-parent families and for citizens born outside Europe, living conditions seem rather to be declining.

CONCLUSION

Family and gender policies are indeed integral and central parts of the Swedish welfare model. The goal of levelling out social and economic inequalities between families with children and families without children became important in the wake of the economic crisis in the 1930s: politicians became increasingly aware of how high unemployment and widespread poverty affected women and men, resulting in an urgent need to politically regulate the family. The social-democratic government appointed the population committee to analyse the devastating consequences of poverty and declining birth rates, and to suggest how to enable (above all) women to become parents, and the result was seen in the introduction of antenatal clinics and child-welfare centres, legal prohibitions against the dismissal of married or pregnant women from workplaces, and means-tested maternity support.

These reforms were all part of the crisis management in the 1930s. The reform of women's living conditions was also embedded in a debate about issues of principle, and how the future of the political regulation of the family should be outlined. The crisis policies during the 1930s thus became an attempt to shape the future. Not all problems, of course, were addressed back then, but the very foundation for how to include family and gender relations in a broader political programme for productivity and economic growth emerged at this time in history, and the development of the 'dual-earner/dual-carer family model' in the postwar period is partly rooted in the crisis management of the 1930s.

The Swedish welfare state came under severe pressure during the economic crisis in the 1990s. Mass unemployment and cutbacks in the social welfare system increased poverty among large parts of the population, above all among families with children. For some years between the early

1990s and 1998, various governments decided to reduce government expenditure, and the idea that a reduced budget deficit, leading to lower interest rates, was the only way to stimulate economic growth and employment became an established fact.

The crisis affected the transfer system for families badly, an obvious result being increasing poverty. The crisis can also be analysed as a backlash for family and gender-equal policy ambitions, as previous policy goals aimed at levelling out inequalities between families were partly abandoned. Even if the system itself was not altered, mass unemployment and the cutbacks in the social welfare system indeed changed living conditions for many families with children. Although a large part of the population was hit by the crisis, three groups were affected worse than others: lone mothers, non-European migrant families and young adults. When the economy recovered and the welfare system was partly reinstalled, living conditions for many families improved. For lone mothers and non-European migrant families, however, the situation has not got any better. On the contrary, poverty figures have increased during the new millennium alongside a growing polarization between rich and poor, which could be an indicator of changing labour and welfare policy goals, including the ambition to level out inequalities between social classes as well as between women and men. This is also a pattern that has been further strengthened throughout the current crisis, indicating that inequalities between different groups are no longer a prioritized target within financial family policy, which poses a challenge to the 'dual earner/dual carer family model'.

REFERENCES

Åmark, Klas (2005), *Hundra år av välfärdspolitik: Välfärdsstatens framväxt i Norge och Sverige*, Umeå, Sweden: Boréa.

Benner, Mats (1997), *The Politics of Growth: Economic Regulation in Sweden, 1930–1994*, Lund, Sweden: Arkiv.

Benner, Mats and Torben Vad (2000), 'Sweden and Denmark', in Fritz Scharpf and Vivien Schmidt (eds), *Welfare and Work in the Open Economy*, vol. 2: *Diverse Responses to Common Challenges in Twelve Countries*, Oxford: Oxford University Press, pp. 399–466.

Bergqvist, Christina and Anita Nyberg (2001), 'Den svenska barnomsorgsmodellen – kontinuitet och förändring under 1990-talet', in Marta Szebehely (ed.), *Välfärdstjänster i omvandling*, Reports of the Government Commissions (SOU) 2001:52, Stockholm: Fritzes, pp. 239–87.

Bergqvist, Christina (ed.) (1999), *Equal Democracies: Gender and Politics in the Nordic Countries*, Oslo: Scandinavian University Press in cooperation with the Nordic Council of Ministers.

Bergström, Villy (1992), 'Party program and economic policy', in Klaus Misgeld,

Karl Molin and Klas Åmark (eds), *Creating Social Democracy: A Century of the Social Democratic Labor Party in Sweden*, University Park, PA: Pennsylvania State University Press, pp. 131–74.
Björklund, Anders, Mårten Palme and Ingemar Svensson (1995), 'Tax reforms and income distribution: an assessment using different income concepts', *Swedish Economic Policy Review*, **2** (2), 229–66.
Borchorst, Anette (2008), 'Woman-friendly policy paradoxes? Childcare policies and gender equality visions in Scandinavia', in Kari Melby, Anna-Birte Ravn and Christina Carlsson Wetterberg (eds), *Gender Equality and Welfare Politics in Scandinavia: The Limits of Political Ambition*?, Bristol: Policy Press, pp. 27–43.
Brandt, Berit and Elin Kvande (2007), 'Care politics for fathers in a flexible time culture', in Diane Perrons, Colette Fagan, Linda McDowell, Kath Ray and Kevin Ward (eds), *Gender Divisions and Working Time in the New Economy: Changing Patterns of Work, Care and Public Policy in Europe and North America*, Cheltenham, UK and Northampton, MA, USA: Edward Elgar, pp. 148–62.
Daly, Mary (2000), *The Gender Division of Welfare: The Impact of the British and German Welfare States*, Cambridge: Cambridge University Press.
Daly, M. (2011), 'What adult worker model? A critical look at recent social policy reform in Europe from a gender and family perspective', *Social Politics*, **18** (1), 1–23.
Ds 2002:32, *Welfare in Sweden: The Balance Sheet for the 1990s*, Stockholm: Socialdepartementet.
Ellingsæter, Anne-Lise and Arnlaug Leira (eds) (2006), *Politicising Parenthood in Scandinavia: Gender Relations in Welfare States*, Bristol: Policy Press.
Ellingsæter, Anne-Lise and Arnlaug Leira (eds) (2007), *Velferdsstaten og familien: Utfordringer og dilemmaer*, Oslo: Gyldendal.
Esping-Andersen, Gøsta (1990), *The Three Worlds of Welfare Capitalism*, Cambridge: Cambridge University Press.
Esping-Andersen, Gøsta (2009), *The Incomplete Revolution: Adapting to Women's New Roles*, Cambridge: Cambridge University Press.
FK Protocol (Första Kammarens [First Chamber] protokoll), number 29, 1937.
Frangeur, René (1998), *Yrkeskvinna eller makens tjänarinna: Striden om yrkesrätten för gifta kvinnor i mellankrigstidens Sverige*, Lund, Sweden: Arkiv.
Government Bill 1937/38:38, *Förslag om ändring i förordningen av moderskapspenning och mödrahjälpen*, Stockholm: Socialdepartementet.
Government Bill 1939/40:114. *Lag om förbud mot arbetstagares avskedande i anledning av äktenskaps ingående, havandeskap och barnsbörd*, Stockholm: Justitiedepartmentet och Socialdepartementet.
Government Bill 1989/90:110, *Om reformerad inkomst- och företagsbeskattning*, Stockholm: Finansdepartmentet.
Haataja, Anita and Anita Nyberg (2006), 'Diverging paths? The dual-earner/dual-carer model in Finland and Sweden in the 1990s', in Anne-Lise Ellingsæter and Arnlaug Leira (eds), *Politicising Parenthood in Scandinavia: Gender Relations in Welfare States*, Bristol: Policy Press, pp. 217–41.
Hammarstedt, Mats (2008), 'Assimilation and participation in social assistance among immigrants', *International Journal of Social Welfare*, **18** (1), 85–94.
Hantrais, Linda (2004), *Family Policy Matters: Responding to Family Change in Europe*, Bristol: Policy Press.

Hatje, Ann-Catrin (1974), *Befolkningsfrågan och välfärden: Debatten om familjepolitik och nativitetsökning under 1930- och 1940-talen*, Stockholm: Allmänna.
Hirdman, Yvonne (1989), *Att lägga livet till rätta: Studier i svensk folkhemspolitik*, Stockholm: Carlssons.
Jonung, Lars (1997), 'Framtidens stabiliseringspolitik – svensk makropolitik igår, idag och i morgon', in Åke E. Andersson (ed.), *Bostadsmarknaden på 2000-talet*, Kristianstad, Sweden: SNS, pp. 39–83.
Karlsson, Gunnel (2001), *Från broderskap till systerskap: Det socialdemokratiska kvinnoförbundets kamp för inflytande och makt i SAP*, Lund, Sweden: Arkiv.
Leira, Arnlaug (2002), *Working Parents and the Welfare State: Family Change and Policy Reform in Scandinavia*, Cambridge: Cambridge University Press.
Leira, Arnlaug (2006), 'Parenthood change and policy reform in Scandinavia, 1970s–2000s', in Anne-Lise Ellingsæter and Arnlaug Leira (eds), *Politicising Parenthood in Scandinavia: Gender Relations in Welfare States*, Bristol: Policy Press, pp. 27–53.
Lewis, J. (1992), 'Gender and the development of welfare regimes', *Journal of European Social Policy*, **8** (2), 159–73.
Lindbom, Arne (ed.) (2001), *Den nya bostadspolitiken*, Umeå, Sweden: Boréa.
Lundberg, Erik (1983), *Ekonomiska kriser förr och nu*, Stockholm: SNS.
Lundqvist, Åsa (2001), *Bygden, bruket och samhället: Om människor och organisationer i brukssamhället Böksholm, 1900–1979*, Lund, Sweden: Arkiv.
Lundqvist, Åsa (2007), *Familjen i den svenska modellen*, Umeå, Sweden: Boréa.
Lundqvist, Åsa (2011), *Family Policy Paradoxes: Gender Equality and Labour Market Regulation in Sweden, 1930–2010*, Bristol: Policy Press.
Morgan, Kimberly (2007), *Working Mothers and the Welfare State: Religion and the Politics of Work-Family Policies in Western Europe and the United States*, Stanford, CA: Stanford University Press.
Myrdal, Alva and Myrdal, Gunnar (1934), *Kris i befolkningsfrågan*, Stockholm: Bonniers.
Nyberg, Anita (2007), 'Economic crisis and sustainability of dual-earner, dual-carer model', in Diane Perrons, Colette Fagan, Linda McDowell, Kath Ray and Kevin Ward (eds), *Gender Divisions and Working Time in the New Economy: Changing Patterns of Work, Care and Public Policy in Europe and North America*, Cheltenham, UK and Northampton, MA, USA: Edward Elgar, pp. 91–103.
Odhner, Carl-Erik (1992), 'Workers and farmers shape the Swedish model: Social Democracy and agricultural policy', in Klaus Misgeld, Karl Molin and Klas Åmark (eds), *Creating Social Democracy: A Century of the Social Democratic Labor Party in Sweden*, University Park, PA: Pennsylvania State University Press, pp. 175–212.
Official Statistics of Sweden, *Statistics – Social Welfare. Social Assistance: 2010. County and Municipal Expenditures*, Stockholm: The National Board of Health and Welfare.
Ohlander, Ann-Sofie (1992), 'The invisible child? The struggle for a Social Democratic family policy in Sweden, 1900–1960', in Klaus Misgeld, Karl Molin and Klas Åmark (eds), *Creating Social Democracy: A Century of the Social Democratic Labor Party in Sweden*, University Park, PA: Pennsylvania State University Press, pp. 213–36.
Olsson, Sven E. (1992), *Social Policy and Welfare State in Sweden*, Lund, Sweden: Arkiv.
Palme, Joakim (2000), 'Socialförsäkringar och kontanta familjestöd', in

Åke Bergmark (ed.), *Välfärd och försörjning*, Reports of the Government Commissions (SOU) 2000:40, Stockholm: Fritzes, pp. 61–86.

Reports of the Government Commissions (SOU 1938:13), *Betänkande angående förvärvsarbetande kvinnors rättsliga ställning vid äktenskap och barnsbörd: Avgivet av befolkningskommitténs betänkande*, Stockholm: Nord. Bokhandel.

Reports of the Government Commissions (SOU 1938:47), *Betänkande ang. gift kvinnas förvärvsarbete m.m. Avgivet av kvinnoarbetskommitténs betänkande*, Stockholm, available at: http://libris.kb.se/bib/888635

Rothstein, Bo (1992), *Den korporativa staten: Intresseorganisationer och statsförvaltning i svensk politik*, Stockholm: Norstedts.

Rothstein, Bo (1996), *The Social Democratic State: The Swedish Model and the Bureaucratic Problem of Social Reforms*, Pittsburgh, PA: University of Pittsburgh Press.

Sainsbury, Diane (ed.) (1999), *Gender and Welfare State Regimes*, Oxford: Oxford University Press.

Sainsbury, Diane (2000), 'Välfärdsutvecklingen för kvinnor och män på 1990-talet', in Åke Bergmark (ed.), *Välfärd och försörjning*, Reports of the Government Commissions (SOU) 2000:40, Stockholm: Fritzes, pp. 87–128.

Salonen, Tapio (2011), *Välfärd, inte för alla: Den ekonomiska familjepolitikens betydelse för barnfattigdomen i Sverige*, Stockholm: Rädda Barnen.

SCB inkomstatistik (2008), *Income Statistics 2008*, Stockholm: Statistics Sweden, available at www.scb.se/Pages/PressRelease____285936.aspx.

Schön, Lennart (2000), *En modern svensk ekonomisk historia: Tillväxt och omvandling under två sekel*, Stockholm: SNS.

Socialförsäkringsrapport 2009:4, Stockholm: Försäkringskassan.

Sommestad, Lena (2001), 'Lovsång till mejerskan: om den föränderliga kvinnligheten', in Ulla Wikander (ed.), *Det evigt kvinnliga: En historia om förändring*, Lund, Sweden: Studentlitteratur, pp. 214–36.

Stanfors, Maria (2007), *Mellan arbete och familj: Ett dilemma för kvinnor i Sverige, 1900–2000*, Stockholm: SNS.

Statistical Yearbook of Sweden (2011), *Statistisk årsbok*, Stockholm: Statistics Sweden.

Therborn, Göran (1989), *Borgarklass och byråkrati i Sverige*, Lund, Sweden: Arkiv.

7. Economic crises as political opportunities

Johannes Lindvall

INTRODUCTION

Economic crises tend to have significant political consequences. The Great Depression of the 1930s led, among other things, to political realignments in Sweden and the United States and the breakdown of democracy in Austria and Germany. More recently, the Great Inflation of the 1970s and 1980s marked the beginning of a long period of austerity in economic and social affairs, resulting in the secular decline of Europe's social-democratic parties. This chapter examines the political consequences of the world-wide financial and economic crisis that began in 2007–08, comparing this 'Great Recession' with the Great Depression, which is arguably its closest historical parallel (although there are many differences, as Bordo and James (2010), and others, have pointed out).

There are at least three good reasons to pay close attention to the political consequences of deep economic crises. First of all, such crises create new political opportunities, and politicians know this well. As Barack Obama's new chief of staff, Rahm Emanuel, put it two weeks after the US presidential election in 2008, 'You never want a serious crisis to go to waste' (*Wall Street Journal* 2008). Second, the effects of deep crises linger. In the United States, the emergence of the 'New Deal Coalition' gave the Democratic Party an upper hand in national politics for decades, and in Sweden, the election of 1932 heralded 40 years of social-democrat hegemony. Third, social scientists can learn a great deal about the effects of political systems on policy responses and economic outcomes when they observe how different states respond to a common shock (Gourevitch 1986, p. 221; see also Katzenstein 1978).

This chapter is mainly concerned with the effects of the Great Recession and the Great Depression on the distribution of power between left-wing and right-wing parties. I argue elsewhere, on the basis of quantitative evidence, that the electoral consequences of the Great Recession and Great Depression were largely similar (Lindvall 2012a): immediately after the beginning of each crisis, right-wing parties did better than left-wing parties, but after approximately three years the playing field was levelled. This chapter uses qualitative evidence on elections and government formation in twenty democratic states in 1929–35 and 2008–12 to develop and extend these arguments. The first section distinguishes between three kinds of political consequences that economic crises can have, and presents a brief discussion of political institutions and public policies. The second section examines the effects of the Great Recession and the Great Depression on the distribution of political power between left-wing and right-wing parties. The third section concludes with a discussion of how to explain the observed patterns.

POLITICAL CONSEQUENCES

It is customary, in political science, to distinguish between the polity (the basic political institutions), politics (the competition between parties, interest groups, and individuals for power, leadership and influence), and policy (legislation, executive orders and other authoritative political decisions). The Great Depression had powerful effects in all three dimensions. The idea of this chapter is to use the Depression era as a benchmark in order to examine the political consequences of the Great Recession. The chapter is primarily concerned with politics (the second dimension), but I would like to begin with a few observations regarding political institutions (the first dimension) and economic policy (the third dimension), placing the main topic of the chapter in context.

The most important political consequence of the Great Depression was the backlash against democracy in Europe and Latin America in the 1930s. For Huntington (1991), the interwar period represents the first 'reverse wave' in the history of democratic government, putting an end to the first, long wave of democratization that began in the 1820s and ended a century later in the aftermath of the First World War. In Huntington's view, the Great Depression was one of the factors behind the rise of anti-democratic political parties and movements in the interwar years (Huntington 1991, p. 18). This claim is backed up by a rich comparative literature on the relationship between prosperity and democratization. Although the precise shape and nature of the relationship between income and democracy is still debated (Boix and Stokes 2003; Przeworski et al. 2000), there is broad agreement in the literature that economic crises put democracy at risk.

Figure 7.1, which relies on data from the Polity Project (Marshall and Jaggers 2012), describes the mean level of democracy among the sovereign states of the world in the interwar period (1919 to 1939) and the period

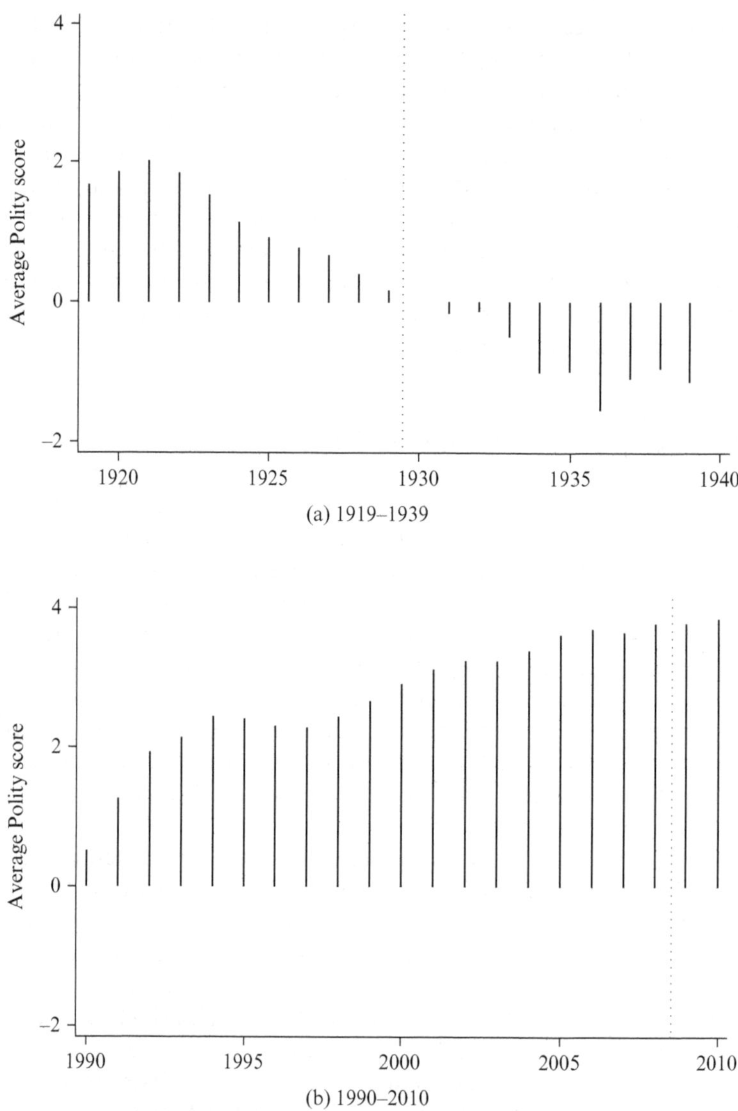

Source: Data from Marshall and Jaggers (2012). The combined, revised Polity score ranges from −10 (pure authoritarianism) to 10 (pure democracy). There were between 62 and 69 states in the data set in 1919–1939 and between 145 and 164 in 1990–2010.

Figure 7.1 Economic crises and democracy: average Polity score in the world

between the fall of the Berlin Wall and the last available measurement (1990 to 2010), identifying the timing of the Great Wall Street Crash (October 1929) and the Lehman Brothers collapse (September 2008) with vertical dotted lines. It is interesting to note that both the Great Depression and the Great Recession occurred less than two decades after major changes in the international system, involving the breakup of empires, the creation of new states and the spread of democracy (the end of the First World War on the one hand, the end of the cold war on the other). It is also interesting to note that just after the Great Wall Street Crash, the average level of democracy in the world shifted into the negative, authoritarian spectrum.

As Figure 7.1a also makes clear, however, democracy was already in retreat when the Great Depression occurred. As Huntington noted, the first 'reverse wave' in the history of democracy began with Benito Mussolini's rise to power in Italy in the early 1920s, almost a decade before the Depression, and fascism was clearly a phenomenon with many causes, not all of them economic (Mann 2004, ch. 2). The Depression may have pushed some countries over the brink, notably Germany and Austria, but if the economic crisis had occurred in more benign circumstances, it is far from certain that it would have had a similarly catastrophic outcome. Those of us who believe strongly in the intrinsic value of democracy can take comfort from the fact that when the Great Recession began, democracy was more firmly established in the world (Figure 7.1b). That said, Figure 7.1a brings the more sinister political developments of the 2010s into relief (notably the rise of far-right parties in many countries and the introduction of new curbs on civil liberties in some European states a few years into the Great Recession).

I now turn to public policy (the third dimension). This topic is explored by many other contributors to this volume. However, since many of those contributions are concerned with medium- to long-term policy consequences in domains such as social policy and environmental policy (see, for example, the contributions by Åsa Lundqvist and Anna Gustafsson), I would like to say something about macroeconomic policy, which, in political science, is the main concern of the rich literature on policy responses to the Great Depression (see especially Gourevitch 1984; Weir and Skocpol 1985).

The macroeconomic policy response to the Great Recession was different from the response to the Great Depression. In most advanced democracies, the policy response to the financial crisis and subsequent recession in 2007–09 had three elements:

1. support measures for ailing banks and financial institutions;
2. expansionary monetary policy, including large interest rate cuts by all major central banks and a policy of 'quantitative easing' and 'credit

easing' by the Bank of England and the US Federal Reserve (Benford et al. 2009; Bernanke 2009); and

3. expansionary fiscal policy, including the Obama administration's signature 'stimulus package' – the American Recovery and Reinvestment Act of 2009, which contained $787 billion in tax cuts and spending increases over three years – and the European Union's Economic Recovery Programme, which, in 2008, called for discretionary stimulus measures in the range of 1.5 per cent of GDP.

These policies were adopted by the governments of the advanced democracies within months after the collapse of Lehman Brothers in September 2008. In the Great Depression, in comparison, the macroeconomic policy response was hesitant and slow when it came to both monetary and fiscal policy.

The relative effectiveness of international organizations in the contemporary world is probably one part of the explanation for the differences between 2008–09 and the Great Depression. The IMF's managing director called for a large, global fiscal stimulus already in the autumn of 2008 (see Spilimbergo et al. 2008, p. 3; IMF 2009, p. 97). Meanwhile, the central banks of the advanced industrialized countries coordinated their monetary policies, and at least before the European sovereign debt crisis deteriorated in 2010–11, the European Union managed to coordinate the economic policies of its member states. In many of the advanced democracies, domestic political conditions were also more conducive to a rapid economic policy response in the Great Recession than in the Great Depression (Lindvall 2012b).

It is important to note, however, that the swift monetary policy response and the adoption and implementation of fiscal stimulus measures in Europe and North America in 2008–10 appear to have been relatively contained and short-term measures. The discussion about how to scale back the new stimulus measures began as soon as the risk of a major macroeconomic disaster – a second Great Depression – was averted. Already in April 2009, seven months after the bankruptcy of Lehman Brothers, the IMF's *World Economic Outlook* observed that several IMF directors held the view that further fiscal stimulus was inappropriate: 'Some Directors considered it premature to pursue further discretionary fiscal easing, pointing to uncertain fiscal policy lags and multipliers and the risk of such policies becoming procyclical once the recovery begins' (IMF 2009, p. 172).

At the time of writing, in 2012, it does not seem likely, therefore, that the 'Keynesian' response to the Great Recession will reshape post-crisis economic policy in the way that the Keynesian revolution transformed policymaking in the 1930s and 1940s. That was a period when many countries developed what Margaret Weir (1992) has called 'social Keynesianism', using macroeconomic policy instruments to further long-term political agendas as opposed to merely using them to deal with the immediate threat of economic collapse. On the other hand, past crises have typically been associated with social and political regime changes (see Lennart Schön's contribution to this volume), and it is too early to tell what the long-term policy consequences of the Great Recession will be.

ELECTIONS AND GOVERNMENT FORMATION IN TWO GREAT CRISES

I turn now to the main topic of this chapter: the effects of the Great Recession and the Great Depression on the distribution of political power between left-wing and right-wing parties.

In Lindvall (2012a), which is based on a statistical analysis of election results, I draw three conclusions:

1. The electoral consequences of the Great Depression and the Great Recession were – perhaps surprisingly – rather similar: the same types of statistical models can account for a significant part of the observed variation in election outcomes in both periods, although the results for the 1930s are more robust.
2. The common view that there was something surprising about the failures of left-wing parties in the Great Recession seems misguided, at least if we take history as our guide, for if anything, left-wing parties did better in the first years of the Great Recession than they did in the first years of the Great Depression.
3. As Achen and Bartels (2005) and Bartels (2011) have shown convincingly, powerful retrospective economic voting mechanisms were at work in both the 1930s and 2000s: where left-wing parties were in power when these crises occurred, right-wing parties were likely to do well, and where right-wing parties were in power, left-wing parties were likely to do well. However, the results in Lindvall (2012a) suggest that left-wing governments were punished harder. At least in the first couple of years of each crisis, voters thus appear to have held incumbents to different standards.

In this chapter, I develop and extend these analyses in three important ways. First, whereas the analysis of the Depression era in Lindvall (2012a) stopped in 1933, when parties on the left and parties on the right appeared to perform equally well, this chapter incorporates evidence on elections in 1934 and 1935, demonstrating that parties on the left did very well between the summer of 1932 and the end of 1935. Second, this chapter relies on qualitative evidence on elections and government formation rather than quantitative data on electoral swings, which means that the analyses presented here tell us more about the distribution of executive power between parties on the left and parties on the right. Third, whereas Lindvall (2012a) only included the first post-crisis election in each country, this chapter examines all the national-legislature elections in the first half of the 1930s in twenty democratic states.

The analysis is based on a systematic comparison of the aftermath of the Great Depression and the aftermath of the Great Recession. The time periods covered in the chapter are 1929–35 (beginning with the fall in stock prices on the New York Stock Exchange on 24 October 1929, and ending on 31 December 1935) and 2008–12 (beginning with the collapse of the American investment bank Lehman Brothers on 15 September 2008, and ending in mid 2012). I include all sovereign states that were democracies in 1929 (when the Great Depression began) and held at least one democratic election between 25 October 1929 and the mid-1930s. According to the Polity data set (Marshall and Jaggers 2012), Australia, Austria, Belgium, Canada, Costa Rica, Czechoslovakia, Denmark, Estonia, France, Germany, Greece, Ireland, Latvia, the Netherlands, New Zealand, Norway, Sweden, Switzerland, United Kingdom and the United States meet these criteria (using a combined, revised Polity score of 6 or more as the benchmark).

Beginning with the Depression era, Tables 7.1 and 7.2 provide evidence on all elections that were held in democratic countries between October 1929 and December 1935, and on the ensuing government formation. The columns 'Government before' and 'Government after' contain the most important evidence, whereas the column 'Notes' provides contextual information on changes in the support for individual parties. If the election resulted in the formation of a government that was to the right of the incumbent government before the election, I have italicized the ideological labels in the 'Government before' and 'Government after' columns. If there was no significant change in the ideological orientation of the government, the labels appear in standard type. If, on the other hand, the election resulted in the formation of a government to the left of the incumbent government before the election, the labels appear in bold type.

It is immediately apparent that elections were more likely to result in a shift to the right in the first half of the period and more likely to result in a shift to the left in the second. In 1929, 1930 and 1931, there were no shifts to the left, with the possible exception of Latvia, but four shifts to the right. In 1932, there were shifts to the left in three countries and shifts to the right

Table 7.1 Elections and government formation 1929–32

Country	Date of election	Government before	Government after	Notes
Czechoslovakia	27 October 1929	Centre-right	Centre-right	Gains for the Social Democrats, losses for the Communists.
Canada	28 July 1930	*Centre*	*Right*	Gains for Conservatives. Losses for Liberals and Progressives.
Germany	14 September 1930	Centre-right	Centre-right	Gains for National Socialists and Communists. Losses for the Social Democrats and the German National Peoples Party.
Norway	20 October 1930	Centre	Centre	Gains for Conservatives and Liberals. Losses for Social Democrats and Communists.
United States	4 November 1930	(Right)	(Right)	Mid-term election. Small losses for Republicans, gains for Democrats.
Austria	9 November 1930	*Centre-right*	*Fascist*	Minor gains for right-wing parties. Transition to Austro-fascism under Dollfuss in 1933–1934.
Latvia	3–4 October 1931	**Right**	**Centre-right**	Social Democrats lose support. Right-wing coup in 1934.
Switzerland	25 October 1931	Mixed	Mixed	Only minor changes from previous election.
United Kingdom	27 October 1931	*Left*	*Centre-Right*	Gains for Conservatives. Large losses for Labour. National Government under MacDonald.
New Zealand	1–2 December 1931	Right	Right	Gains for Labour Party, but National Party remains in power.
Australia	19 December 1931	*Left*	*Right*	Gains for Country Party and United Party. Losses for Labor.

Table 7.1 (continued)

Country	Date of election	Government before	Government after	Notes
Costa Rica	14 February 1932	Centre	Centre	New president appointed by parliament.
Ireland	16 February 1932	Right	Right	Large gains for Fianna Fáil. Losses for Labour Party and Cumann na nGaedheal.
France	1 and 8 May 1932	**Centre-right**	**Centre-left**	Gains for centre-left parties, who win a majority of the seats in the Chamber of Deputies.
Estonia	21–23 May 1932	*Centre*	*Centre-right*	Gains for centre-right and Russian-speaking parties, losses for centre-left parties.
Germany	31 July 1932	Non-partisan	Non-partisan	Gains for National Socialists and Communists. Losses for Social Democrats.
Sweden	17–18 September 1932	**Centre-right**	**Left**	Gains for Social Democrats and Agrarians. Losses for Conservatives and Liberals.
Greece	25 September 1932	*Centre*	*Right*	Losses for Liberal Party.
United States	8 November 1932	**Right**	**Centre**	Franklin D. Roosevelt (Democrat) defeats Herbert Hoover (Republican). House and Senate: big losses for Republicans, gains for Democrats.
Denmark	16 November 1932	Centre-left	Centre-left	Small gains for Social Democrats and Conservatives. Losses for Liberals and Social Liberals.
Belgium	27 November 1932	Centre-right	Centre-right	Gains for Catholics, Social Democrats and Communists.

Table 7.2 Elections and government formation 1933–35

Country	Date of election	Government before	Government after	Notes
Ireland	24 January 1933	Right	Right	Fianna Fáil wins overall majority.
The Netherlands	26 April 1933	Centre-right	Centre-right	Only small changes since previous election.
Greece	5 March 1933	Right	Right	Gains for right-wing parties.
Norway	16 October 1933	**Centre-right**	**Left**	Big gains for Social Democrats, who go on to form a government in 1935.
Australia	15 September 1934	Right	Right	Gains for Labor and Communists, but Country Party and United Party remain in government.
United States	6 November 1934	(Centre)	(Centre)	Mid-term election. Democrats increase their majority in the House and the Senate.
Czechoslovakia	19 May 1935	Centre-right	Centre-right	Large gains for fascist Sudeten German party. Losses for old German-speaking parties. Minor losses for most moderate parties.
Canada	14 October 1935	**Right**	**Left**	Split within the Conservative Party puts the Liberals in government in spite of small losses.
Denmark	22 October 1935	Centre-left	Centre-left	Big gains for Social Democrats.
Switzerland	27 October 1935	Mixed	Mixed	Many new, small parties. Minor changes in support for main parties.
United Kingdom	14 November 1935	Right	Right	Labour gains, but Conservatives remain in majority.
New Zealand	27 November 1935	**Right**	**Left**	Big gains for Labour Party.

in two countries (both of which would turn to authoritarianism within a few years). In 1933, 1934 and 1935, there were no shifts to the right, but several shifts to the left. The first few years of the Great Depression were clearly a difficult period for the left, whereas the mid-1930s were a difficult period for the right (at least in countries that remained democratic).

In the first two years after the beginning of the Great Depression, the only democratic countries where the left made relative electoral gains were Czechoslovakia and the United States (where the changes were quite small) and New Zealand (where the incumbent right-wing government stayed in power in spite of gains for the Labour Party). Meanwhile, centre-left parties did badly in many countries. The Liberals in Canada and the Labour parties in Australia, Norway and the United Kingdom all suffered significant electoral losses, resulting in the formation of new right-wing governments in Australia and Canada, and also in the United Kingdom, where the former Labour leader Ramsay MacDonald agreed to lead a National Government based on the Conservative majority in the House of Commons. In Austria, the parties on the right made minor gains in 1930 in what proved to be the last free election of the First Republic (which fell to Fascism under Dollfuss in 1933–34), and in Germany, the slight increase in Communist Party support in 1930 was offset by big losses for the main left-wing party, the Social Democrats.

In 1932, the centre-left continued to do badly in some countries: in Estonia and Greece, incumbent governments that included left-wing or centrist parties were defeated by right-wing opposition parties; in Germany, the Social Democrats continued their decline; and in Ireland, the Labour vote declined sharply in two subsequent elections (although it should be noted that the Labour Party's losses were associated with the rise of Éamon de Valera's Fianna Fáil, which ran on a relatively progressive platform, compared with the incumbent party Cumann na nGaedheal, which had been in power since independence).

From mid-1932 until 1935, in contrast, centre-left parties did well in almost all democratic elections. In May 1932, the French socialist parties won a clear majority. In September, Per-Albin Hansson's Social Democrats won the Swedish general election and formed a minority government that later solidified its support through cooperation with the Farmers' Party. In November 1932, Franklin D. Roosevelt defeated Herbert Hoover in the presidential election and the Democrats won a clear majority in both houses of Congress (they then increased their majority further in 1934). In Belgium, both the Social Democrats and Communists made electoral gains in 1932. In Denmark, the incumbent Social Democrats increased their support in the election of 1932, staying in government, and they also went on to win the 1935 election. In Norway, the Social Democrats increased their support greatly in 1933 and went on to form a government in 1935 through cooperation with Norway's agrarian party. In Australia, the Country Party and United Party remained in government after the 1934 election, but electoral support increased for both Labor and the Communists. In the United Kingdom, the Conservatives remained in the majority after the 1935 election, but the Labour Party recovered somewhat from the defeat of 1931. In Canada, the Liberals formed a new government after the election of 1935 (in spite of a slight decrease in their vote share). In New Zealand, finally, the Labour Party won the 1935 election and formed a new government.

Confirming these patterns, Figure 7.2 describes the proportion of left-wing and right-wing Prime Ministers in a sample of countries between 1920 and 1939. As the figure shows, the proportion of left-wing Prime Ministers was at an all-time high on the eve of the Great Depression. The proportion declined in the next two years, only recovering in 1935 (the years 1936–39 display clear evidence of a social-democratic breakthrough in the years just prior to the Second World War).

If history serves as our guide, then, it was wrong to expect the left to capitalize immediately on the economic crisis in the wake of the recession of 2008–2009 (see, for example, Judt 2010 and *The Economist* 2009), for centre-left parties were also unable to win elections in the immediate aftermath of the Great Depression, which remains the greatest crisis of capitalism that the world has ever seen. It is an open question whether centre-left parties will be able to repeat the comeback that they had in the mid to late 1930s.

Now consider the Great Recession period (Tables 7.3 and 7.4). The evidence is limited, since my analysis stops in September 2012, four years after the beginning of the crisis. The pattern is largely similar, however, the main difference being that in the first two years of the Great Recession, parties on the left did relatively better than they did in the Great Depression, even defeating incumbent right-wing governments in the United States (2008) and Greece (2009) (as well as in Japan and other countries not included in this study).

Overall, however, the first two years after the beginning of the Great Recession was a difficult period for left-wing parties, just as the first two years after the beginning of the Great Depression. In Australia, Austria, the Czech Republic, Finland, Germany, the Netherlands, New Zealand, Sweden and the United Kingdom, and in the United States 2010 mid-term elections, centre-left parties experienced significant electoral losses, and in five countries – Germany, the Netherlands, New Zealand, Slovakia, and the United Kingdom – centre-left parties either lost power outright or were forced to leave governing coalitions. But it is noteworthy that in

(a) Percentage of Left-Wing Prime Ministers

(b) Percentage of Right-Wing Prime Ministers

Note: The dotted vertical line marks the date of the Great Wall Street Crash. The dotted trend lines estimate a locally weighted smoothing functions.

Figure 7.2 Prime Ministers in interwar democracies: (a) percentage of left-wing Prime Ministers; (b) percentage of right-wing Prime Ministers

Table 7.3 Elections and government formation 2008–10

Country	Date of election	Government before	Government after	Notes
Austria	28 September 2008	Centre	Centre	Losses for Social Democrats and Christian Democrats. Big gains for far-right parties.
Canada	14 October 2008	Right	Right	Losses for Liberal Party. Gains for Conservatives and Greens.
United States	4 November 2008	**Right**	**Centre**	Barack Obama defeats George W. Bush and Democrats win majority in Congress.
New Zealand	8 November 2008	*Left*	*Right*	Losses for Labour Party. Gains for National Party.
Norway	14 September 2009	Left	Left	Gains for Social Democrats and Conservatives. Losses for Left Party.
Germany	27 September 2009	*Centre*	*Right*	Big losses for Social Democrats. Gains for Free Democratic Party, Left Party, Greens.
Greece	4 October 2009	**Right**	**Left**	Gains for PASOK. Big losses for New Democracy Party.
Costa Rica	7 February 2010	Centre	Centre	Small increase in support for the social democratic president's party, Partido Liberación Nacional.

Table 7.3 (continued)

Country	Date of election	Government before	Government after	Notes
United Kingdom	6 May 2010	Left	Right	Big losses for Labour Party. Gains for Conservatives.
Czech Republic	28–29 May 2010	*Caretaker*	*Centre-right*	Big losses for Social Democrats. Two new right-wing parties.
The Netherlands	9 June 2010	*Centre*	*Centre-right*	Losses for Christian Democrats, Socialist Party. Gains for Liberals, D66, and Freedom Party.
Slovakia	12 June 2010	*Centre-left*	*Centre-right*	Gains for Social Democrats, new right-wing parties. Losses for nationalists and communists.
Belgium	13 June 2010	Centre	Centre	Small gains for Parti Socialiste. Losses for far-right parties.
Australia	21 August 2010	Left	Left	Losses for Labor. Gains for all others, especially Greens.
Sweden	19 September 2010	Centre-right	Centre-right	Losses for Social Democrats. Gains for Conservatives and far-right Sweden Democrats.
Latvia	2 October 2010	Right	Right	Increased support for governing parties.
United States	2 November 2010	(Centre)	(Centre)	Mid-term election. Large gains for Republicans.

Table 7.4 Elections and government formation 2011–2012

Country	Date of election	Government before	Government after	Notes
Ireland	25 February 2011	**Centre-right**	**Centre**	Big gains for Fine Gael and Labour. Massive losses for Fianna Fáil.
Estonia	6 March 2011	Centre-right	Centre-right	Losses for centrists and Greens. Gains for right-wing parties and Social Democrats.
Finland	17 April 2011	Centre-right	Centre-right	Big gains for the populist party True Finns. Losses for all other parties.
Canada	2 May 2011	Right	Right	Gains for Conservatives and New Democratic Party. Losses for Liberals and Bloc Québécois.
Denmark	15 September 2011	**Right**	**Centre-left**	Gains for Social Liberals and Unity. Losses for Conservatives and Danish People's Party.
Latvia	17 September 2011	Right	Right	Parliament dissolved by referendum. Large support for Reform Party, formed by President Zatler.
Switzerland	13 October 2011	Mixed	Mixed	Gains for Green Liberal Party. Losses for People's Party.
New Zealand	26 November 2011	Right	Right	Gains for National Party and Green Party; losses for Labour.
Slovakia	10 March 2012	**Centre-right**	**Left**	Social Democrats win absolute majority in parliament.
Greece	6 May and 17 June 2012	*Non-partisan*	*Right*	After two elections, the leader of the New Democracy Party is able to form a new government.
France	10–17 June 2012	**Right**	**Left**	Following François Hollande's win in the presidential election, Socialists win majority.
Netherlands	15 September 2012	**Centre-right**	Mixed	Purple coalition formed.

2011, some 2½ years into the crisis, the tide appeared to turn, just as it did in the spring and summer of 1932 (2½ years into the Great Depression). In Ireland, the centre-right Fine Gael and the Irish Labour Party defeated the incumbent Fianna Fáil government in February 2011, forming a new, more centrist coalition government (all but destroying Fianna Fáil, which had been Ireland's dominant party). The September 2011 election in Denmark resulted in the defeat of the incumbent Liberal–Conservative government, which had governed Denmark for a decade, and the formation of a new centre-left coalition. In 2012, finally, left-wing parties won elections in France and Slovakia.

CRISES AS POLITICAL OPPORTUNITIES

In this chapter, I have explored several different ways in which deep economic crises can provide politicians and policy entrepreneurs with new political opportunities. Anti-system parties and movements can exploit crises for sinister ends, as we know from the Great Depression, when several democracies succumbed to authoritarianism. For policy entrepreneurs, crises open 'windows of opportunity' (Kingdon 2003 [1984]) that enable them to put new ideas on the political agenda. The main section of this chapter, however, has been concerned with the constraints and opportunities that political parties and governments face during deep economic crises. I have shown that both in the Great Recession and the Great Depression, the first few years were a difficult period for parties on the left, whereas the second phase of each crisis was a difficult period for parties on the right. I will end this chapter with a few reflections on possible explanations for this pattern.

As I discuss at length in Lindvall (2012a), the dominant idea in the literature on elections in economic crises is the *punishment hypothesis*, according to which voters simply punish any government that happens to be in power during a deep economic downturn. This argument is made in two papers by Achen and Bartels (2005) and Bartels (2011), who find a great deal of support for what Bartels (2011) calls a 'simple model of retrospective voting', in which citizens 'tended to reward their governments when their economies grew robustly and to punish their governments when economic growth slowed'. Looking at Tables 7.1 to 7.4, it is easy to see that this mechanism was at work in both the Great Depression and the Great Recession – particularly in the Great Recession – but it does not seem to tell the whole story, for if we look at the evidence from 1929–31 and 2008–10, it was predominantly centrist and left-wing governments that were punished in this manner, not right-wing governments, whereas the opposite happened in 1933–35 and 2011–12. These 'double standards' call for an explanation.

One potential explanation, as I also discuss in Lindvall (2012a), is that voters become less altruistic in hard times, rendering the political climate less hospitable for left-wing parties, which is something that James Alt (1979) has argued on the basis of the British experience in the 1960s and 1970s. Alt's hypothesis is also consistent with empirical work by Durr (1993, p. 167), who demonstrates that voters in the United States tend to become more liberal in good times and more conservative in bad times. Again, however, one part of the puzzle remains unsolved, for when centre-left parties began to recover – some 2½ years after the Wall Street Crash and the Lehman Brothers collapse, respectively – the Great Depression and the Great Recession were far from over, so it is not clear why altruism should have recovered at those points in time.

The two theories that I have just reviewed thus appear to provide important pieces of the puzzle, but they are not enough. In my view, the most promising way forward is to examine the interests of particular groups of voters in different phases of economic crises. Specifically, I would like to propose two ideas that, in my view, warrant further investigation. The first idea is that in the initial phase of a deep, global, economic crisis, when the crisis is widely understood as a threat to the established economic order, the interests of pivotal voters in the middle of the income distribution are more likely to be aligned with the rich (and hence with conservative parties) than with the poor. The second idea is that once an economic crisis ceases to be regarded as a systemic threat, political circumstances favour the formation of centre-left electoral alliances and governing coalitions, since widespread and persistent economic hardship is likely to affect the middle class as well as the poor.

REFERENCES

Achen, Christopher H. and Larry M. Bartels (2005), 'Partisan hearts and spleens: retrospection and realignment in the wake of the Great Depression', paper for presentation at the Annual Meeting of the Midwest Political Science Association, Chicago, 7–9 April.

Alt, James E. (1979), *The Politics of Economic Decline*, Cambridge: Cambridge University Press.

Bartels, Larry M. (2011), 'Ideology and retrospection in electoral responses to the Great Recession', available at: www.princeton.edu/~bartels.

Benford, James, Stuart Berry, Kalin Nikolov, Chris Young and Mark Robson (2009), 'Quantitative easing', *Bank of England Quarterly Bulletin*, **49** (2), 90–100.

Bernanke, Ben S. (2009), 'The crisis and the policy response', Stamp Lecture, London School of Economics, 13 January.

Boix, Carles and Susan C. Stokes (2003), 'Endogenous democratization', *World Politics*, **55** (4), 517–49.

Bordo, Michael and Harold James (2010), 'The Great Depression analogy', *Financial History Review*, **17** (2), 127–40.

Durr, Robert H. (1993), 'What moves policy sentiment?', *American Political Science Review*, **87** (1), 158–70.

Economist, The (2009), 'The European elections: swing low, swing right', 11 June.

Gourevitch, Peter (1984), 'Breaking with orthodoxy', *International Organization*, **38** (1), 95–129.

Gourevitch, Peter (1986), *Politics in Hard Times*, Ithaca, NY: Cornell University Press.

Huntington, Samuel P. (1991), *The Third Wave: Democratization in the Late Twentieth Century*, Norman, OK: University of Oklahoma Press.

International Monetary Fund (IMF) (2009), *World Economic Outlook April 2009*, Washington, DC.

Judt, Tony (2010), 'Ill fares the land', *New York Review of Books*, **57** (7).

Katzenstein, Peter J. (ed.) (1978), *Between Power and Plenty*, Madison, WI: University of Wisconsin Press.

Kingdon, John W. (2003), *Agendas, Alternatives, and Public Policies*, London: Longman.

Lindvall, Johannes (2012a), 'The electoral consequences of two great crises', unpublished manuscript, Lund University, Sweden.

Lindvall, Johannes (2012b), 'Politics and policies in two crises', in Nancy Bermeo and Jonas Pontusson (eds), *Coping with the Crisis*, New York: Russell Sage Foundation.

Mann, Michael (2004), *Fascists*, Cambridge: Cambridge University Press.

Marshall, M-G. and K. Jaggers (2012), 'Polity IV Project: Political Regime Characteristics and Transitions, 1800–2010', College Park, MD: University of Maryland.

Przeworski, Adam, Michael E. Alvarez, José Antonio Cheibub and Fernando Limongi (2000), *Democracy and Development*, Cambridge: Cambridge University Press.

Spilimbergo, Antonio, Steve Symansky, Olivier Blanchard and Carlo Cottarelli (2008), 'Fiscal Policy for the Crisis', *IMF Staff Position Note*, 29 December (SPN/08/01).

Wall Street Journal (2008), 'In crisis, opportunity for Obama', 21 November, p. A2.

Weir, Margaret (1992), *Politics and Jobs*, Princeton, NJ: Princeton University Press.

Weir, Margaret and Theda Skocpol (1985), 'State structures and the possibilities for "Keynesian" responses to the Great Depression in Sweden, Britain, and the United States', in Theda Skocpol, Peter B. Evans, and Dietrich Rueschemeyer (eds), *Bringing the State Back In*, Cambridge: Cambridge University Press.

8. The 'new new deal' as a response to the euro-crisis

Bengt-Åke Lundvall

INTRODUCTION

While the eurozone was originally designed to protect member countries from economic instability, it has now turned into a major source of instability for the world as a whole. Currently European leaders bring Europe ahead in the direction of a European Federation not because it is part of their vision, but because it seems to be the only way to avoid triggering a global depression.

When the EMU was established there were warning voices that a monetary union without a common fiscal policy would be vulnerable to external shocks. The total budget of the EU is only a few per cent of GNP and cannot play the same role as the federal budget in the US as automatic stabilizer. This is especially problematic for a currency union bringing together countries at very different levels of economic development. There were elements in the Lisbon Strategy that could have reduced the gaps between the North and South of Europe. But the turn toward more neo-liberal solutions that took place around 2005 undermined its capacity to function as a scaffolding for the eurozone (Lundvall and Lorenz 2011).

In this chapter I show that the countries in the eurozone now most exposed to financial speculation are the ones that have the weakest industrial structure with the biggest proportion of workplaces directly exposed to competition with emerging economies. On this background I will argue that, standing alone, neither Austrian austerity nor Keynesian policies can help establish a sustainable eurozone. There is a need to design Keynesian policies coordinated at the European level in such a way that they promote deep institutional change in education, labour market and industrial policy in the South of Europe. Public expenditure needs to be allocated to stimulate the learning capacity where it is weakest – this is why the solution may be referred to as a 'new new deal'. It is about redistributing learning capacities.

INNOVATION AND THE DIVISION OF LABOUR

The following analysis builds upon a simple theoretical model linking to each other 'innovation as an interactive process' and the dynamics of the division of labour (Lundvall 2006). According to Adam Smith the extension and deepening of the division of labour is the major mechanism behind economic growth. On the other hand innovation is the most important mechanism behind the evolving division of labour. New products and processes give rise to new and more developed forms of specialization. The more developed division of labour opens up new interfaces for interactive learning that may stimulate further innovation. It also enhances diversity that opens up for 'new combinations' of 'distant elements'. Such new combinations are at the very core of the innovation process.

But specialization may also raise barriers between professions and disciplines, between theorists and practical people and, not least, it may reproduce social distance between workers and bosses. One way to interpret the results to be presented below is that a mix of theory and practice at school and democracy/participation at work reduce both barriers and social distance and thereby enhance the opportunities for interactive learning and for absorbing quickly and efficiently new ideas in the production system.

In order to intervene wisely in this process it is important to understand the role of different kinds of 'differences' for the performance of innovation systems. While high degrees of diversity in people's experiences and in sources of knowledge give a rich foundation for innovations, high degrees of inequality hamper the interaction and communication that is crucial for successful innovation. A crucial policy challenge is to combine the potential of egalitarian learning systems with open inter-cultural dialogue and high degrees of diversity.

THE LEARNING ECONOMY

The learning economy refers to acceleration in the rate of economic and technical change imposing a strong transformation pressure on open economies (Lundvall and Johnson 1994). Behind the acceleration of change lie shorter product life cycles and intensified global competition as well as politically driven deregulation. At the level of the firm, the acceleration of change is registered as an intensification of competition. At the level of the individual it is experienced as a need permanently to renew skills and competences in order to remain 'employable'. Change and learning are two sides of the same coin. The speed-up of change confronts people and organizations with new problems and to tackle the new problems requires new skills (OECD 1996). The selection by employers of more learning-oriented employees and the market selection in favour of change-oriented firms accelerates further innovation and change.

In an open economy the key to economic success is to constantly transform the economy so that exposed activities are either upgraded or substituted for by new activities that make more intensive use of competence. It is a major task for policy to design institutions that regulate education and labour markets so that they promote processes of learning and the formation and diffusion of learning organizations in the private and public sectors. As will be demonstrated in the next section, it is not sufficient to promote R&D efforts and the training of scientists and engineers.

MODES OF INNOVATION AND INNOVATION PERFORMANCE

In Johnson et al. (2002) we linked the distinction between codified and tacit knowledge to innovation and learning. In Jensen et al. (2007) we introduced two modes of learning related to this distinction. Using survey and register data from around 700 Danish firms we demonstrated that firms that combine R&D efforts (STI learning) with organizational learning and interaction with customers (DUI learning) are the most innovative.

In order to find out how the different aspects of establishing a learning organization tend to be combined with the capacity to handle scientific and codified knowledge, we pursued a clustering across firms using latent class analysis. The first cluster is a static- or low-learning cluster and encompasses about 40 per cent of the firms. Firms belonging to the second cluster, which we refer to as the STI cluster, comprise about 10 per cent of the firms. They have activities that indicate a strong capacity to absorb and use codified knowledge. The third cluster, which we refer to as the DUI cluster, is characterized by an over-average development of organizational characteristics typical for the learning organization but without activities that indicate a strong capacity to absorb and use codified knowledge. The fourth cluster includes firms using mixed strategies that combine the DUI and STI modes. It includes one-fifth of the firms.

In order to examine the effect of the learning modes on the firm's innovative performance we use logistic regression analysis as reported in Table 8.1. The dependent variable for this exercise is whether or not the firm has introduced to the market a new product or service (P/S innovation) over the last three years. The independent variables in the Model 1 specification are binary variables indicating whether or not the firm belongs to a particular cluster. In the Model 2 specification we include

Table 8.1 Logistic regression of learning clusters on product/service innovation

Variable	Model 1 (without controls)		Model 2 (with controls)	
	Odds ratio estimate	Coefficient estimate	Odds ratio estimate	Coefficient estimate
STI cluster	3.529	1.2611**	2.355	0.8564**
DUI cluster	2.487	0.9109**	2.218	0.7967**
DUI/STI cluster	7.843	2.0596**	5.064	1.6222**
Business services			1.433	0.3599
Construction			0.491	–0.7120*
Manufacturing (high tech)			1.805	0.5905*
Manufacturing (low tech)			1.250	0.2229
Other services			0.747	–0.2923
100 and more employees			1.757	0.5635*
50–99 employees			0.862	–0.1481
Danish group			0.859	–0.1524
Single firm			0.521	–0.6526*
Customized product			1.378	0.3203
Pseudo R^2	0.1247	0.1247	0.1775	0.1775
N	692	692	692	692

Notes: ** = significant at the 0.01 level; * = significant at the 0.05 level.

control variables to account for the effects of industry, firm size, ownership structure and whether the firm produces customized or standard products.

Overall, the results of the logistic analysis show that adopting DUI mode-enhancing practices and policies tends to increase firm innovative performance. Further, they support the view that firms adopting mixed strategies combining the two modes tend to perform better than those relying predominantly on one mode or the other.

Our results strongly suggest a need for realignment of policy objectives and priorities, given the tendency to develop innovation policy with a one-sided focus on promoting the science base of high-technology firms. Actually both a strategy that promotes organizational learning in STI firms and one that promotes STI learning in DUI firms may have more effect on innovation than the standard solution of promoting R&D in high-tech firms that are already experienced in pursuing it.

Thinking in terms of the two modes and their evolution in the learning economy may also have implications for policy coordination and institution-building. If the main responsibility is given to a ministry of science then the STI bias in innovation policy is reinforced. The best solution might be to establish a council with a secretariat at the level of the Prime Minister's office with the mandate to coordinate 'innovation and competence-building' nationwide.

HOW EUROPE'S ECONOMIES LEARN

Lorenz and Valeyre (2005) develop an original and informative EU-wide mapping of how employees work and learn in the private sector. In Arundel et al. (2007) international comparisons show that there is a positive correlation between the national share of employees engaged in advanced forms of learning at the workplace and the percentage of private sector enterprises successful in the forms of innovation requiring high levels of in-house creative activity.

Cluster analysis is used to identify four different systems of work organization:

- Discretionary-learning (DL)
- Lean
- Taylorist
- Traditional forms.

Two of these, the discretionary-learning and lean forms, are characterized by high levels of learning and problem-solving in work. The principal difference between the discretionary-learning and the lean clusters is the relatively high level of discretion or autonomy in work exercised by employees grouped in the former. Task complexity is also higher in the discretionary-learning cluster than in the lean cluster.

Discretionary learning thus refers to work settings where a lot of responsibility is allocated to the employee who is expected to solve problems on his or her own. Employees operating in these modes are constantly confronted with 'disequilibria' and as they cope with these they learn and become more competent. But in this process they also experience some of their earlier insights and skills becoming obsolete.

Lean production also involves problem-solving and learning but here the problems are more narrowly defined and the set of possible solutions less wide and diverse. The work is highly constrained and this points to a more structured or bureaucratic style of organizational learning that corresponds rather closely to the characteristics of the Japanese-inspired 'lean production' model.

The other two clusters are characterized by relatively low levels of

Table 8.2 National differences in organizational models (percentage of employees by organizational class)

	Discretionary learning	Lean production learning	Taylorist organization	Simple organization
North				
Netherlands	64.0	17.2	5.3	13.5
Denmark	60.0	21.9	6.8	11.3
Sweden	52.6	18.5	7.1	21.7
Finland	47.8	27.6	12.5	12.1
Centre				
Austria	*47.5*	21.5	13.1	18.0
Germany	*44.3*	19.6	14.3	21.9
Luxembourg	*42.8*	25.4	11.9	20.0
Belgium	*38.9*	25.1	13.9	22.1
France	*38.0*	33.3	11.1	17.7
West				
United Kingdom	34.8	40.6	10.9	13.7
Ireland	24.0	37.8	20.7	17.6
South				
Italy	30.0	23.6	20.9	25.4
Portugal	26.1	28.1	23.0	22.8
Spain	20.1	38.8	18.5	22.5
Greece	18.7	25.6	28.0	27.7
EU-15	*39.1*	*28.2*	*13.6*	*19.1*

Source: Adapted version based on Lorenz and Valeyre (2006).

learning and problem-solving. The Taylorist form leaves very little autonomy to the employee in making decisions. In the traditional cluster there is more autonomy but learning and task complexity is the lowest among the four types of work organization. This cluster includes employees working in small-scale establishments in personal services and transport where methods are for the most part informal and non-codified.

Table 8.2 shows that people working in different national systems of innovation and competence work and learn differently. Discretionary learning is most widely diffused in the Netherlands, the Nordic countries and to a lesser extent in Austria and Germany. The lean model is most in evidence in the UK, Ireland and Spain. The Taylorist forms are more present in Portugal, Spain, Greece and Italy, while the traditional forms are similarly more in evidence in these four southern European countries.[1] The share of discretionary learning is higher in Germany than in the UK or in France.

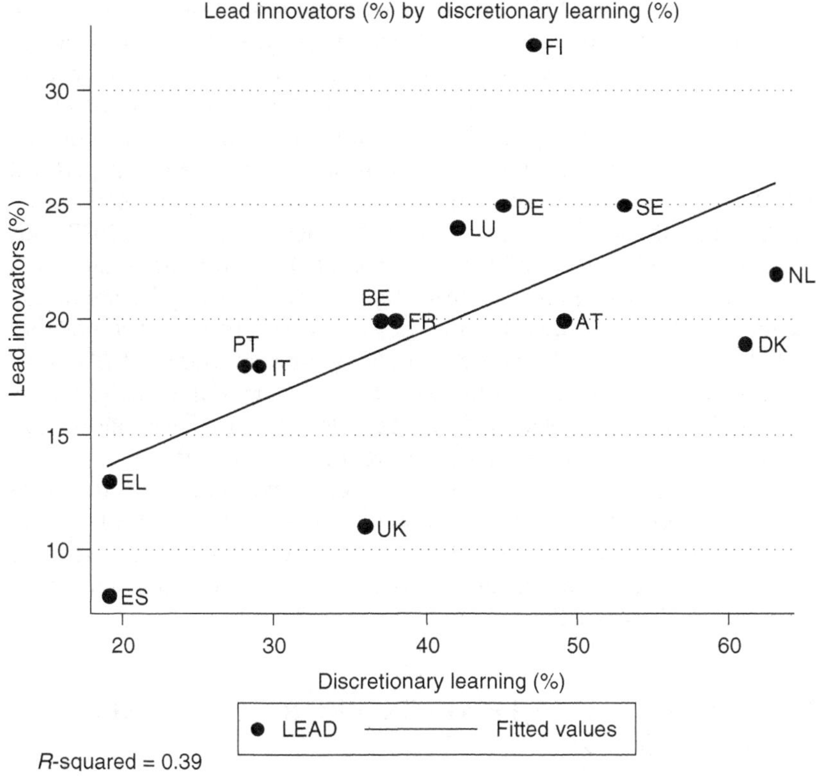

Source: Based on Arundel et al.2007.

Figure 8.1 Percentage lead innovators by percentage discretionary learning

Table 8.2 indicates unequal access to learning at work across different parts of Europe. The three Nordic countries, together with the Netherlands, have few Taylorist jobs left in the economy while a majority of employees operate in jobs that are demanding both in terms of skills and in terms of autonomy.

When comparing and ranking national innovation systems the focus is normally on STI indicators. For instance the European innovation scoreboard does not include any indicator reflecting organizational learning. The analysis pursued here shows that differences in how people work and learn across Europe are even more dramatic than differences in R&D efforts or in the intensity of training of scientific personnel.

Figure 8.1 is from Arundel et al. (2007). Drawing on the results from the Third Community Innovation Survey it shows the positive correlation between the national share of employees engaged in advanced forms of learning at the workplace and the percentage of private sector enterprises doing more radical forms of innovation. *Lead innovators* are those enterprises that have demonstrated a capacity for developing new-for-the-market innovations, and the category includes both firms that perform R&D on a continuous basis and those that do not perform R&D at all or that only do so occasionally. In the Arundel et al. study (2007) this group of highly creative innovators is separated out from non-innovators as well as from less ambitious firms that innovate mainly by modifying technology developed by other firms or organizations (*modifiers*) or that introduce innovations developed entirely by external sources (*followers*).

Figure 8.1 shows that countries with wide participation in discretionary learning have a bigger share of firms that develop their own innovations and innovations new to the market. Here it is notable that the UK stands out from the northern and most of the continental nations both for its low level of discretionary learning and its low percentage of lead innovators. These results are compatible with other studies showing that firms with learning-organization characteristics tend to be more innovative (Lundvall and Nielsen 2007).

EDUCATION AND TRAINING FOR LEARNING ORGANIZATIONS

Since discretionary learning depends on the capacity of employees to undertake complex problem-solving tasks it can be expected that nations with a high frequency of these forms will have made substantial investments in education and training. In what follows we compare tertiary education in universities and other institutions of higher education with the continuing vocational training offered by enterprises.

Tertiary education develops both problem-solving skills and formal and transferable technical and scientific skills. While most of the qualifications acquired through third-level education will be relatively general and hence transferable in the labour market, the qualifications an employee acquires through continuing vocational training will be more firm-specific. Some of this training will be designed to renew employees' technical skills and knowledge in order to respond to the firm's requirements in terms of ongoing product and process innovation.

Figure 8.2 shows the correlations between the frequency of the discretionary learning forms and two of the four measures of human resources for innovation used in Trendchart's innovation benchmarking exercise:

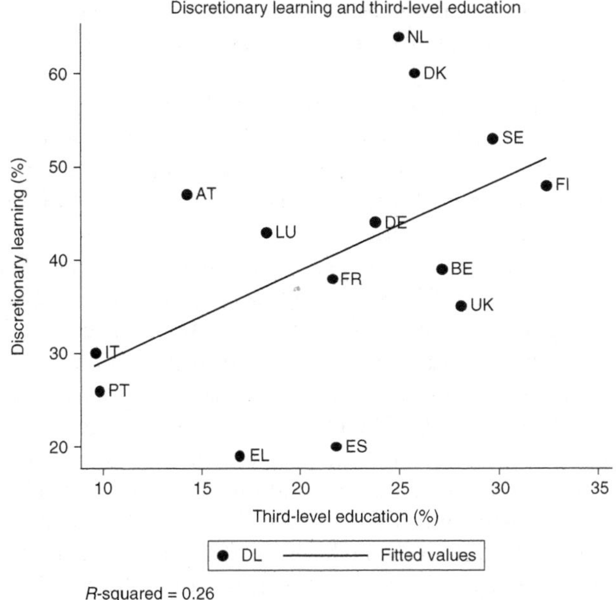

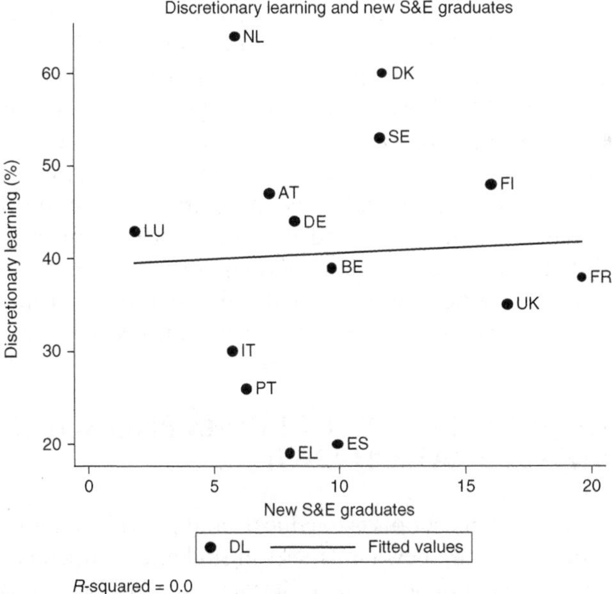

Figure 8.2 Discretionary learning and tertiary education

the proportion of the population with third-level education and the number of science and engineering graduates since 1993 as a percentage of the population aged 20–29 years in 2000.

The results show a modest positive correlation (R-squared = 0.26) between the discretionary-learning forms and the percentage of the population with third-level education, and no discernible correlation between the discretionary-learning forms and the measure of the importance of new science and engineering graduates.

Figure 8.3 shows that there are fairly strong positive correlations (R-squared = 0.75 and 0.52 respectively) between the frequency of discretionary learning and two measures of firms' investments in continuing vocational training: the percentage of private-sector firms offering such training and the participants in continuous vocational education as a percentage of employees in all enterprises.[2] The results suggest that these forms of firm-specific training are key complementary resources in the development of the firm's capacity for knowledge exploration and innovation. The diagram also points to a north/south divide within Europe. The Nordic countries are characterized by relatively high levels of vocational training and by relatively high-level use of the discretionary-learning forms. This may be a factor that contributes to their relative success in the learning economy.

These results indicate that national educational systems where the emphasis is on the formal training of scientists and engineers while neglecting the broader forms of vocational training may be vulnerable in the context of the learning economy. It is notable that Portugal, Spain, Italy and Greece, which have all made considerable strides in increasing the number of science and engineering graduates, but stand out for their low levels of investment in continuing vocational training, rank the lowest on the discretionary learning scale. The more drastic the status difference and distinction between theory and practice in education programmes, the more difficult it will be to install participatory learning in the private sector. The strong element of vocational training in the Nordic countries contributes to engaging workers more actively in processes of change.

SKILL REQUIREMENTS IN FIRMS ENGAGED IN ORGANIZATIONAL CHANGE

Since one major role of schools is to educate and provide qualified labour, it is important to capture new tendencies in skill and competence requirements. In a socio-economic context characterized by rapid change it is especially interesting to analyse in what directions organizations engaged in change specify change in skill requirements. In this section we take a

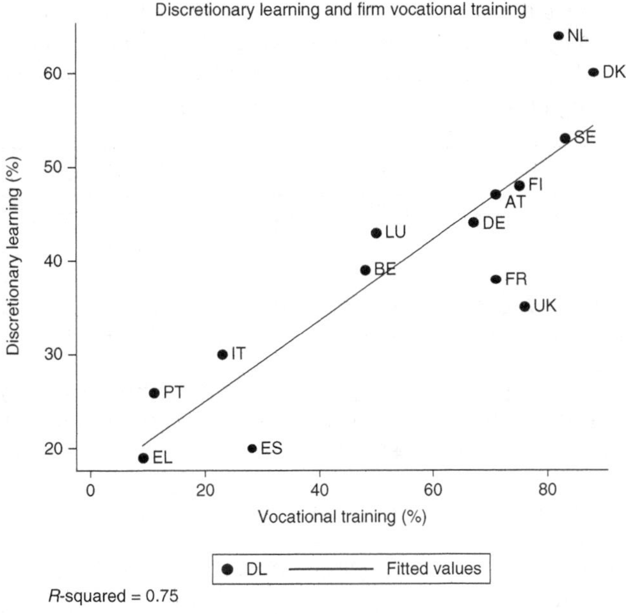

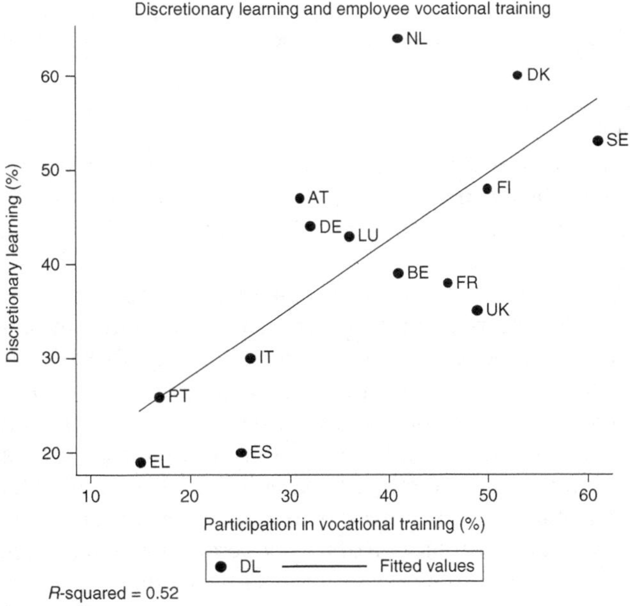

Figure 8.3 Discretionary learning and employee vocational training

Table 8.3 Changes in task content for employees in the period 1993–95 for firms that have made organizational changes (outside the parentheses), compared with firms that have not made organizational changes (in parentheses)

	More	Less	Unchanged	No answer
(a) Independence in work	72.6 (37.1)	4.2 (2.7)	21.2 (56.3)	2.0 (3.8)
(b) Professional qualifications	56.4 (36.3)	7.5 (5.3)	33.3 (53.8)	2.8 (4.4)
(c) Degree of specialization	33.9 (26.2)	20.8 (7.8)	39.3 (58.4)	6.0 (7.5)
(d) Routine character of tasks	5.6 (8.2)	41.8 (15.5)	45.0 (67.1)	7.7 (9.1)
(e) Customer contact	51.6 (29.3)	5.1 (3.1)	37.2 (59.9)	6.1 (7.6)
(f) Contact with suppliers	34.9 (18.0)	7.1 (4.3)	46.4 (62.0)	11.6 (15.6)
(g) Contact with other firms	24.7 (14.0)	5.5 (4.3)	56.8 (68.9)	13.0 (13.7)
(h) Cooperation with colleagues	59.1 (27.1)	5.8 (4.5)	31.8 (63.3)	3.2 (5.0)
(i) Cooperation with management	64.9 (28.6)	5.9 (4.2)	26.1 (62.2)	3.1 (4.9)

Note: Management representatives in 4000 Danish private firms, excluding agriculture, were asked 'Did the firm introduce a non-trivial change in the organisation in the period 1993–95?'. The response rate was close to 50 per cent. For more detailed information see Lundvall (2002).

Source: Lundvall (2002).

closer look into how management in a selection of Danish firms refer to changes in their demand for skills. The focus is upon changes in the competences demanded within firms that have engaged in organizational change (Lundvall 2002).

A series of surveys of the Danish national innovation system (the DISKO surveys) showed among other results that organizational change involves a shift in the relative importance of tasks. Table 8.3 reveals substantial differences in the pattern of answers (percentage share of firms giving respectively more or less emphasis to each specific category of tasks) between the firms that have introduced new forms of organization and those that have not (numbers in parenthesis). The demand for general skills (independence in the work situation, cooperation with external partners, especially customers, and for cooperation with management and colleagues) has grown in both categories of firms. But it has grown much more strongly in those that have pursued organizational change. There are correspondingly large differences between the two types of organization in the rate of occurrence of a *reduction* in routine work. This response pattern gives an indication of the future direction of skill requirements.

Therefore education systems should be designed in such a way that they promote general skills in terms of communication, cooperation and creativity (to solve non-routine problems). This points to teaching methods that are democratic and interactive rather than authoritarian and unidirectional. Collective creativity may be stimulated by engaging students in team-work and in solving unstructured problems with the teacher as coach.

As illustrated by Table 8.3 (see line d) the general tendency among the firms is that the amount of routine work is shrinking while the demand for independent, creative and cooperative workers is increasing. While this points to a need for education to contribute to creativity, many tasks still require a capacity to pursue routine work, based upon discipline-organized knowledge and with a high degree of precision in solving tasks. This is true even for the core of 'creative professions' such as architects and artists. Therefore education systems should not abandon traditional teaching methods and individual training to solve well-structured problems. On balance, however, national education systems need to give more room for stimulating both collective and individual creativity in order to cope with change and build a learning society.

THE ROLE OF UNIVERSITIES IN THE LEARNING ECONOMY

When it comes to linking universities to economic development the main emphasis is currently on how universities may serve industry through direct flows of information from ongoing research. To illustrate, in a recent book with the title *How Universities Promote Economic Growth*, edited by World Bank economists (Yusuf and Nabeshima, 2007), the only dimension covered is the formation of university–industry links related to research. We believe that this narrow agenda, where the role of higher education is neglected, reflects a biased interpretation of the sources of innovation (as STI-driven) as well as an underestimation of the importance of transmitting tacit knowledge embodied in people (Lundvall 2008).

On the basis of the data presented in the last two sections above there may be a need to consider how well teaching programmes prepare students for the transfer and practical use of scientific knowledge. Innovation is a process requiring close interaction between individuals and organizations. Therefore, while skills in mathematics and language are fundamental, they need to be combined with social skills that make it possible to cooperate vertically in hierarchies as well as horizontally with experts with a different educational background.

This implies that teaching at universities needs to be adjusted in order to prepare the students for communication and cooperation with other categories of workers and experts. Traditional learning forms such as mass lectures do not prepare students to use the theory and methods in a real-life context and neither does it replicate the kind of learning that is required in a future professional life. In professional life most learning takes place through problem-solving, often in a context of collaboration with others with a different background. *Problem-based learning and combining theoretical work with periods of practical work are obvious responses to these problems.*

The transition to a learning economy has important *implications for higher education.* One major implication is that education institutions need to be ready to support *continuous and life-long learning.* Especially in fast-moving fields of knowledge there is a need to give regular and frequent opportunities for experts to renew their professional knowledge. The proliferation of executive education programmes in business schools may be seen as indicating the growing insight among individuals and in management that continuously renewing competences is of great importance. But so far opportunities for upgrading professional skills have been offered mainly in relation to management functions. Similar programmes are needed in other areas where effective demand is less strong.

Finally, rapid change in science and technology and the need to move quickly from invention to innovation present a strong argument for keeping a reasonably *close connection between education and research* in higher education. Teachers who have little or obsolete knowledge about what is going on in current research are not helpful when it comes to giving students useful insights into dynamic knowledge fields.

LINKING MODES OF LEARNING TO MEASURES OF EMPLOYMENT AND UNEMPLOYMENT SECURITY

EU member nations display large differences in systems of employment and unemployment protection. Systems combining high levels of unemployment protection with relatively low levels of employment protection may have an advantage in terms of the adoption of the forms of work organization that promote learning and 'new-to-the-market' innovation. Organizations that compete on the basis of strategies of continuous knowledge exploration tend to have relatively porous organizational boundaries so as to permit the insertion of new knowledge and ideas from the outside. Job tenures tend to be short because careers are often structured around a series of discrete projects rather than advancing within an intra-firm hierarchy (Lam and Lundvall 2006).

While the absence of legal restrictions on hiring and firing will not necessarily result in the forms of labour market mobility that contribute to a continuous evolution of the firm's knowledge base, strong systems of employment protection may prove to be an obstacle. Well-developed systems of unemployment protection, on the other hand, may contribute to the development of fluid labour markets. The security such systems provides encourages individuals to commit themselves to what would otherwise be perceived as unacceptably risky forms of employment and career paths, and such forms of protection contribute to accumulation of knowledge for particular sectors or regions, since in their absence unemployed workers would be under greater pressure to relocate.

Evidence in support of the view that systems of flexicurity promote the DL forms of work organization is provided in Figure 8.4. Graph (a) shows that there is a fairly strong positive relation (R-squared = 0.52) between a measure of the level of unemployment protection in a nation and the frequency of discretionary learning. Graph (b) shows a negative relation (R-squared = 0.36) between a measure of the level of employment protection and the frequency of the DL forms. Graph (c) in Figure 8.4 shows an index of flexicurity constructed from the measures of employment and unemployment protection. The index is constructed so that a nation combining intermediate levels of both unemployment and employment security will score higher than a nation combining a high level of unemployment security with a high level of employment security, or a nation combining a low level of employment security with a low level of unemployment security.[3] The assumption is that the positive effects of a high level of unemployment protection (low level of employment protection) cannot compensate for the negative effects of a high level of employment protection (low level of unemployment protection). Rather, as the literature on flexicurity suggests, what is required is rather the right mix of flexibility and security. The index is positively correlated (R-squared = 0.48) with the frequency of the DL forms of work organization.

In Holm et al. (2010) we have taken one further step towards addressing this research agenda by using multi-level logistic regression to explore the relation between individual level outcomes and national systems of labour market flexibility and regulation. The results confirm that the way work is organized is nation-specific and that it varies with the degree of labour market mobility and with the way labour markets are regulated. Again flexicurity goes hand in hand with discretionary learning at the workplace.

Discretionary learning and unemployment protection

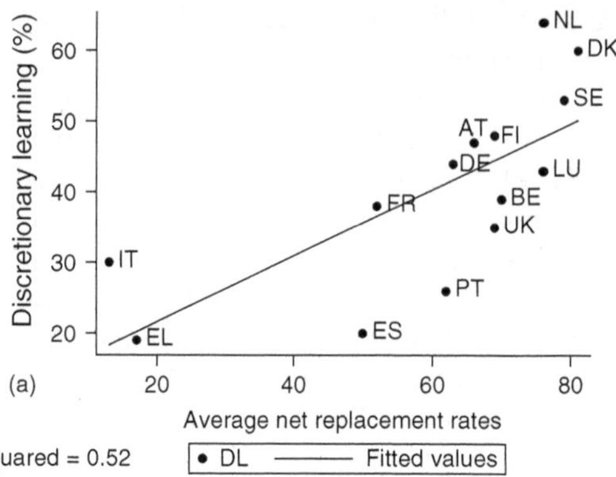
Discretionary learning (%)
Average net replacement rates
NL
DK
SE
AT
FI
DE
LU
FR
BE
UK
IT
PT
ES
EL
(a)
R-squared = 0.52
DL
Fitted values

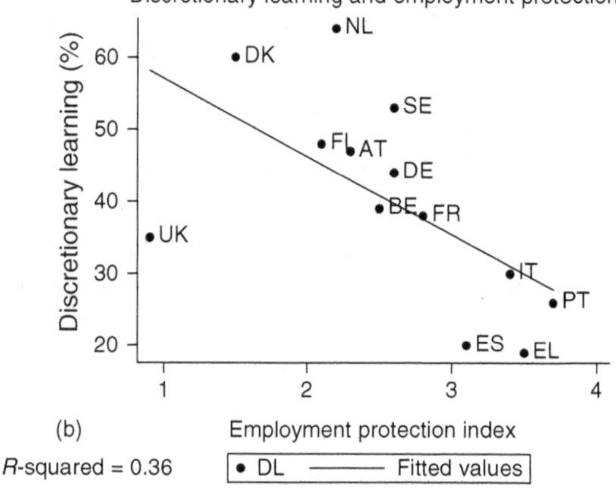
Discretionary learning and employment protection
Discretionary learning (%)
Employment protection index
NL
DK
SE
FI
AT
DE
BE
FR
UK
IT
PT
ES
EL
(b)
R-squared = 0.36
DL
Fitted values

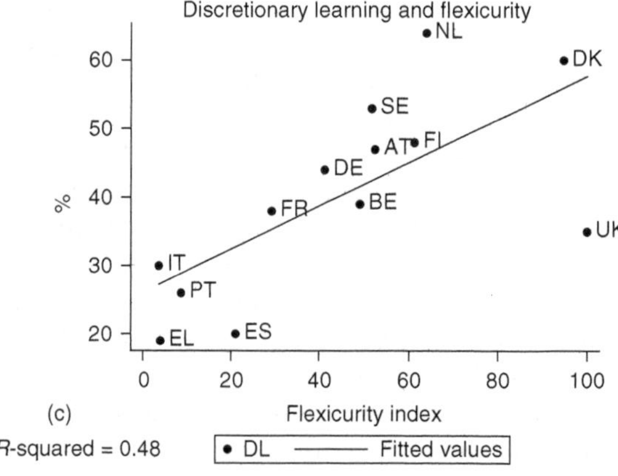
Discretionary learning and flexicurity
%
Flexicurity index
NL
DK
SE
AT
FI
DE
FR
BE
UK
IT
PT
EL
ES
(c)
R-squared = 0.48
DL
Fitted values

Note: The unemployment protection measure shown is the average net replacement rate of in-work income over 60 months averaged across four family types and two income levels including social assistance in 1999. See OECD, *Benefits and Wages* (2002, p. 40). The employment protection measure is the OECD's overall employment protection index for the late 1990s. See OECD (2000, ch. 2).

Source: Lundvall and Lorenz (2011).

Figure 8.4 Correlations between discretionary learning and systems of social protection

DEGREE OF INEQUALITY IN ACCESS TO ORGANIZATIONAL LEARNING IN EUROPE

An egalitarian income distribution might not be the most important dimension of social equality. If it is combined with growing gaps in competence between skilled and low-skilled workers it might result in underemployment of the low-skilled. The data referred to above on organizational models of learning in different European countries makes it possible to find indicators of such more adequate measures of inequality. In Table 8.4 we present an indicator for the social distribution of workplace learning opportunities. We distinguish between 'workers' and 'managers' and we compare their access to discretionary learning in different national systems.[4]

Table 8.4 shows that employees at the high end of the professional hierarchy have more easy access to jobs involving discretionary learning. This is true for all the countries listed. But it is also noteworthy that the data indicate that the inequality in access to learning is quite different in different countries. In the Nordic countries and Netherlands the inequality in the distribution of learning opportunities is moderate while it is very substantial in the less-developed south. For instance, the proportion of the management category engaged in discretionary learning in Portugal is almost as high as in Finland (62 per cent in Finland and 59 per cent in Portugal), but the proportion of workers engaged in discretionary learning is much lower in Portugal (18.2 per cent versus 38.2 per cent).

The Nordic countries are egalitarian not only in terms of income distribution. Also when it comes to access to workplace learning the distribution is more equal than in the south of Europe. The combination of welfare states offering basic security, equal income distribution and low social distance is reflected in high degrees of trust and in broad participation in change. While there are tendencies toward polarization in the current context also in the Nordic countries, they still benefit from 'social capital' reducing social distance and other barriers to communication and

Table 8.4 National differences in organizational models (percentages of employees by organizational class)

	Discretionary learning	Share of managers in discretionary learning	Share of workers in discretionary learning	Learning Inequality index*
North				
Netherlands	64.0	81.6	51.1	37.3
Denmark	60.0	85.0	56.2	35.9
Sweden	52.6	76.4	38.2	50.3
Finland	47.8	62.0	38.5	37.9
Centre				
Austria	47.5	74.1	44.6	39.9
Germany	44.3	65.4	36.8	43.8
Luxembourg	42.8	70.3	33.1	52.9
Belgium	38.9	65.7	30.8	53.1
France	38.0	66.5	25.4	61.9
West				
UK	34.8	58.9	20.1	65.9
Ireland	24.0	46.7	16.4	64.9
South				
Italy	30.0	63.7	20.8	67.3
Portugal	26.1	59.0	18.2	69.2
Spain	20.1	52.4	19.1	63.5
Greece	18.7	40.4	17.0	57.9

Note: *The index is constructed by dividing the share of 'workers' engaged in discretionary learning by the share of 'managers' engaged in discretionary learning and subtracting the resulting percentage from 100. If the share of workers and managers was the same, the index would equal 0, and if the share of workers was 0 the index would equal 100.

Source: Lundvall et al. (2008).

interaction in processes of change and innovation. On the other hand we can see that the major reason for the low share of discretionary-learning jobs in the South reflects that workers – as opposed to management – do not have access to such jobs.

So, while it might be true that higher education fosters people who contribute directly to innovation, it seems to be when those people interact with broader segments of the workforce in promoting or coping with change that the innovation system as a whole turns out to be most efficient. The broader participation in change reflected in more equal access to discretionary learning may reflect not only the increased income security offered by welfare state initiatives.

THE EURO-CRISIS AND EUROPE'S UNEVEN DEVELOPMENT

The euro-crisis was triggered by the financial crisis of 2007. But it is rooted in the uneven development of the countries belonging to the eurozone. We have seen how uneven development is reflected in differences in how people work and learn at work. The differences between the South and the North are dramatic. We have also shown that the institutional characteristics of especially labour markets and education systems are highly interdependent with the frequency of the workers' access to workplace learning.

The crisis and the fear of getting the national economy into the searchlight of financial speculators force individual national governments to pursue budget cuts and make attempts to weaken trade unions and lower taxes for business. This is also the kind of 'competitive-response' that German Chancellor Merkel has insisted upon as a solution for Europe as a whole. But while this kind of policy might be legitimate for a small open economy such as Ireland with potential problems with the external balance, for Europe as a whole this 'small-country strategy' is self-defeating.

Not only will it cement long-term unemployment and lead to a prolonged recession. Budget cuts related to education, training and active labour market policies will contribute to making the uneven development of Europe even more serious. Deepening inequality at the national and international level will undermine social capital and interactive learning. The current version of the competitiveness/stabilization pact will aggravate rather than solve the structural crisis for the eurozone. There is a need for a completely different approach that attacks directly the uneven development in Europe. The strategic aim of this alternative strategy should be to enhance the learning capacity in Europe with emphasis upon southern Europe.

POLICY RECOMMENDATIONS

On the basis of the analysis in this chapter we recommend policy initiatives aiming at promoting innovation through reforming education systems, labour markets and working life in the south of Europe:

1. Education systems should be made robust to cope with radical unforeseen change and prepare students for participatory life-long learning.
2. Higher education should stimulate problem-based learning and combine traditional learning of disciplines with their application to real problems.

3. Universities should become more open to interaction with society and students should spend more 'learning time' outside their classroom.
4. Education systems should establish porous borders between theoretical–academic programmes and more practical–professional programmes.
5. Labour market policy should establish strong incentives for both employers and employees to upgrade skills.
6. New training programmes for those with the weakest positions in the learning society (low-skilled workers and certain ethnic minorities) should be developed.
7. A new social contract should be developed where employees respond to enhanced economic security and skill-upgrading by more active participation in change.
8. Managers and employees, as well as their organizations, should be engaged in the diffusion of good practice for organizational learning.
9. At the national level the Prime Minister should act as de facto chair for a new National Council for Competence Building and Innovation.

Such changes would require the engagement and positive participation of all segments of society. Government should play the role of the main driver and coach of the reform process.

THE ROADS AHEAD FOR EUROPE

The Lisbon Strategy may be seen as an attempt to establish regional and political convergence in Europe with the ultimate aim of building a strong and cohesive union built upon the principle of solidarity. But the implementation, with emphasis on 'best-practice' and benchmarking in specific policy areas, was both too technocratic and too weak in terms of the instruments used to implement it. Neither was the strategy successful in stimulating popular participation in the project. To mobilize citizens for the European project there is a need for a vision that goes beyond the common market and 'structural reform'.

In a seminal paper written at the occasion of the conference on 'The European Identity in a Global Economy' in preparation for the Lisbon Summit under the Portuguese Presidency, Manuel Castells argued that there is a need for 'a common European identity on whose behalf citizens around Europe could be ready to share problems and build common solutions' (Castells 2002, p. 234). After rejecting common religion and culture he pointed to 'shared feelings concerning the need for universal social protection of living conditions, social solidarity, stable employment, workers' rights, universal human rights, concern about poor people around the world, extension of democracy to regional and local levels . . .' He proposed that if European institutions promoted these values probably the 'project identity' would grow (Castells 2002).

To mobilize popular support, to reconstruct the EMU and to attack uneven development in Europe there is a need to recognize the 'social dimension' and to transform it into an Economic and Social Union (ESU). There is also a need for a shift where the fear of state intervention and blind belief in markets is changed into a pragmatic perspective, where governments are allowed to take on the tasks necessary to promote stable economic growth. Among the most important tasks we would emphasize a redesign of all institutions and sector policies so that they respond to the fact that we are in a new phase where knowledge is the most important resource and learning the most important process.

NOTES

1. Lorenz and Valeyre (2006) use logit regression analysis in order to control for differences in sector, occupation and establishment size when estimating the impact of nation on the likelihood of employees being grouped in the various forms of work organization. The results show statistically significant 'national effect' also when controlling for the structural variables, thus pointing to considerable latitude in how work is organized for the same occupation or within the same industrial sector.
2. It is also worth observing that there are fairly strong positive correlations between the frequency of leading innovators and the two measures of vocational training, R-squared = 0.47 and 0.45 respectively.
3. The index is constructed by reversing the scoring on the employment protection index such that high values correspond to low levels of protection and multiplying this reversed score by the unemployment index. The resulting flexicurity index has then been rescaled so that the maximum score is 100.
4. The class of managers includes not only top and middle management but also professionals and technicians (ISCO major groups 1, 2 and 3) The worker category includes clerks, service and sales workers as well as craft, plant and machine operators and unskilled occupations (ISCO major groups 4 through 9).

REFERENCES

Arundel A., E. Lorenz, B.-Å. Lundvall and A. Valeyre (2007), 'How Europe's economies learn: a comparison of work organization and innovation mode for the EU-15', *Industrial and Corporate Change*, **16** (6), 1175–210.

Castells, M. (2002), 'The Construction of European Identity' in Maria Joan Rodrigues (ed.), *The Knowledge Economy in Europe*, Cheltenham, UK and Northampton, MA, USA: Edward Elgar.

Holm, J.R., E. Lorenz, B.-Å. Lundvall and A. Valeyre (2010), 'Organisational learning and systems of labour market regulation in Europe', *Industrial and Corporate Change*, **19** (4), 1141–73.

Jensen, M.B., B. Johnson, E. Lorenz and B-Å. Lundvall (2007), 'Forms of knowledge and modes of innovation', *Research Policy*, **36** (5), 680–93.

Johnson, B., E. Lorenz and B-Å. Lundvall (2002), 'Why all this about codified and tacit knowledge?', *Industrial and Corporate Change*, **11** (2), 245–62.

Lam, A. and B.A. Lundvall (2006), 'The learning organisation and national systems of competence building and innovation', in E. Lorenz and B.A. Lundvall (eds), *How Europe's Economies Learn: Coordinating Competing Models*, Oxford: Oxford University Press.

Lorenz, E. and A. Valeyre (2005), 'Organisational innovation, HRM and labour market structure: a comparison of the EU-15', *Journal of Industrial Relations*, **47** (4), 424–42.

Lorenz, E. and A. Valeyre (2006), 'Organisational forms and innovative performance: a comparison of the EU-15', in E. Lorenz and B- Å. Lundvall (eds), *How Europe's Economies Learn: Coordinating Competing Models*, Oxford: Oxford University Press.

Lundvall, B-Å. (2002), *Innovation and Social Cohesion: The Danish Model*, Cheltenham, UK and Northampton, MA, USA: Edward Elgar.

Lundvall, B-Å. (2006), 'Interactive learning, social capital and economic performance', in D. Foray and B. Kahin (eds), *Advancing Knowledge and the Knowledge Economy*, Cambridge, MA: Harvard University Press.

Lundvall, B-Å. (2008), 'Higher education, innovation and economic development', in J.Y. Lin and B. Plescovic (eds), *Higher Education and Economic Development*, Washington, DC: World Bank.

Lundvall, B-Å and Johnson, B. (1994), 'The learning economy', *Journal of Industry Studies*, **1** (2), 23–42.

Lundvall, B-Å and E. Lorenz (2011), 'From the Lisbon Strategy to EUROPE 2020', in N. Morel, B. Palier and J. Palme (eds), *Towards a Social Investment Welfare State? Ideas, Policies and Challenges*, Bristol: Policy Press, pp. 333–51.

Lundvall, B-Å. and P. Nielsen (2007), 'Knowledge management and innovation performance', *International Journal of Manpower*, **28** (3–4), 207–23.

Lundvall, B-Å., P. Rasmussen and E. Lorenz (2008), 'Education in the learning economy: a European perspective', *Policy Futures in Education*, **6** (2), 681–700.

Organisation for Economic Co-operation and Development (OECD) (1996), *Transitions to Learning Economies and Societies*, Paris.

Organisation for Economic Co-operation and Development (OECD) (1999), *OECD Science, Technology and Industry Scoreboard 1999: Benchmarking Knowledge-Based Economies*, Paris.

Organisation for Economic Co-operation and Development (OECD) (2000), *Employment Outlook 1999*, Paris.

Organisation for Economic Co-operation and Development (OECD) (2002), *Benefits and Wages*, Paris.

Yusuf, S. and K. Nabeshima (eds) (2007), *How Universities Promote Economic Growth*, Washington, DC: World Bank.

9. A cultural political economy of crisis responses: the turn to 'BRIC' and the case of China

Ngai-Ling Sum

This chapter uses cultural political economy to examine the emergence of the 'BRIC' (Brazil, Russia, India, China) economic imaginary as an ensemble of discourses and practices that provided a sense of 'hope' and 'strength' after 11 September 2001 and that was recontextualized and sedimented after the 2007 financial crisis. It also presents a case study of the appropriation and recontextualization of this imaginary in China. Cultural political economy (hereafter CPE) makes a 'cultural-linguistic' turn in critical political economy to explore the coevolving semiotic-material bases of capital accumulation, its crisis tendencies, and crisis management capacities (Sum 2005; Sum and Jessop 2006; Sum 2010). Discursive processes are especially prominent during crises, when diverse actors, for different reasons, seek to construe and explain the crisis, to attribute blame and exonerate other factors and actors, and to imagine diverse routes to recovery (see Jessop, this volume, Chapter 12).

My contribution has three main parts. The first examines how transnational actors constructed and promoted the BRIC imaginary as one response to emerging signs of crisis in the US and Europe. The next part examines how the 'BRIC' discourses are being recontextualized in China in terms of 'four golden brick countries' and how this is being used to signify China's new 'strength' and 'greatness at last'. The third and last part explores China's response to the North Atlantic financial and economic crisis through a vast stimulus package to 'protect its 8 per cent GDP growth rate' and showcase its strength. It also explores aspects of the 'dark side' of the Chinese 'success' story and the counter-hegemonic discursive and material responses that it has triggered.

THE CONSTRUCTION OF HOPE/STRENGTH: THREE STAGES IN THE TURN TO 'BRIC'

Drawing on Gramscian and Foucauldian concepts, cultural political economy explores the relations among discourse, power and structural materialities. Applied to the present case, it asks questions such as:

1. Where do a particular economic imaginary (e.g. BRIC) and its related discursive networks originate?
2. Which actors are involved in the discursive networks that construct and promote objects of 'hope'/'strength'?
3. What ideas are selected and mobilized to recontextualize and hybridize the referents of these objects?
4. How are these imaginaries normalized, translated and negotiated?
5. What knowledging technologies are involved in the constitution of the corresponding subjectivities and identities?
6. How do these ideas enter policy discourses and everyday practices?
7. What impacts does this have across different sites and scales?

'BRIC' discourse builds on the idea of 'emerging markets', a term coined in 1981 by a senior official, Antoine van Agtmael, at the International Finance Corporation (part of the World Bank), who later founded Emerging Markets Management. The term identified some Third World and post-socialist economies as sites of 'new opportunities' with 'high risks' but potentially high returns. The 'BRIC' economies were identified as a subset of the 'large emerging markets' after 9/11 and have since been narrated in three overlapping stages: investor story, investor–consumer story, and investor–consumer–lender story. Each stage is associated with nodal actors who construct 'hope'/'strength' via 'knowledging' instruments and technologies (on these, see Dean 1999; Miller and Rose 2008) (Table 9.1).[1]

Stage One: Investor Story

Contrary to the fluid origin of most discourses, the BRIC idea has a clear start date. It was invented when Goldman Sachs's chief economist, Jim O'Neill, watched the televised collapse of the World Trade Centre on 11 September 2001. For him, this event meant that further progress in globalization would have to go beyond Americanization and the Northern–Western world (Tett 2010). His Goldman Sachs team then identified some useful 'non-western others' with strong growth potential. By 30 November 2001, these 'others' were called the 'BRIC' in Goldman Sachs Global Economic Paper no. 66, 'Building better global economic BRICs'.

Table 9.1 The production of 'hope'/'strength': three overlapping stages in the production of 'BRIC' knowledge

Stages	Major actors and institutions	Major discourses and knowledge tools	Knowledging technology
Stage 1: 2001– present 'BRIC' as investor story	International investment banks (e.g. Goldman Sachs) Chief Economist (e.g. Jim O'Neill) and colleagues; fund managers, sales teams, rating agencies, financial press . . .	• 2001 Invented the category in the report on 'Building better global economic BRICs' • 2003 Research report, 'Dreaming with BRICs: the path to 2050' • Other reports, books, webtours, indexes, etc. (see Table 9.2)	Technology of identification Technology of investability
Stage 2: 2004–present 'BRIC' as investor–consumer story	Economists, investment consultants, business media (Bloomberg, *The Economist*, CNN, blogs, etc.), international organizations (e.g. World Bank, IMF)	Decoupling theses • Transatlantic economies in recession owing to subprime crisis and its fallout. Other regions, esp. the BRIC, will grow in downturn – strong consumption • 'Decoupling 2.0' article (*The Economist*)	Technology of identification
Stage 3: Late 2008–present 'BRIC' as an investor–consumer–lender story	International organizations (WB, IMF, G20, BRIC Summit, etc.), national leaders, foreign policy analysts and mass media	• BRIC IMF Bond Programme • Buying IMF SDRs (e.g. USD 50bn by China) • Shifting global economic balance of power (e.g. from G8 to G20 or even G2)	Technology of agency

Source: Author's own compilation.

Extrapolating GDP growth rates until 2050, the BRIC economies were constructed as the new object of 'hope' with '*each set to grow again by more than the G7*' (2001: S.03; my italics). China and India would become the dominant global suppliers of goods and services respectively while Brazil and Russia would become key suppliers of food, raw materials and energy.

This construal of BRIC as a new 'hope' object for investors initially found mixed responses. While Goldman Sachs's corporate clients, who were seeking new markets, backed it, other banks and investors worried that the BRICs were politically unstable and vulnerable to changing commodity prices. O'Neill's team continued to supply clients with 'hope'. For example, a 2003 report, 'Dreaming with BRICs: the path to 2050', announced:

> The relative importance of the BRICs as an engine of new demand growth and spending power may shift more dramatically and quickly than expected. Higher growth in these economies could offset the impact of greying populations and slower growth in the advanced economies.
>
> Higher growth may lead to higher returns and increased demand for capital. The weight of the BRICs in investment portfolios could rise sharply. Capital flows might move further in their favour, prompting major currency realignments. (Wilson and Purushothaman 2003, p. 2)

By 2050 this imagined four-cylinder 'engine of growth' could make China's GDP 30 per cent higher than US output; India's could be four times Japan's; and Brazilian and Russian GDP could each be 50 per cent bigger than the UK. References to economic attributes such as size and rates of growth exemplify, in neo-Foucauldian terms, a technology of identification. Thus the BRICs are singled out, made knowable, and visibilized as the largest 'emerging economies', embarking on high-growth paths with potentially 'high returns' for investors. With continuing neoliberal globalization and China's 2001 entry into the WTO, ever more corporations and financial organizations were seeking new markets and sites for profitable investment. New discursive networks began to form, appropriating and circulating the BRIC imaginary as an object of investment and strategic action. After the 2003 paper, reports Tett (2010), Goldman economists entered what O'Neill described as 'briclife' as some of its clients (e.g. Vodafone, BHP Billiton, IKEA and Nissan) swamped the team with enquiries and placed their hopes in the BRIC imaginary and, more significantly, invested their capital in the four economies.

Goldman sustains the BRIC imaginary and its 'briclife' by churning out more knowledge products (many in several languages), ranging from reports and renewed forecasts to books, videos and webtours (Table 9.2). This story was occasionally challenged by other economists and investment

Table 9.2 Major BRIC knowledge products from Goldman Sachs

Name of knowledge products	Nature of product (year/month)	Ways of constructing hope and strength
'Building better global economic BRICs'	Report, November 2001	• Invented the BRIC category • Outlined healthier outlook in BRIC with combined GDP growth rate of 12% in next decade
'Dreaming with BRICs: the path to 2050'	Report, October 2003	• Mapping BRIC's GDP growth until 2050 • Postulating BRIC economies could be larger than G6 in 40 years' time
'How solid are the BRICs?'	Forecast, December 2005	• Updating the 2003 forecast • BRIC grow more strongly than projection
'Web tour: the BRICs dream' (in English, Arabic, Chinese and Japanese)	Webtours, May 2006	• Video on the BRIC • Dreaming about BRIC in post-9/11 world • China would overtake the USA in 2050 • Growth of middle classes in BRIC as major consumers of cars and energy
'India's urbanization: emerging opportunities'	Report, July 2007	• Framing boom in city life • Identifying investment opportunities in urban infrastructure and fast accumulation of financial assets
BRICS and Beyond	Book, November 2007	• Updating the 2001 report • Postulating rise in BRIC's equity markets • Moving beyond BRIC to other emerging economies (e.g. N-11)

Table 9.2 (continued)

Name of knowledge products	Nature of product (year/month)	Ways of constructing hope and strength
Interview with Jim O'Neill	Video, February 2008	• Keeping BRIC's share of global GDP as 15% • Advising individual BRIC countries (e.g. India needs more FDI) • Arguing for the sustainability of BRIC • Growing international role of BRIC states
Building the World: Mapping Infrastructure Demand	Report, April 2008	• Identifying increase infrastructure demand • Arguing China will provide one-half to three-quarters of incremental demand • Growing pressure on commodity markets
'Ten things for India to achieve its 2050 potential'	Report, June 2008	• Advising on improved governance and the need to control inflation • Promoting liberalization of financial market • Supporting improvement for agricultural productivity
'BRICs lead the global recovery'	Report, May, 2009	• BRIC can lead stabilization of world market • Promoting BRIC as a driving force in the export-driven recovery
'The BRICs as drivers of global consumption '	Report, August 2009	• Arguing G3 countries face slow and difficult recovery • Maintaining that BRIC can lift global domestic demand through higher consumption

'The BRICs Nifty 50: The EM & DM winners'	Report and stock baskets, November 2009	• Stating good consumption and infrastructural demand from BRIC • Identifying two BRIC Nifty 50 baskets to help investors to access the BRIC market
'BRICs at 8: strong through the crisis, outpacing forecasts'	Video, March 2010	• BRIC weathered global crisis very well • On pace to equal the G7 in size by 2032
'BRICs remain in the fast lane'	Report, June 2011	BRICs continue to climb ladder of global economic prominence by size faster than expected but living standards lag far behind developed world
'A progress report on the building of the BRICs'	Report, July 2011	Infrastructure has improved notably but investment must accelerate based on private as well as public investment

Source: Author's own compilation based on materials from Goldman Sachs's 'Our Thinking > BRIC' website.

consultants, who asked why some emerging economies were excluded (e.g. South Korea and Turkey) and others included (e.g. Russia and Brazil). New acronyms were proposed for the BRIC or BRIC-plus (e.g. CRIB or BRICK) or to divert attention elsewhere (e.g. CIVET)[2] to negotiate its meanings and appeals but the BRIC imaginary remained hegemonic based on the extrapolation of individual growth rates but also on the purported complementarity and coherence of BRIC as an asset/investment form.

Major international banks and other investment banks and hedge funds bundled stocks, shares and bonds and marketed many new funds under the BRIC label. Among early entrants were '4 Year MYR HSBC BRIC Markets Structured Investment', 'Templeton BRIC Fund' (Singapore), and the 'iShares MSCI BRIC Index Fund'. Investment consultancies such as Investment U (e.g. Daltorio 2009) narrated several funds as excellent investable choices (see Table 9.3). Their investability was framed in terms of their positive financial practices: spreading risks through a broad portfolio of stocks; placing funds in the biggest BRIC economy (China-Hong Kong) and in giant companies in strong lines of business (e.g. telecoms, resources); strong profit forecasts; and management by established 'emerging market' gurus. Armed with these investment products, financial sales teams and other intermediaries marketed them to potential clients through print and audio-visual ads, glossy brochures, financial journalism, phonecalls, home visits, etc. In neo-Foucauldian terms, this technology of investability (a) constructs strength, profitability and confidence by narrating these funds as sound asset choices; (b) directs investor subjects to put their money in these economies; and (c) normalizes BRICs as investment objects.

Benefiting from the general search for new investment objects, the inflow of equity funds to BRIC increased almost twelvefold between 2002 and 2007. BRIC's share was about two-thirds of total inflow into emerging markets between 2003 and 2007 (see Table 9.4). Within the BRIC group, China gained most in 2006 and India in 2007. The credit crunch led to a sharp general fall in inflow in 2008, with China the exception with a positive inflow of US$ 3.7 billion.

Stage Two: 2004–Present: Investor–Consumer Story

The BRIC-as-investor story gained a consumption dimension in the mid-2000s. The initial sign was a Goldman team report on *The BRICs and Global Markets: Crude, Cars and Capital* (2004) that identified an 'emerging middle class' demanding more commodities, consumer durables and capital services. This BRIC 'dream' was echoed by economic strategists

Table 9.3 BRIC Investment funds and their construction of strength and profitability

Name of recommended fund	Reasons for choice	Breakdown of ETF* by country	Top 10 components consist of giant firms
iShares MSCI BRIC Index Fund First choice	A portfolio of about 175 stocks from the BRIC countries. Despite a gain in excess of 40% year-to-date, the fund is still down over 30% over the past 52 weeks, so valuations are still not back to pre-crisis levels	China and Hong Kong: 42%, Brazil: 32%, India: 13% and Russia: 13%	China Mobile, Gazprom, Reliance Industry, Petrobras, Vale, Itau Unibanco, HDFC Bank, China Life Insurance, Lukoil, and Industrial & Commercial Bank of China
Templeton Emerging Markets Fund Second choice	The fund is managed by emerging market guru, Mark Mobius. Mobius has been with the Templeton since 1987 and has blazed the trail for emerging markets investors	China and Hong Kong: 23%, Brazil: 23%, India: 10%, Russia: 9%, Thailand: 8%, Turkey and South Korea: 7% each	Petrobras, Vale, Petrochina, Akbank, Denway Motors, Itau Unibanco, Sesa Goa, Banco Bradesco, Aluminum Corp of China and SK Energy

Note: * Exchange Traded Fund

Source: Adapted from Daltorio (2009) to fit a tabular form.

Table 9.4 Net inflows of portfolio equity to the BRIC economies 2002–08 ($ billion)

Country	2002	2003	2004	2005	2006	2007	2008
China	2.2	7.7	10.9	20.3	42.9	18.5	3.7
India	1.0	8.2	9.0	12.1	9.5	35.0	–15.0
Brazil	2.0	3.0	2.1	6.5	7.7	26.2	–7.6
Russia	2.6	0.4	0.2	–0.2	6.1	18.7	–15.0
BRIC	*7.8*	*19.3*	*22.2*	*38.7*	*66.2*	*98.4*	*–33.9*
Developing countries	5.5	24.1	40.4	68.9	104.8	135.4	–57.1

Source: Adapted from World Bank (2008, 2010).

such as Clyde Prestowitz, a former Reagan Administration official, who reached a wider audience in his book *Three Billion New Capitalists*. He projected that by 2020, 'the annual increase in dollar spending by the BRIC will be twice that of the G6' (2005, p. 227).

This BRIC-as-consumer story resonated strongly as the 2007 financial crisis emerged and intensified, prompting the search for new signs of 'hope' and new objects of recovery. This new stage attributed a further locomotive role to the BRIC based on their consumer-led demand, which would defer recession and create recovery opportunities for recession-ridden advanced economies.

This narrative was enthusiastically circulated and/or negotiated by economists, business and the general media (e.g., Bloomberg, *Newsweek*, *Wall Street Journal* and CNN) and international bodies (e.g. IMF) under the rubric of the 'decoupling thesis'. This asserts that the BRIC economies can expand on the basis of their own investment and consumption, despite recession in more advanced economies. Bloomberg reported Jim O'Neill as saying that 'the BRIC consumer is going to rescue the world' (Marinis 2008) and 'since October 2007, the Chinese shopper alone has been contributing more to global GDP growth than the American consumer' (Mellor and Lim 2008). The technology of identification was deployed again and BRIC was reinvented as a 'decoupled' object whose consumption power could save the world from recession.

Apart from O'Neill, this story was popularized by discursive networks of top investment advisers and fund managers (e.g. Todd Jacobson from Lord Abbett and Co.) (Shinnick 2008; Lordabett.com 2009) in the mass and Internet media. For example, Peter Schiff, author and president of Euro-Pacific Capital Inc, was a prominent proponent of this thesis and his position was echoed in many YouTube videos, blogs, articles and news items. A typical statement in his book *Little Book of Bull Moves in Bear Markets* argues:

> I'm rather fond of the word decoupling, in fact, because it fits two of my favorite analogies. The first is that America is no longer the engine of economic growth but the caboose. [The second is w]hen China divorces us, the Chinese will keep 100 per cent of their property and their factories, use their products themselves, and enjoy a dramatically improved lifestyle. (Schiff 2008, p. 41)

The 'decoupling thesis' is also negotiated in different ways. First, some financial analysts, economists and international/regional organizations, such as the World Bank and Asia Development Bank, cautiously noted that trade was contracting rather than decoupling. For example, in April 2008, citing reduced exports, the World Bank lowered its growth forecast for China to 6.5 per cent. Second, a different kind of caution was expressed in June 2008, when the IMF released its study *Convergence and Decoupling*. This argued that decoupling could coexist with integration. Since 1985 globalization has stimulated greater trade and financial integration and this, in turn, has produced tighter coupling of business cycles among countries with similar per capita incomes. Nonetheless, history also shows that some (groups of) countries have decoupled from the global economy at various stages of their development. Third, another concern was expressed by the British foreign affairs think tank Chatham House in the wake of the collapse of Merrill Lynch and Lehman Brothers in September 2008. Its briefing paper *Synchronized Dive into Recession* argued:

> Will a severe OECD recession engulf the rest of the world? Up to mid-2008, the emerging markets remained strong – 'decoupling' did work. Now the crisis has deepened, no region will remain immune to shock waves. (Rossi 2008)

In spite (or perhaps because) of these views and the ambiguity of '(de) coupling', the thesis continued to circulate. Indeed, O'Neill reinforced it in *Newsweek* in March 2009:

> Who said decoupling was dead? The decoupling idea is that, because the BRICs rely increasingly on domestic demand, they can continue to boom even if their most important export market, the United States, slows dramatically. The idea came into disrepute last fall, when the U.S. market collapse started to spread to the BRICs, but there's now lots of evidence that decoupling is alive and well. (O'Neill 2009)

This was echoed by *The Economist* in an article, 'Decoupling 2.0', on 21 May 2009. This interpreted decoupling as 'a narrower phenomenon, confined to a few of the biggest, and least indebted, emerging economies' such as China, India and Brazil. These have strong domestic markets and prudent macroeconomic policies and also enjoy growing cross-trade – and, more recently, have begun to use their own currencies to settle this trade. In an interview, Michael Buchanan, Goldman Sachs' Asia-Pacific Economist in Hong Kong, increased the stakes:

> For the last couple of months, data have revealed a growing divergence between western economies and those in much of Asia, notably China and India . . . One reason for this divergence is that the effects of the financial crisis hit Asia much later. While the American economy began slumping in 2007, Asian economies were doing well until the collapse of Lehman Brothers in September. What followed was a rush of stimulus measures – rate cuts and government spending programs. In Asia's case, these came soon after things soured for the region; in the United States, they came much later though on a much bigger scale.

> In addition, developing Asian economies were in pretty good financial shape when the crisis struck. The last major crisis to hit the region – the financial turmoil of 1997–98 – forced governments in Asia to introduce overhauls that ultimately left them with lower debt levels, more resilient banking and regulatory systems and often large foreign exchange reserves. (Buchanan 2009)

This argument creatively reinterpreted the BRIC-decoupling thesis by limiting it to China and, to a lesser extent, India. In highlighting the 'new decoupling' thesis, this step construed them as 'useful others' with large foreign exchange reserves, buoyant fiscal positions and financial stimulus packages. In November 2009, the World Bank raised its 2010 economic forecast for China's GDP growth to 8.4 per cent. These economies offer 'hope' through their good investment markets, robust middle-class consumption and relative large stimulus packages (see Table 9.5). This scaling down of BRIC to China and India was reinforced within the policy circuit by Roger Scher (2009), whose question 'From BRIC to BIC . . . or even IC??' cast doubt on Russia's strength and Brazil's prospects. Others introduced the term 'BriC' to highlight China's position (see below).

Stage Three: Investor–Consumer–Lender Story

As the crisis in advanced countries deepened and the hopeful search for objects of recovery continued, more attention went to the BRIC quartet's geopolitical significance. Policymakers, international organizations, think tanks, foreign policy analysts and others now played a greater role in constructing 'hope'. This trend was illustrated by the UK Prime Minister, Gordon Brown, when he was coordinating an IMF rescue package for the global economy in October 2008. He stated:

> China . . . has very substantial reserves. There are a number of countries that actually can do quite a lot in the immediate future to make sure that the international community has sufficient resources to support countries that get themselves into difficulties. (Sanderson 2008)

This plea was reiterated as Brown prepared for the G20 meeting in London in April 2009, when China was expected to contribute US$40 billion to the rescue package. Accompanying these specific policy initiatives, foreign policy rhetoric emphasized the emergence of a 'multipolar world order' and 'comprehensive interdependence' among countries. These new geopolitical imaginaries became more credible when Russia held the first BRIC Leaders' Summit in Yekaterinburg in June 2009 and Brazil, China and India hosted the second, third and fourth summits in April 2010,

April 2011 and March 2012 respectively. These served as arenas for BRIC leaders to perform and confirm their collective identity as well as envisage their future. Inter alia, this would balance Russia's push to go beyond a global economy dominated by the dollar with China's drive to diversify reserves away from US Treasury bonds.[3]

Thus, in reaction to Brown's 2009 call for them to back the IMF rescue package, the BRIC governments agreed to contribute to a more diversified international monetary system. Influenced by Stiglitz's UN Commission on Reforms of the International and Monetary Systems and discussions around the UN Conference on the Global Financial and Economic Crisis, the BRIC summit advocated 'Special Drawing Rights' (SDRs) as a new 'global currency' that could increase liquidity. The IMF would issue SDR-denominated bonds that the BRIC economies could purchase for their reserves. This new approach was backed at the G20 Summit in April 2009, when the then IMF managing director, Dominique Strauss-Kahn, announced the issue of US$250 million SDR-denominated bonds. The IMF Executive Board confirmed this on 1 July 2009, China pledged to buy US$50 billion, and Russia, Brazil and India would each gradually purchase US$10 billion.

In contrast to conventional IMF loan facilities, this form of financing involved new kinds of lender and governance relations that favoured the BRIC economies. As lenders to the IMF, the strength of this quartet was reconfirmed symbolically via: (1) the developed economies' recognition that they should be part of the solution to the crisis by subscribing to these SDR-denominated bonds; (2) their general unwillingness to commit funds on a long-term basis until the IMF reallocated country quotas; and (3) their specific demand for an increase in their voting shares within the IMF governance structure from 5 to 7 per cent of the total.[4] Despite these signs of 'hope'/'strength', some observers commented that the new SDR bonds would only absorb a small proportion of the BRIC's foreign reserves and, therefore, did not really challenge the role of the US dollar (Kelly 2009).

This (negotiated) amalgam of 'BRIC' discourses and practices (and their continued reworking and rearticulation over three overlapping stages) has helped to sediment and naturalize BRIC as a complex object of 'hope'/'strength'. It deferred the recession by offering investment opportunities for frustrated investors, generating consumer demand that can facilitate recovery and growth, and making reserves available to finance international lending. The BRIC discourse also led to successive BRIC summits and some concerted economic, financial and political actions. Thus the quartet has supposedly graduated from 'emerging markets' to 'emerging global powers'. This shift illustrates what neo-Foucauldians call a technology of agency (Cruikshank 1999). It is based in this case on the coexistence of participation and control in the international arena. Using the power shift from G8 to G20 as an example, the BRICs were encouraged to participate as 'we' in the new multipolar world order. However, while the BRICs' increasing roles in the G20 allowed their participation, it also steers the manner of their engagement, e.g. as engines of consumption, lenders to the IMF, and so forth. Such participation, coordination and steering of the BRIC economies in arenas such as the G20 allows for the emergence of a broader 'discussion forum' to address crisis-related issues as well as producing directives to international organizations such as the IMF. This engagement steers the BRIC economies towards discussions around crisis management that may rebuild and renegotiate the neoliberal agendas (e.g. the dollar–yuan exchange policy, BRIC as consumers and economic opportunities, US dollar hegemony, etc.).

BRIC-ING OF CHINA AND ITS 2008 STIMULUS PACKAGE

The (re)making of the BRIC regime as an object of 'hope'/'strength' was not a smooth process. The BRIC identity and its boundaries are constantly (re) negotiated by (trans)national actors. Some global market strategists and economists asked why some emerging economies were excluded while Russia was included. Some foreign policy analysts questioned the coherence of the quartet, leading one to use 'BRIC-à-Brac' to convey their diverse, toothless nature (Drezner 2009).[5] More prosaically, others warned of a 'BRIC bubble', arguing that, even if their GDP continued to expand, this might not guarantee higher stock market returns (Tasker 2010; Evans-Pritchard 2011).

In the Sinophone world, the term 'BRIC' is translated as '*bricks*' and has been recontextualized, initially in Taiwan and then more widely, as '*the four golden brick countries*' (金磚四國). The 'golden bricks' imaginary has been embraced by China's financial and official communities as a symbol of 'strength' and sign of 'greatness-at-last'. This reinforces China's longstanding construction of 'national strength' under a one-party authoritarian regime. Many headlines in its official newspaper, the *People's Daily*, adopted BRIC-related discourses such as 'Shining, golden "BRIC"' (6 September 2006) and 'BRIC set to build golden brick' (16 June 2009). This 'golden' metaphor helps to signify the strength and pride of the Chinese nation, especially after its long history of foreign invasion and national humiliation. In particular, this claim to strength is expressed quantitatively in terms of a 'shining BRIC' that can 'protect 8 per cent GDP growth rate'. It is worth noting here the cultural significance of the number eight, because it is a homonym for 'prosperity' – a source of output legitimacy for the Chinese state.

Table 9.5 The central–local government's share of the stimulus package and sources of finance in China 2008–10

Level of government	Amount (trillion RMB)	% of total	Major sources of finance
Central government	1.2	29.5	• Direct grants • Interest-rate subsidies
Regional–local governments	2.8	70.5	• Loan-based finance • Policy loans • Local government bonds issued by the central government (around 200 billion RMB) • Corporate bonds (130 billion RMB were issued 2008.Q4) • Medium-term notes (25 billion RMB were issued in March 2009) • Bank loans

Source: Window of China (2009); Naughton (2009).

With the onset of the 2007 financial crisis and North Atlantic economic recession, Chinese exports fell sharply, unemployment rose dramatically, and social unrest increased. Central government responded proactively to the crisis to reprofile itself nationally and internationally. It reiterated its 'protection of 8 per cent GDP growth rate' as a signal to project strength and justify a vast stimulus package of RMB4 trillion (USD586 billion) implemented from November 2008. While well-received globally, the stimulus measures affect national–local social relations unevenly, especially fiscal relations between central and local governments. The package was narrated officially as supporting ten major industrial sectors (e.g. steel, shipbuilding, electronics, and petrochemicals), building infrastructural projects (e.g. high-speed rail, the electric grid), boosting consumer spending, developing the rural economy, and encouraging education and housing (Tong and Zhang 2009). However, based on fiscal practice since the late 1990s, only around a third of the package was financed centrally; the rest was to come from regional–local governments, regional government ministries, and state-owned enterprises (Table 9.5). To enable this borrowing, the central government loosened credit policies and abolished credit ceilings for commercial banks.

China's Stimulus Package, 'Property Bubble' and the 'Subaltern' South

Regional ministries and local governments were eager to seize this opportunity and get their pet infrastructure projects approved (Naughton 2009). Given the prevailing central–local fiscal arrangements since the 1990s, local governments have to provide matching funds. This is hard because (1) they must channel 60 per cent of their revenue to Beijing; (2) the economic downturn reduced revenue from business taxes; and (3) they have no formal mandate to borrow money. This resulted in a funding gap. A 2009 National Audit Office survey reported that local governments in eighteen provinces were failing to provide the expected level of 'matching funds', with the weakest province sending only 48 per cent of the required amount (Xi et al. 2009).

Formally, this shortfall can be filled by financial resources from a mix of local government bonds issued by central government, corporate bonds, medium-term notes and bank loans (Table 9.5). However, as China's bond market is not well developed, local governments seek their own sources of finance. One source is intensified use of land to generate income. Under China's land leasehold market established in the late 1970s, urban land is state-owned but land-use rights can be leased for fixed periods (e.g. 70 years for housing) and leases are tradable (Hsing 2010, p. 36). This encourages local officials to convert rural land, which still belongs to rural 'collectives', into urban land by compensating (at least in principle) dispossessed village communities.

Local governments can commodify land in two main ways: to lever loans and raise revenue. First, although they have accumulated land, licences and equity investments, these assets cannot be translated into cash because the Budget Law prohibits these authorities from raising funds directly. So they set up related investment companies to raise loans from state-owned banks (e.g. Bank of China, China Construction Bank) and use land-use rights as collateral. With the easy availability of credit and the close relationship between local governments and state-owned banks, local government debt rose five times between 2008 and 2009 from RMB1 trillion (US\$146 billion) to an estimate of RMB5 trillion (US\$730 billion) by the end of 2009 (Zhang 2010). Concurrently, Bank of China and China Construction Bank reported that profits rose 26 and 15 per cent respectively for 2009 (*Business Weekly* 2010).

Second, land-right leases are auctioned to private and state-owned developers (e.g. China Poly Group, China Resource Group and China Merchant Group) for property projects, generating government revenue and stimulating growth. In 2009, the Ministry of Land and Resources reported local governments generated RMB1.6 trillion (US\$233 billion) –

an increase of 60 per cent over 2008 – with 84 per cent of revenues coming from property development (*China Daily* 2010). Property development is a major source of fiscal revenues for local governments and, in addition, state-owned and private property developers (and their local government partners) can earn high profits from selling housing units, especially when easy credit is available from state-controlled banks.

This process has strengthened the emerging social attitude that property ownership is a source of economic security, a hedge against inflation, a lender of social status, a family safety net and a provider of personal pride. The business press, ordinary media, and peer pressures help to reinforce these views in everyday life. Given the limited outlets to invest savings, continuously rising property values over the last decade have suggested that real estate offers higher returns; indeed, low interest rates and the absence of a national property tax allowed speculative property to be purchased and held relatively cheaply. Thus real estate came increasingly to be seen as an object of investment, ownership and/or speculation. This underpins the central government focus on high growth rates, local government dependency upon land and/or real estate for revenue, and the drive of real-estate developers for profit. Such land-induced accumulation is fuelling real-estate inflation and fears of a 'property bubble'. According to Colliers International, residential prices in 70 large and medium cities across China rose in 2009, with 50 to 60 per cent increases in Beijing and Shanghai. Such increases reduce housing affordability with the conventionally calculated income-to-price ratio in Beijing at 1 to 22 (Smith 2010; Powell 2010; FlorCruz 2009). This means that housing prices for a standard unit are 22 times average annual family incomes.

This inflationary rise has added a political dimension to the housing question. Premier Wen Jiabao acknowledged this on 27 February 2010, remarking that 'property prices have risen too fast' and this 'wild horse' has to be tamed. Central government leaders have tried to dampen the market (e.g. tightening credit; raising deposits for purchase of new land to 50 per cent; enabling state-owned developers whose core business is not property to exit the sector; taxing residential housing, etc.). However, banks have found other ways to raise money (e.g. selling off loans to state-owned trusts and asset management companies; turning loans into investment products for private investors, etc.). These practices are supported by those with vested interests in the property boom, such as jobs and perks for officials, income and growth statistics for ministries and local governments, profit and/or investment for state-owned banks and related investment vehicles as well as state-owned or private property developers, and, of course, benefits to property owners (on the real-estate coalition, see Sum 2011).

However, overinvestment in real estate and infrastructural projects destabilizes the economy with very uneven impacts on the socio-economic positions of ordinary citizens and the 'subaltern south'. While many issues are relevant (e.g. land seizures, peasant protests, isolated 'nail houses' whose owners resist buyout offers so that their homes stick up like nails on a flat floor, etc.), I will discuss two social issues: housing affordability and the plight of migrant workers in rural towns.

First, rising prices are based on and reinforce the view that property ownership provides personal security and capital gains. This underpins the stimulus–loan–property boom and its socio-economic base but also causes social unrest over resettlement compensation, land clearance, housing and education costs, conditions for migrant workers, inflation, and petty and major corruption. These issues are reflected and popularized in countless newspaper columns, documentaries, policy speeches and appeals for action.

This plight was depicted sharply by a TV sitcom entitled *Dwelling Narrowness (Snail House)* (蜗居) in 2009. It highlighted the struggle of two sisters to buy user rights to an apartment during a property boom in a fictional city that could well be Shanghai. To obtain the purchase money, one sister begins an affair with a wealthy and corrupt official, who later falls from grace because of a scandal over the diversion of pension funds into property deals (He 2009). The story resonated among ordinary people, especially regarding the impact of high property prices on families and young couples as well as the uneven distribution of wealth between property-owning and non-property-owning groups. In spite (or perhaps because) of its popularity, the series disappeared from the airwaves; *Southern Metropolitan News* explained that its transmission was suspended for 'technical reasons'. The series is still available on the Internet and in DVD format in the black market. Up to December 2009, it had been viewed 41 million times on the Internet and even government officials admitted to watching it.[6] This series echoes the everyday life of 'house slaves' (房奴). These are the white-collar employees who, in the midst of soaring property prices propelled by an easy-credit and over-investment stimulus package, slave to save the deposit for flats and to pay their mortgage, and who struggle to balance domestic budgets. It seems as if it is not these workers who own their flats or houses, but their houses and flats that own them and dictate their working lives and family relationships.

China's uneven development is also reflected in the plight of migrant workers in rural towns on the periphery of cities. These workers are a significant part of the reserve army of labour and a bedrock of the booming Chinese export economy. Although they have no opportunity to become 'house slaves', they risk displacement by the same property boom dynamic. This accelerates land clearance in rural towns to make way for real-estate projects, displacing workers and increasing accommodation costs. This has prompted social unrest over land appropriation, undercompensation for land and property seizures, corruption, and rising prices. In October 2010, a blogger called 'Blood Map' used Google Maps to map sites where land conflicts have occurred, violence has been used against residents, and people have resisted illegal land grab and property demolitions.[7]

Land appropriation and clearance also affect migrant families. Lacking *hukou* (long-term residency) in urban areas, their children attend cheap, privately run schools set up in slums in these rural towns. Urban clearance threatens such affordable education owing to school closures. In addition to the threat of closure, some schools are categorized as 'illegal' (and hence receive no compensation for closure) by the local authorities (Li 2010). Some children are locked out from schools, some are rehoused in makeshift schools, and some must return to their home villages to be cared for by their grandparents or other relatives. There are currently some 20 million such 'left-behind children' in China.[8]

This also raises more general issues concerning the 'rights of migrant workers' and a *hukou* system that creates second-class citizens. In response to these challenges, on 2 March 2010 13 regional newspapers throughout China issued a joint call for the abolition of the 'outdated' *hukou* system,[9] but this call was quickly diverted. The authorities continually talk of reorienting policies and putting more resources into the social agenda (e.g. housing, education, healthcare, etc.). However, as the stimulus package is largely land-led, the injection of funds into healthcare and social housing tends to grow more slowly than economic expansion tied so closely to the vested interests of regional–local governments, the property-owning elite, state-owned banks, state-owned and/or private-property developers, infrastructure-related departments and organizations, etc. There have been recent calls to tighten credit by suspending home loans to buyers purchasing a third housing unit, and acknowledge the need for social development, etc. These measures are likely to be counteracted by these groups and their continual push for growth and investment. The resulting tensions are expressed on different levels. Socially, there is the rise in social unrest (e.g. Wukan peasant riot) and the demand for the return of land. Economically, the central government's push for tightening credit has simply intensified shadow banking in hotbed sites such as Wenzhou and Anyang.

CONCLUDING REMARKS

CPE highlights the discursive moments (including subjectivities, identities, economic and political categories, knowledge production, modes of calculation, and structures of feeling) of economic and political relations and their connection with structural factors such as social forms, class relations, contradictions, and crisis-tendencies. This chapter applies this approach to three overlapping stages in the construction of the BRIC economies since 2001 as a (trans)national object of 'hope' and/or 'strength'. These stages were not arbitrary but related to major new material conjunctures – notably the 9/11 attacks and the unfolding of the North Atlantic financial crisis from 2007. In response to these conjunctures, diverse actors experimented with discourses and practices that would reorient their interpretations and actions. Some of these discourses (e.g. the 'decoupling thesis') have been negotiated, selected, deepened, sedimented and naturalized as efforts to manage the security and financial crises have continued. In addition, a CPE approach would examine how: (1) these processes have been mediated by discursive networks that include international investment banks, economic strategists, business media, think tanks, international organizations and foreign policymakers; and (2) governmental knowledging technologies of power, such as identification, investability and agency, were deployed to privilege and naturalize the BRIC economies as objects of 'hope'/'strength' relevant for the imagined recovery of the global political economy. This chapter has shown how this BRIC imaginary is negotiated and appropriated diversely by examining the case of China. In the Sinophone world, the BRIC imaginary is recontextualized as 'the four golden brick countries' that symbolize China's 'strength' and act as a sign of its 'greatness-at-last' through its capacity to 'protect an 8 per cent GDP growth rate'. With the onset of the 2007 financial crisis, the promotion of its vast economic stimulus package has intensified some deep-rooted tensions within China's national–local political economy. Growing social tensions and unevenness represent the 'dark side' of the stimulus package that is too often narrated in the (trans)national arena in terms of 'hope' and 'strength' to the neglect of local subaltern social sites, everyday resistance, and peasant riots.

NOTES

1. After 2008, a fourth stage emerged, involving the construction of 'fear' regarding Chinese and Indian competitiveness vis-à-vis the US (Schmidt 2010).
2. CIVET refers to Colombia, Indonesia, Vietnam, Egypt, and Turkey.
3. Because China's currency reserves are still invested largely in US Treasury bonds, China is more cautious, at least in the short term, than its BRIC partners regarding the dominance of the dollar. Russia's call to challenge the US dollar failed to gain China's support at the first BRIC Summit (*China Daily* 2009).
4. In the G20 Pittsburgh Meeting (September 2009), European governments – notably France and the UK – blocked discussion of IMF governance reform because they feared

losing influence at the IMF. On 25 April 2010, China's voting power in the World Bank increased from 2.78 to 4.42 per cent.

5. The fundamental differences among the BRIC include diverse political systems and dissimilar views on key policy issues such as free trade and energy pricing.
6. Viewing data are available at: http://chinasilicon.blogspot.com/2009/12/40-million-views-of-sitcom-housing-for.html (accessed 8 April 2012).
7. See 'Elusive "blood map" founder speaks out', available at: http://observers.france24.com/content/20101119-china-evictions-violence-blood-map-google-founder-speaks-out (accessed 8 April 2012).
8. Rural migrants without the right *hukou* permit in urban areas cannot access public housing, schooling, or local pension and healthcare benefits. This system is changing but it still favours the educated migrant communities.
9. 'Editorial calls for abolition of *hukou* system', available at: http://chinainsight689.com/chinese-domestic-news/editorial-calls-for-abolition-of-hukou-system/ (accessed 8 April 2012).

REFERENCES

Buchanan, Michael (2009), 'Decoupling is happening for real', 10 July, available at: www.chartwelletfadvisor.com/etf-newsletters/vol06-iss096.pdf (accessed 21 February 2010).

Business Weekly (2010), 'China Construction Bank 2009 profit up 15 percent', 28 March, available at: www.businessweek.com/ap/financialnews/D9EO1OQ00.htm (accessed 8 April 2012).

China Daily (2009), 'BRIC mum on reserve currencies', 17 June, available at: www.chinadaily.com.cn/bizchina/2009-06/17/content_8294061.htm (accessed 8 April 2012).

China Daily (2010), 'China's land sales revenue close to $ 233 bln in 2009', 2 February, available at: www.chinadaily.com.cn/china/2010-02/02/content_9417378.htm (accessed 8 April 2012).

Cruikshank, Barbara (1999), *The Will to Empower*, Ithaca, NY: Cornell University Press.

Daltorio, Tony (2009), 'Profit from the "new decoupling"', available at: www.investmentu.com/IUEL/2009/July/decoupling-emerging-markets.html (accessed 8 April 2012).

Dean, Mitchell (1999), *Governmentality: Power and Rule in Modern Society*, Thousand Oaks, CA: Sage.

Drezner, Daniel W. (2009), 'BRIC-a-brac', available at: http://drezner.foreignpolicy.com/posts/2009/06/17/bric_a_brac (accessed 8 April 2012).

The Economist (2009), 'Decoupling 2.0', May 21.

Evans-Pritchard, Ambrose (2011), 'Goldman Sachs shuns the BRICs for Wall Street', www.telegraph.co.uk/finance/economics/8265175/Goldman-Sachs-shuns-the-BRICs-for-Wall-Street.html (accessed 8 April 2012).

FlorCruz, Jaime (2009), 'Will the China property bubble pop?', available at: www.cnn.com/2009/BUSINESS/12/30/china.property.bubble/index.html (accessed 8 April 2012).

Goldman Sachs (2001), 'Building better global economic BRICS', global economic paper no. 66, available at: www.goldmansachs.com/our-thinking/topics/brics/brics-reports-pdfs/build-better-brics.pdf (accessed 13 September 2011).

Goldman Sachs (2004), 'The BRICs and the global markets: crude, cars and capital', issue 2004-9, available at: www.goldmansachs.com/ceoconfidential/CEO-2004-09.pdf (accessed 13 September 2011).

He, H-F. (2009), 'Rumours swirl as top TV series blacked out: smash hit about perils of buying a flat allegedly axed for cutting too close to bone', *South China Morning Post*, 26 November.

Hsing, You-Tien (2010), *The Great Urban Transformation: Politics of Land and Property in China*, Oxford: Oxford University Press.

Kelly, Brendan (2009), 'Brazil, Russia, India and China (the BRICs) throw down the gauntlet of the International Monetary System', 28 June, available at: www.eastasiaforum.org/2009/06/28/brazil-russia-india-and-china-the-brics-throw-down-the-gauntlet-on-monetary-system-reform/ (accessed 19 March 2010).

Li, Rex (2010), 'Schools' demise forces migrant children home', available at: www.scmp.com/portal/site/SCMP/menuitem.2af62ecb329d3d7733492d9253a0a0a0/?vgnextoid=9bcaf2f9bae86210VgnVCM100000360a0a0aRCRD&ss=China&s=News (accessed 3 March 2010).

Lordabett.com (2009), 'Why decoupling should benefit international investors', available at: www.lordabbett.com/articles/wp_why_decoupling_should.pdf (accessed 3 March 2010).

Marinis, Alexandre (2008), 'BRIC Consumers Can't Hold Off World Recession', Livemint.com, available at: www.livemint.com/2008/12/18211911/Bric-consumers-can8217t-hol.html (accessed 8 April 2012).

Mellor, William and Le-Min Lim (2008), 'BRIC shoppers will "rescue world" Goldman Sachs says', available at: www.bloomberg.com/apps/news?pid=newsarchive&sid=a3aTPjYcw8a8 (accessed 8 April 2012).

Miller, Peter and Nik Rose (2008), *Governing the Present*, Cambridge: Polity.

Naughton, Barry (2009), 'Understanding the Chinese stimulus package', *Chinese Leadership Monitor* no. 28, Spring, available at: media.hoover.org/sites/default/files/documents/CLM28BN.pdf (accessed 8 April 2012).

O'Neill, Jim (2009), 'The new shopping superpower', available at: www.newsweek.com/2009/03/20/the-new-shopping-superpower.html (accessed 13 April 2010).

Powell, Bill (2010), 'China's property: bubble, bubble, toil and trouble', 22 March, available at: www.time.com/time/magazine/article/0,9171,1971284,00.html (accessed 8 April 2012).

Prestowitz, Clyde (2005), *Three Billion New Capitalists*, New York: Basic Books.

Rossi, Vanessa (2008), 'Synchronized dive into recession', International Economic Programme, October 2008, IEP BP 08/04, available at: www.chathamhouse.org.uk/files/12340_bp1008recession.pdf (accessed 8 April 2012).

Sanderson, Henry (2008), 'China wants more say in global financial bodies', available at: www.usatoday.com/money/economy/2008-10-29-2068576087_x.htm (accessed 8 April 2012).

Scher, Roger (2009), 'From BRIC to BIC . . . or even to IC?', available at: http://risingpowers.foreignpolicyblogs.com/2009/06/08/from-bric-to-bic%E2%80%A6or-even-ic/ (accessed 8 April 2012).

Schiff, Peter D. (2008), *Little Book of Bull Moves in Bear Markets*, London: Wiley.

Schmidt, Eric (2010), 'Erasing our innovation deficit', available at: www.washingtonpost.com/wp-dyn/content/article/2010/02/09/AR2010020901191.html (accessed 8 April 2012).

Shinnick, Richard (2008), 'Decoupling thesis intact', available at: http://seekingalpha.com/article/63886-decoupling-thesis-intact (accessed 8 April 2012).

Smith, Charles Hugh (2010), 'Global economy's next threat: China's real estate bubble', available at: www.dailyfinance.com/story/global-economys-next-threat-chinas-real-estate-bubble/19302329/# (accessed 8 April 2012).
Sum, Ngai-Ling (2005), 'Discourses, material power and (counter-)hegemony', available at: www.lancaster.ac.uk/cperc/publications.htm (accessed 1 February 2010).
Sum, Ngai-Ling (2010), 'The production of hegemonic policy discourses: "competitiveness" as a knowledge brand and its (re-)contextualizations', *Critical Policy Studies*, **3** (1), 50–76.
Sum, Ngai-Ling (2011), 'Financial crisis, land-induced financialization and the subalterns in China', in Christoph Scherrer (ed.), *China's Labour Question*, Berlin: Springer, pp. 199–208, retrieved from www.global-labour-university.org/fileadmin/books/CLQ_full_book.pdf (accessed 12 December 2011).
Sum, Ngai-Ling and Bob Jessop (2006), 'Towards a cultural international political economy: post-structuralism and the Italian School', in Marieke de Goede (ed.), *International Political Economy and Post-Structural Politics*, Basingstoke: Palgrave Macmillan, pp. 157–76.
Tasker, Peter (2010), 'Beware the lure of GDP when seeking stocks in Brics', available at: www.ft.com/cms/s/0/18f2c282-ff1b-11de-a677-00144feab49a.html (accessed 8 April 2012).
Tett, Gillian (2010), 'The story of the Brics', available at: www.ft.com/cms/s/2/112ca932-00ab-11df-ae8d-00144feabdc0.html (accessed 15 March 2010).
Tong, Sarah Y. and Yang Zhang (2009), China's responses to the economic crisis, EAI Background Brief no. 438, National Singapore University, available at: www.eai.nus.edu.sg/BB438.pdf (accessed 13 April 2010).
Wilson, Dominic and Roopa Purushothaman (2003), 'Dreaming with the BRICs: the path to 2050', Goldman Sachs Global Economic Research Website, global economic paper no. 99, available at: www.goldmansachs.com/our-thinking/brics/brics-reports-pdfs/brics-dream.pdf (accessed 8 April 2012).
Window of China (2009), 'China updates details of stimulus fund', 21 May, available at: http://news.xinhuanet.com/english/2009-05/21/content_11415559.htm (accessed 8 April 2012).
World Bank (2008), *Global Development Finance 2008*, Washington, DC: World Bank.
World Bank (2010), *Global Development Finance 2010*, Washington, DC: World Bank.
Xi, Si, Xiangdong Zhang and Zhiyun Cheng (2009), 'Mitigating debt bomb for Chinese local governments', Economic Observer, 1 June, available at: www.eeo.com.cn/ens/finance_investment/2009/06/01/138892.shtml (accessed 8 April 2012).
Zhang, M. (2010), 'CBRC beefs up measures', *Shanghai Daily*, 25 February, available at: www.china.org.cn/business/2010-02/25/content_19472067.htm (accessed 8 April 2012).

10. The metaphor challenge of future economics: growth and sustainable development in Swedish media discourse

Anna W. Gustafsson

INTRODUCTION

Right from the beginning of the current financial crisis voices were heard declaring the death of growth capitalism – a capitalism incorporating a thought of continuous growth that can be discussed as 'the master narrative' (Friman 2002) of a modern society. The ongoing climate crisis and the food crisis contributed to an intensification of the critique of the thought of constant or long-term economic growth as the motor of society and as an underlying axiom for societal development.

As a response to the challenges caused by economic growth and financial crisis, climate crisis and the inequality of the distribution of food, health and development in a global perspective, the concept of 'sustainable development' was introduced. It envisions a world where economics, ecology, social justice and equality live together in harmony. This means that the discussion of sustainability and more specifically sustainable development is future-oriented and tries to bring together and negotiate between world views and discourses that sometimes collide; the discussion of future economics is a melting pot of ideas as well as of discourses expressing these ideas. It is therefore interesting and fruitful to study the discourse of growth and sustainability in the media during the latest financial crisis (2008 onwards) – especially in financial journalism and in political debate. These are genres that have a wide distribution, reaching many readers, and therefore can be said to reflect and affect views circulating in society.

The theoretical background for this study is found in critical discourse analysis (CDA). The discourse analytical toolbox of CDA is aimed at studying how reality is constructed in discourses, which are realized with linguistic means in texts. How then does the use of central concepts and metaphors contribute to a certain understanding of reality – and of the financial crisis?

Following this introductory section, the first part of the main text of this chapter discusses the conceptualization of growth and economic development as reflected in the use of metaphors in media discourse before and during the first years of the crisis (2008–10) – using the methodology of critical metaphor analysis. The second part discusses the meaning and use of the Swedish translation of the concept of sustainability, *hållbarhet* (which is also a metaphor). Researchers have pointed out that 'sustainability' has become a buzzword – a fashionable word used to make a good impression or provide a key to a certain discourse exploited by corporate interests (Parr 2009). In a quantitative corpus study as well as a qualitative case study the discursive use of the concept of sustainable development in economic and political media discourse during the first years of the crisis will be discussed.

Metaphors have the power to affect our conceptualization of reality. They are powerful rhetorical tools. In a concluding discussion the role of metaphor in the discourses of growth and sustainability will be discussed in a rhetorical and future-oriented perspective.

Analysing Metaphors

Growth and sustainability are both metaphors. As metaphors they contribute to the organization of our experience: they help us understand abstract processes, but at the same time they create realities (Lakoff and Johnsson 1980). Conceptual metaphor theory (CMT) stresses this function of metaphors. CMT deals with the underlying mappings, that is the systematic correspondences between the conceptual domain we try to understand and the conceptual domain the metaphor is taken from.[1] Recent CMT theory distinguishes between metaphors that are realized – linguistic metaphors – and metaphors that structure our thought – conceptual metaphors (see Deignan 2005, p. 14).

One example of a conceptual metaphor is 'good is up'. This conceptualization is visible in linguistic realizations such as: 'Things went downhill for a while, but now we're on our way up again.' The vast majority of metaphors are mappings of a concrete domain onto an abstract one. Using our physical experience from the concrete one we can transfer that experience to the abstract domain. Another example of a metaphor using a domain that we have experience from is the following, about the financial crisis: 'The global contagion is unavoidable.'

Seen in this perspective, metaphor is no longer considered a simple figure of speech, with a decorative function, but as having a more profound function for our conceptualizations. Therefore, metaphor in public discourse not only plays an ornamental role, but also is used to capture the reader's attention, to stress certain aspects of reality via conceptual mechanisms. Metaphor use is potentially ideological: metaphors can be used 'to present a particular interpretation of situations and events' (Deignan 2005, p. 23). Metaphors highlight certain aspects of topics and hide others (Lakoff and Johnsson 1980, pp. 10–14). By studying the metaphors used in talk about a certain topic, and by discussing alternative metaphors and the entailments of these, we can gain access to a certain community's interpretation of the world.

Critical metaphor analysis (CMA) combines the conceptual metaphor theory with corpus methodology and critical discourse analysis (CDA) (Charteris-Black 2004, 2005, 2006).[2] CMA stresses the potential of a metaphor to influence and change thinking and behaviour. As in CDA, one focus when studying metaphors is 'the ideological and political import of particular metaphors, and conflict between alternative metaphors' (Fairclough 1992, p. 77).

Analysing Word Meaning

As stated above the meaning and use of the concepts of sustainability and sustainable development will be explored in a quantitative corpus study as well as a qualitative case study using a corpus of Swedish texts from before and during the first years of the financial crisis. The focus on word meaning is important from a CDA perspective, since the articulations of meaning and the definitions and combinations of words in texts helps to articulate particular world views and ideologies. Fairclough suggests that 'particular structurings of the relationships between words and the relationships between the meanings of a word are forms of hegemony' (Fairclough 1992, p. 77). In the analysis of word meaning, lexicographic information only helps to a certain point. Words can be filled with new meanings and new connotations in use in specific contexts, and only by analysing the usage of the words in actual texts can we start uncovering the implications of the discourse. In this study, I use 'concept' when referring to a word or expression as a bearer of complex political-ideological meaning, and 'word' when referring to the actual word or lexicographical unit.

Where discourses with different world-views and different definitions of central concepts collide there is antagonism, and a discursive struggle about certain central concepts takes place. In this article the concept of 'sustainability' is seen as such an arena for struggle; different actors fill it with different meaning. The Brundtland Report (discussed in the second part of this chapter) can be described as an effort to produce an articulation of the concept aimed at uniting antagonistic discourses.

Corpus of Texts

For the purpose of studying the metaphors in counter-discourses as well as the distribution of the concepts, a corpus was created: four periods before and during the crisis were scanned for texts using the words *hållbar* (sustainable), *hållbarhet* (sustainability), *tillväxt* (growth) and *finanskris* (financial crisis). The first period, April 2008, represents the time before the acute crisis; the second period, October 2008, represents the acute phase of the bank crisis; the third period, October 2009, was chosen to see if one year of crisis had changed the discourse of growth and sustainability; the fourth period (April 2010) was the latest possible period at the time the study was performed.

The texts were selected from different genres of the political-economic discourse: political debates and economic analyses in newspapers and on internet debate sites, reports by the National Institute of Economic Research and the Riksbank (Bank of Sweden), political party blogs and parliamentary debate (details are given in the appendix to this chapter).

METAPHORS IN THE DISCOURSES OF THE FINANCIAL CRISIS

'Growth' is what Lakoff and Johnsson would call an ontological metaphor, which draws upon our experiences as human beings. Earlier studies of metaphors for growth have demonstrated the wide range of metaphors for growth and economic development. The growth metaphor is productive and systematic and together with associated metaphors it constitutes a rich and coherent lexical field (White 2003, p. 148). The abundance of growth metaphors, where growth is conceptualized as natural and good, and correspondingly the absence of growth is conceptualized as bad, all signify the naturalness of the thought of growth.[3] We may even have difficulties in conceptualizing a society not built upon growth; this is visible in our language.

Metaphors for Growth and Crisis

In a first attempt to capture the role of the growth concept an online press archive, *Presstext*,[4] was used to collect metaphors conceptualizing ideas about growth and crisis before and during the financial crisis. *Tillväxt* (growth) is often conceptualized as a friend:

> Economic growth is the best friend of the environment.
> (*Ekonomisk tillväxt är miljöns bästa vän.*) (Gotlands Allehanda 0110)[5]

Other metaphors clearly reflect that growth is seen as a fundamental driving force of societal development. They focus on the move forward, and growth can be conceptualized as the vehicle that transports us:

> Oil will become glowing hot when growth in the world accelerates.
> (*Oljan kommer att bli glödhet när tillväxten i världen tar fart.*) (Dagens Nyheter 0110)

But growth is also perceived as the motor itself. The metaphors help us in conceptualizing growth as a fundamental driving force of societal development:

> Since Chinese growth has been a great motor in the global recovery.
> (*Eftersom den kinesiska tillväxten varit en stor motor i den globala återhämtningen.*) (Veckans Affärer 0110)

Although the organic sphere, the original source domain for the growth metaphor, does not seem as productive to describe economic development any more in these texts, it is productive in the discourse about the financial crisis, which is often conceptualized as winter or storms:

> A good buy the day trade hits the bottom – otherwise a strong yield company to overwinter with.
> (*Ett bra köp den dag börsen slår i botten - annars ett utdelningsstarkt bolag att övervintra med.*) (Privata Affärer 0408)

The conceptualization of the financial crisis as an illness also belongs to a more organic sphere:

> The global contagion is unavoidable, and the effects of the stock market strike right into the real market transactions.
> (*Den globala smittan är oundviklig, och börsens effekter slår rakt in i de reala affärerna*) (VA 1008)

Financial crisis and economic decline can, just like growth, be seen as a living organism. But whereas growth was described as a friend, financial crisis is conceptualized as an enemy:

> As long as that group increases and as long as every fourth youngster is unemployed it is hard to explain the battle against the financial crisis to be won.

> (*Så länge den gruppen ökar och så länge var fjärde ungdom går arbetslös är det svårt att förklara slaget mot finanskrisen vunnet.*) (Göteborgsposten 0110)

This pilot study illustrates the naturalness of the thought of growth. But what then about the counter discourses – or rather, what about discourses promoting alternative views on economic development, and their use of metaphors?

Metaphors of Growth Critique

A search in the corpus (see the appendix to this chapter) for texts using the concept of *hållbar utveckling* (sustainable development) was performed to find metaphors in discourses shifting the perspective on growth. The aim was to elucidate what kinds of framings and metaphors were used to question the conceptualization of growth as a natural good. What counter-discourses can be reflected in the metaphor use in financial journalism and political debate?

Negative discourse

Texts discussing sustainable development sometimes negate growth with concepts like no-growth or de-growth – and thus negate a profoundly positive concept. In the corpus the concept of *nolltillväxt* (zero-growth) is used quite frequently in the beginning of the crisis, but not as often as the crisis unfolds.[6] But the concept is mostly used in financial journalism (describing the absence of growth), supported with metaphors like the following:

> If we compare with [the competitor's] fourth quarter on 33 per cent the zero growth of Alfa Laval stands out as even more noteworthy. The seemingly disquieting calm . . .
> (*Jämför vi med [konkurrentens] fjärde kvartalet på 33 procent framstår Alfa Lavals nolltillväxt än mer anmärkningsvärd. Det fjärde kvartalets till synes oroväckande stiltje . . .*) (Veckans affärer 0408)

Zero-growth is here conceptualized in a somewhat contradictory metaphor as 'disquieting calm', thus actualizing a sailing ship becalmed on the sea (which is coherent with the metaphoric construction of growth discussed above). Also in political debate (in the corpus), zero-growth is seen entirely as a negative feature. But the use of it in the corpus echoes other growth-critical voices,

> Zero-growth is no eco-friendly, harmonious, ideal state. It is only dirty, dreary and dangerous.
> (*Nolltillväxt är inget miljövänligt, harmoniskt idealtillstånd. Det är bara smutsigt, trist och farligt.*) (Ekdal, DN 1008)

In this corpus, no actor claims that zero-growth is something to strive for – it is a goal that is only attributed to others.

'De-growth' (*nerväxt*) is used only a couple of times in the corpus as something positively connected. But the overall impression is that these concepts are seldom used, and then only in their negative sense as a symptom of an economic crisis.

The counter-discourses often discuss various forms of limits. It seems that what we can do is to limit the costs for nature and people, to limit emissions and so on.

> The most rational is to impose a ceiling on the emissions and the use of resources, and then continue to develop an economy under that ceiling.
> (*Det mest rationella är att sätta ett tak för utsläppen och resursförbrukningen, och sedan utveckla en ekonomi under detta tak.*) (Borgnäs, Newsmill 0410)

In the example above these thoughts are linguistically realized with the metaphor 'impose a ceiling on' – which rests upon the conceptual metaphor 'limits are ceilings' and is consistent with the metaphor of growth (i.e. growth is an upward movement).

Problematic to apocalyptic situation There are also many examples of apocalyptic descriptions of the situation: climate catastrophe, ecological and financial collapse, and so on. In the following example the situation is described as *rovdrift* (ruthless exploitation). The bestial character of humans is described: we are beasts of prey engaged in a ruthless exploitation of the planet. In the example you can see the underlying conceptual metaphor 'natural resources are a prey':

> There already exists one animal species that has conquered, colonized and impoverished the planet – *Homo sapiens sapiens*. We ourselves commit a ruthless exploitation of resources, as though we thought that we have some reserve planets to switch to when we have depleted this one.
> (*Det finns redan en djurart som erövrat, koloniserat och utarmat planeten –* Homo sapiens sapiens. *Vi själva bedriver en rovdrift på resurser, som om vi tror att vi har några reservplaneter att byta till när vi förbrukat den här.*) (Carlsson, Newsmill 0410)

In texts about sustainable development these kinds of framings are used to support the idea of the acute need for change. But framing climate crisis as an apocalyptic situation can also be said to express fatalism that might foster compliance to the trends that generate it, as Eileen Christ (2007) fears. Apocalyptic discourse can also frighten the reader off instead of getting the attention intended (Nerlich and James 2008).

Switchover

Omställning (switchover) is a conventional metaphor for change. It is often used in the discourse of sustainability. A conventionalized metaphor can become a living metaphor again, as in the following example, where the mechanical source domain is enhanced with the word *vridmoment* (torque):

> The public sector can be the driving force, and that which creates a torque in the switchover. Private enterprises and individual citizens can never manage to adjust systems on their own. Universities and municipal energy and housing companies are important actors in the switchover.
> (*Det offentliga kan vara drivkraften och det som skapar ett vridmoment i omställningsarbetet. Privata företag och enskilda medborgare klarar aldrig att ställa om systemen på egen hand. Universiteten och de kommunala energi- och bostadsbolagen är viktiga aktörer i omställningen.*) (Fagerlund, Blog 0410)

The switch metaphor describes the issue of a sustainable lifestyle as an issue that is mainly mechanistic and technical. In the text cited, it is used in a co-text that discusses technical innovations. But using the switch metaphor can also be discussed as a possible legitimizing strategy for 'business as usual': if we by technical, rational means can make our lifestyle less threatening to Earth, there is no need to change our way of living in a deeper sense (Christ 2007).

Climate change discourse metaphors

Discourse metaphors are key framing devices within a particular discourse (like 'sustainability' itself, and maybe 'switch'). The difference between a discourse metaphor and a conceptual metaphor is that discourse metaphors are consciously chosen and that the meaning of them has been negotiated in the discourse. In climate change discourse we find creative discourse metaphors such as *växthuseffekt* (greenhouse effect). Another is 'ecological footprint'. They have in common a high degree of complexity: the interpretation does not yield itself without effort and is more a result of active learning than of a similarity relation that is accessible to the reader. But also these metaphors are mostly used to describe and make understandable the negative impact on the planet of our lifestyle.

A SUSTAINABLE DISCURSIVE STRUGGLE?

The first growth-critical work is often claimed to be *The Affluent Society* (1958) by John Kenneth Galbraith. His work inspired the early critics of growth among American theorists in the 1960s (Friman 2002, p. 142). But the most influential critique of growth for the debate to follow was probably a group of international scholars called the Club of Rome (Mitcham 1995, p.314). In *The Limits to Growth* (Meadows 1972) the group discussed continuous (and exponential) growth in relation to the finite resources of the world. The book had significant impact on the discussions of environmental issues and their relation to growth in the decades to follow (Victor 2008).

The concept of 'sustainable development' was introduced around 1980 and discussed in the *World Conservation Strategy* (IUCN 1980). Important for the definition of the concept is the UN *Report of the World Commission on Environment and Development: Our Common Future* (1987; 'the Brundtland Report'). In the report, sustainability is seen as threefold: economical, social and ecological sustainability. The report can be seen as an effort to bridge no-growth environmentalists and pro-growth groups stressing economic development in the Third World (Mitcham 1995).

The concept of sustainable development is now widely used by politicians and policymakers, inscribed in school curriculums and municipal policy documents. It is also a core principle for the global green movement.

Sustainability: Lexicographic Word Meaning and Metaphor

'Sustainability' is a metaphor. Apart from using metaphors unconsciously (see above), we also use them consciously to help the reader and direct the reader towards an understanding of abstract reasoning. Another important observation is that metaphors enhance specific aspects of words with a wide meaning potential.

The English noun 'sustainability' stems from the verb 'sustain'. The verb 'sustain' is a transitive verb, with a concrete and basic physical meaning of 'upholding' and 'supporting'. It has a metaphorical meaning in the sense of 'supporting' (for example an argument) as well as in the sense of 'maintaining', 'keeping up' and 'persevering in'. These metaphorical meanings can be regarded as fairly conventional and salient for most language users.[7]

If we look instead at the derivation 'sustainable', we find that it has two important meanings:

1. Capable of being upheld or supported; maintainable.
2. Capable of being maintained at a certain rate or level.

The first sense can be both literal (the physical sense) and metaphorical (as in 'a sustainable argument'). The second sense is metaphorical. In contemporary dictionaries, the ecological sense of 'able to continue without causing damage to the environment' is treated as the most common and salient meaning. And for the word 'sustainability', no other explanation than the ecological is given.[8]

Let us now turn to the Swedish translation of the sustainability concept: *hållbarhet*. The noun is a derivation of the adjective *hållbar* (durable). The salient meaning for Swedish language users of the adjective *hållbar* would be that of 'durable' – in a physical way, that is, something constructed to be resistant. *Hållbarhet* (durability) is thus an inherent value or characteristic. This means that the English and Swedish concepts do not have the same meaning potential.[9]

The Brundtland Report – A Bridging Articulation

We looked above at semantic aspects of the concept of *hållbar utveckling* (sustainable development). In this section we take a closer look at the definition of the concept in the UN report (see 'A sustainable discursive struggle?', above).

In the report, 'sustainable development' is defined as a development that is possible to sustain without jeopardizing the social, economical or ecological stability of the world, without running risk of wars, crises, or the emptying of natural resources. The report argues that these things are all intertwined. To meet the basic needs of a growing population we need growth. To achieve long-term growth without venturing the needs of future generations we need to preserve the environment. Ecological sustainability is thus crucial. Social sustainability is about all humans being able to fulfil their basic needs, about fighting poverty and evening out income distribution globally. Economical sustainability is about gaining growth that is as strong as possible without hazarding ecological and social sustainability.

In the Swedish translation of the Brundtland Report, the concept of sustainable development was translated into *hållbar utveckling* (durable development).[10] But the ideological concept of 'sustainable development' is not only about durability. Thus, even though a great many books and articles in Swedish try to define the concept of *hållbar utveckling*, there are conflicting senses in the concept and the salient everyday use of the word that seem to make the concept more difficult to grasp.

This means that there is a kind of unstable meaning in the Swedish phrases *hållbar utveckling* (sustainable development) and *hållbar tillväxt* (sustainable growth). Do we mean development or growth that can be sustained at a certain level (in the long term), or do we mean development or growth that has the inherent characteristic of being resistant towards crises or other threats (that is, the most salient meaning to most language-users who are not up to date with the political and ideological use of the word)? What do we really mean when we say *Vi strävar mot en hållbar tillväxt* (We strive for a sustainable/durable growth)? Do we mean that growth should be resistant to crises or do we mean that it should be possible to sustain at a certain level in a long-term perspective?

The same degree of unstable meaning does not seem to exist in English, yet the concept is difficult to grasp in its complexity. In both languages, the surrounding context of the word – or the 'co-text' – needs to support the political-ideological sense of the word to make it salient for a reader unfamiliar with the concept as a carrier of complex meanings.

A possible positive effect of the inherent ambivalence of the concept has been suggested: that this might make possible a bridging between pro-growth and no-growth concerns (Mitcham 1995). Even if the two sides mean different things when using the concept, at least they talk – and communication is a prerequisite for change. But the confusion about the concept persists, as Rydin points out:

> There remains considerable confusion about exactly what is meant by 'sustainable development', particularly among those 'at the coalface' charged with changing their practices in order to achieve it. In addition, sustainable development does not have much resonance with the general public. It is perhaps surprising that, some 15 years since the publication of the Brundtland Report in 1987, such confusion and ambivalence still persists. Policy makers and politicians have found it easier and politically more prudent to rely on the inherent ambiguities of the concept rather than risk finding themselves tied to a clear and precise definition. (Rydin 2003, p. 2)

Rydin thus points out that the concept does not have much resonance with the general public. Two text genres that do meet the public are economic analysis and political debate articles in newspapers. Below, the use of the concept of 'sustainable development' in these media genres during the first years of the financial crisis is examined. But first a quantitative analysis will be made to gain an understanding of the use of the concepts in relation to growth and to spot different discursive patterns in different genres.

The Discursive Use of *hållbarhet*: a Quantitative Corpus Analysis

The following section of this chapter will account for a corpus study where the use of the word *hållbar* and related concepts in Swedish economical and political discourse is examined (see this chapter's appendix for details of the corpus). The distribution of the concepts in the texts, their collocations and important clusters will be examined. The corpus is analysed with AntConc, a computing tool for textual analysis (Anthony 2005).

Table 10.1 Collocations and clusters of 'hållbar*' *(sustainable*) and* 'tillväxt*' *(growth*)*

Word	Corpus hits	Collocations	Clusters
*Hållbar**	608	*'Utveckling', 'långsiktigt', 'vi', 'skapa', tillväxt, ska, samhälle*	*'Hållbar utveckling', 'långsiktigt hållbar', 'hållbart samhälle', 'hållbar tillväxt'*
'Sustainable'*		'Development', 'long term', 'we', 'create', 'growth', 'will', 'society'	'Sustainable development', 'long-term sustainable', 'sustainable society', 'sustainable growth'
*Tillväxt**	1729	*'Procent', 'ekonomisk', 'år', 'vi', 'BNP', 'ökad', 'jobb', 'sysselsättning'*	*'Ekonomisk tillväxt', 'BNP-tillväxt', 'ökad tillväxt', 'stark tillväxt', 'tillväxt och sysselsättning', 'hållbar tillväxt'*
'Growth'*		'Per cent', 'economic', 'year', 'we', 'GNP', 'increased', 'work', 'employment'	'Economic growth', 'GNP-growth', 'increased' 'growth', 'strong' 'growth', 'growth' 'and' 'employment', 'sustainable', 'growth'

Note: The asterisk is used in corpus searches to produce hits on terms and their variations (thus '*hållbar**' also renders '*hållbara*', '*hållbart*', '*hållbarhet*' etc.).

One way to study word meaning is to see how words are combined and structured and how meanings are created in this process. By looking at collocations (co-variation with words)[11] one can get a picture of which senses of the words are created in discourse. Let us start by looking at the most common collocations and clusters (the most common expressions) of variations of *hållbar* (durable) in the corpus as a whole. In Table 10.1 they are contrasted with the most common collocations and clusters of *tillväxt* (growth); if sustainability is part of a growth critique it is interesting to see whether the concepts seem compatible or whether they seem to 'collide' in the texts.

The table illustrates that long-term development is important when discussing sustainability, as well as the conceptualization of it as something that we can create. 'Growth' and 'sustainable' often co-vary. A closer examination proves that such co-variations happen in political debate articles (0408, 1008), in parliamentary debate (1008, 1009) and in political blogs (1009). The co-variation does not happen in economic analyses in newspapers or in the reports by the National Institute of Economic

Research or the Swedish Riksbank. Discussing sustainability in relation to growth seems to belong to political debate in one form or another.

'Growth' co-varies more often with 'per cent' and 'economic' (as growth is measured as a percentage of GNP). Among important clusters in Table 10.1 we see 'increased' and 'strong growth'. Growth co-varies with 'economic', 'increased' and 'employment' in political debate articles, but with 'per cent', 'GNP', 'continuous', 'strong' and 'prognosis' in the economic analyses. In parliamentary debate 'employment' and 'development' are important collocations (but interestingly for the last period, 0410, 'economic', 'per cent' and 'increased' are common collocations also there). In the reports by the National Institute of Economic Research and the Swedish Riksbank, 'GNP' and 'per cent' are common collocations, but the last period is different. The differences might be explained by the different agendas in the text genres: in political debate growth of all kinds is connected to politics and society, hence treated in an instrumental way, whereas (increased) growth in economic analysis is presupposed to have an inherent value.

A study of collocations and clusters thus makes clear that the connection of 'sustainability' and 'growth' belongs to political debate, but not to economic analyses or financial reports. But how does the use of the concepts change over time during these first years of crisis?

The word 'sustainable' and related forms are most common during the last period (see the chapter appendix). This may support the idea that sustainability is used as a sort of rescue or exit from crisis. But the distribution of *hållbar* (sustainable) and related forms of it in different genres is uneven: it is most common in political debate, but almost absent in other genres. There seems to be an increasing political debate about sustainability but in the acute phase of the crisis sustainability issues are less debated. In economic analyses there are 23 hits before the crises, but almost none in later periods. A closer analysis of the corpus thus reveals that even though sustainability issues seem to have affected economic analysis in newspapers before the crisis, financial journalists had other foci as the crisis unfolded.

'Growth' on the other hand is most common in economic analyses and financial reports, especially before the crisis started. Interestingly, in parliamentary debate the concepts of sustainability and growth are equally common throughout the period.

The results reflect the fact that the corpus consists of text genres with different goals and different rationalities.

The Discursive Use of 'Sustainable Development'

The analysis above predicts that different actors will use the Swedish word *hållbar* and related words in different ways. Moreover, it implies that the salient and most-used meaning of the word in some constellations 'works against' the ideological meaning of the sustainability concept. The concept thus becomes for the public vague and difficult to conceptualize (see Rydin 2003). But different actors also exploit this vagueness. To gain a better understanding of this, a case study of the use of the concept of *hållbar utveckling* (see above) during these first years of crisis has been performed.

The concept is most frequently used in political blogs, parliamentary debate and political debate in the press. In those genres it is used throughout the period. In the reports by the National Institute of Economic Research as well as the reports from the Riksbank it is not used at all. This case study has therefore been limited to a comparison between the use of the concept in media discourse, in economic analyses and political debate articles.

Sustainable development in economic analyses

The concept of *hållbar utveckling* is used 12 times in the economic analyses from before the crisis (0408) but only once (1008) in the following periods. If the concept is an effort to unite pro-growth and no-growth concerns, one would expect it to become more present during times of crises, when the idea of a growth society is shaken. But instead the idea of sustainability seems to be 'forgotten' by financial journalists in those first years of crisis. Instead, they focus on negative effects of the crisis. As noticed above, the concept is also absent in other economic genres, which seems to indicate that the rationality expressed in economic text genres in the media and in official reports has not yet incorporated the thought of sustainability – or at least suppressed it during those first years of crisis. But it is intriguing that the concept has twelve hits in the corpus from 0408. A closer look at those examples leads to the following conclusions:

The concept *sustainable development* is mostly used in articles about companies. There is a political pressure on firms to adhere to climate goals and regulations, which is sometimes referred to in the texts. Some of the hits in the corpus are hits on titles, as for example *chef för hållbar utveckling* (senior vice president of sustainability; e24 0408).

An interesting example is an interview with the president of the World Business Council for Sustainable Development. He points out that sustainable development is of strategic importance and stresses that Swedish companies have to become as active in promoting sustainable development as international businesses. The reason for doing this is clearly stated in the following example:

> Björn Stigson about . . .
> . . . his own organization, the World Business Council for Sustainable Development: We will be the progressive voice of the business sector in the

> global debate. If companies fail to handle the questions of sustainable development, we are at risk of having constraints imposed on us that threaten our freedom to operate our businesses.
> (*Björn Stigson om . . .*
> *. . . den egna organisationen, Näringslivets internationella råd för hållbar utveckling: Vi ska vara näringslivets progressiva röst i den globala debatten. Om företagen inte kan hantera frågorna om uthållig utveckling, riskerar vi att få inskränkningar i friheten att driva affärsverksamhet.*) (DN 0408)

The strategic work for sustainable development must be done, it seems, if companies are to be able to continue business as usual, when new regulations and climate goals are imposing constraints.

The only example from economic analyses in the corpus later than April 2008 is an article from October that year, reporting from the Asia–Europe meeting in China where sustainability issues (among others) were discussed. The Swedish Prime Minister, Fredrik Reinfeldt, there states the importance of keeping the focus on climate questions in spite of the current financial crisis. The aim of the meeting is described as discussions of 'cultural interchange, food security, world economy and sustainable development (climate)' (e24 1008). The use of the concept *hållbar utveckling* is restricted to the ecological sense of the word, which is marked linguistically with the explanation in parenthesis.

These examples are very few but they indicate that in economic discourse sustainable development is treated as a strategic means for making industry prosperous. One can also see a clear tendency for the meaning of the concept to be limited to climate goals.

From a linguistic point of view, an analysis of the use of the concept in the corpus also reveals that the concept is not defined but is introduced as one that is already known.

Sustainable development in political debate articles

In the political debate articles in the corpus, the concept of *hållbar utveckling* is used 19 times. In most debate articles the concept is used as a political ideological concept. But often only one aspect of the three-legged concept in the Brundtland Report occurs in the texts.

In the midst of the crisis, Eskil Johnsson, who introduces himself as a researcher in economics for a sustainable development (SvD 1008) attacks the Chicago School of economics, arguing that their models obstruct sustainable development and have failed to provide a long-term economic model that rewards responsibility. Even though the concept of sustainable development is not defined in the text it becomes evident that it is primarily used for *social* sustainable development – a development that does not create increasing global social cleavages.

One year after the acute crisis (October 2009) more actors are entering the debate about sustainable development. The opposition leaders are discussing the balance between economic and social values, as well as ecological ones, and seem to have Brundtland's definition in mind when using the concept. They discuss such goals as green growth, social justice and the fair distribution of wealth and resources, and in their article all parts of the political-ideological concept are inscribed in the text (GP 1009). But in most of the political debate articles, actors belonging to different governmental or non-governmental organizations stress different parts of the ideological concept of *sustainable development* depending on what kind of organization they represent. The Swedish Society for Nature Conservation, for example, stresses ecological sustainability. Even if poverty, developing countries and economic conditions are mentioned, the focus is on climate:

> That the developing countries manage to rise from poverty in a climate-smart way is in our own interest. The companies now active and ready for Copenhagen are leading the way. A powerful climate deal is good for economy and business, they say to Reinfeldt, Borg, Olofsson and Carlgren.
> (*Att u-länderna lyckas komma ur fattigdom på ett klimatsmart sätt ligger i vårt egenintresse. De företag som nu engagerar sig inför Köpenhamn antar ett stort ledarskap. Ett kraftfullt klimatavtal är bra för ekonomin och affärerna säger de till Reinfeldt, Borg, Olofsson och Carlgren.*) (GP 1009)

It is also interesting to note that by referring to and giving voice to companies working for a climate deal, the society stresses that a powerful climate agreement will be beneficial for the economy and for business – thus legitimizing climate politics with reference to 'rational goals' (where rational can be defined as that about which we have a consensus).

Other actors use the concept of sustainable development rather vaguely, as something good to strive for that is not further defined or hinted at in the text. This is demonstrated in an article from the last period in the corpus (0410) where actors from Amnesty International, the Swedish Peace and Arbitration Society, Christian organizations and UNA-Sweden discuss Swedish weapons exports:

> Peace, democracy, human rights and a sustainable development are fundamental values that must never be compromised.
> (*Fred, demokrati, mänskliga rättigheter och en hållbar utveckling är grundläggande värden som aldrig får kompromissas med.*) (GP Debatt 0410)

Here, 'sustainable development' is treated as a fundamental value, and hence as something already known and agreed upon.

The analysis of *hållbar utveckling* and its uses in two different media genres shows us that the articulations of sustainable development are very diverse in the political debate, but the most striking result of this corpus study is the absence of the concept in economic discourse. To some extent, the discourse of financial journalism seems to display its own rationality; sustainability in economic analyses might only be legitimized if it can be defined as instrumental, that is if it can be used to preserve the presupposed axiom of a capitalistic society – growth is good.

ROUNDING UP

The latest financial crisis is not an isolated crisis about finance. Globalization and the ongoing climate crisis are also important aspects of this crisis. But it is also to some extent a discursive crisis, a struggle about how to categorize, how to explain and how to persuade. This means that it is necessary to acknowledge and understand the role our language plays in framing reality before we can understand what actually happens.

In this article the political debate, and the press coverage of issues related to growth and sustainable development in different genres during the first part of the latest financial crisis, have been the foci of analysis. The analysis of the role that metaphor plays in framing our understanding of this crisis as well as the discursive use of central concepts has given rise to the following conclusions and reflections:

- Metaphors constructing economic growth as something inherently positive – and financial crisis as something inherently negative – permeate our language. The idea of continuous growth thus seems self-evident and natural. This can be seen as a hegemonic construction of meaning – and it means that critics of the thought of growth have a linguistic challenge to meet.
- In texts discussing sustainability or questioning growth there seem to be a lack of supportive metaphors or framings as direct or as easy to conceptualize as the growth metaphors: on the contrary, the metaphors and framings used are more complex and abstract, and they are mostly negative or have an apocalyptic character (Friman 2002; Christ 2007).
- The results of the corpus analysis indicate that discussing sustainability in relation to growth belongs to political debate. Even though sustainability issues seem to have affected economic analysis in newspapers before the crisis, financial journalists had other foci as the crisis unfolded: the restoring of growth. In other economic

genres, such as reports from the National Institute of Economic Research, there is no use of the concept of sustainability at all during this period.

- The case study of the discursive use of 'sustainable development' reveals that economic journalists frame the concept as a tool: sustainability might only be legitimized if it were defined as instrumental, that is, used to preserve the presupposed axiom of a capitalistic society: growth is good. In articles involving political debate, on the other hand, the concept of sustainable development is used in different ways, stressing different parts of its meaning.
- It is often unclear whether the word *hållbar* refers to the political ideological concept or is used in its everyday sense as 'durable' or even as 'defendable' with vague connotations of what is good for the climate. In this way it can function as a rhetorical argument also in other discourses – it becomes a buzzword. It can be argued that the vagueness and inherent ambivalence of the concept is a prerequisite for a 'bridging' of discourses; were the vagueness not there then the potential of the word as a facilitator for consensus-making might be lost. But the risk of miscommunication is obvious.

This chapter has not attempted to examine theories of growth or sustainability, but rather to expand the discussion of these concepts in terms of perception: if our language is based upon perceiving growth as a natural good, then trying to put forward (and make understandable) alternative views will become problematic. If our consensus about sustainable development is built on an ambiguous or equivocal concept – if the bridge between discourses with (at least to some extent) different rationalities is that fragile – how can we really meet? And how can the public, the readers of the text genres studied in this chapter, understand these complex issues if they meet the concepts only as vague buzzwords?

Thus, acknowledging the rhetorical potential of metaphors as tools to persuade, tools to make abstract phenomena understandable, it must be concluded that if we want to change the way we understand growth and economic development, if we want to make the idea of sustainability understandable (where growth is but a part of a bigger picture) we need metaphors with persuasive power that are easy to conceptualize. These might be metaphors using source domains in which balance, harmony or stability is important.

Perhaps one possibility would be to build upon the powerful 'growth' metaphor and use it in other directions, such as 'cultivating' or 'gardening' – where harmony and balance in the garden is of course better than excessive growth. The gardening metaphor allows for a discussion of natural cycles and it involves a gardener – someone who cares for, fertilizes and harvests the fruits.

NOTES

1. In a metaphorical expression such as 'The X Company is safe to overwinter *with*' the target domain would be 'financial crisis' and the source domain 'winter'. The systematic correspondences between the two could be for example: 'periods of time', 'cyclical periods', 'the need to take precautions to survive'.
2. There is an ongoing debate among metaphor researchers whether another theory of metaphor, 'blending theory', is more compatible with critical discourse analysis (O'Halloran 2007; Hart 2008), where some researchers suggest that CMT does not allow metaphors to be treated as discourse. In this study, however, these theoretical questions will not be further discussed.
3. In Chapter 1 in this volume, Schön uses the metaphorical conceptualizations of 'long waves' and 'big waves' to capture economic development. Also these metaphors stress the organic nature of economy and economic development.
4. The archive is a database consisting of full-text articles from about 40 Swedish newspapers and magazines.
5. References to the articles in the press archive will be made with month and year; thus 0110 = January 2010.
6. See Friman (2002, pp. 147–9) for an overview of the history of this concept in Swedish political debate.
7. The lexicographic sources used here are *Merriam-Webster's Dictionary* (online), *Longman Dictionary of Contemporary English* and *Collins Cobuild.*
8. A complicating factor in English is that the expression 'sustained growth', important in economics and used by the Nobel prizewinner Simon Kuznets in the 1970s, actually uses the first sense – so there are two very closely related concepts, which might interfere with each other.
9. There is also a difference in agency. The English words 'sustainable' and 'sustainability' stem from a transitive meaning of the verb – as in '*x* sustains *y*'. That implies that in some way, an agent is present when we speak about 'sustainable development', 'sustainable growth' and 'sustainability'. *We* are striving for a development, a growth, a town that *we* can sustain in ecological, economical and social meaning. In *hållbar*, though, no agent is present.
10. Other translations have later been suggested as better to encapsulate the meaning of sustainable (e.g. *uthållig, bärkraftig* etc.).
11. The AntConc programme was instructed to look for collocations four words before and after the instance of the word (in this case *hållbar**, including forms of the word: *hållbara, hållbar, hållbarhet* etc.).

REFERENCES

Anthony, Laurence (2005), 'AntConc: Design and development of a freeware corpus analysis toolkit for the technical writing classroom', *Proceedings of Professional Communication Conference*, University of Limerick, Ireland, 10–13 July, pp. 729–37.

Charteris-Black, Jonathan (2004), *Corpus Approaches to Critical Metaphor Analysis*, Basingstoke: Palgrave Macmillan.

Charteris-Black, Jonathan (2005), *Politicians and Rhetoric: The Persuasive Power of Metaphor*, Basingstoke: Palgrave Macmillan.

Charteris-Black, Jonathan (2006), 'Britain as a container: immigration metaphors in the 2005 election campaign', *Discourse & Society*, **17** (6), pp. 563–82.

Christ, Eileen (2007), 'Beyond the climate crisis: a critique of climate change discourse', *Telos*, 141, 29–55.

Deignan, Alice (2005), *Metaphor and Corpus Linguistics*, Amsterdam, the Netherlands and Philadelphia, PA: John Benjamins.

Fairclough, Norman (1992), *Discourse and Social Change*, Cambridge: Polity.

Friman, Eva (2002), 'No limits: the 20th century discourse of economic growth', dissertation, Umeå University, Sweden.

Galbraith, John Kenneth (1958), *The Affluent Society*, New York: Mentor.

Hart, Christopher (2008), 'Critical discourse analysis and metaphor: toward a theoretical framework', *Critical Discourse Studies*, **5** (2), 91–106.

International Union for Conservation of Nature and Natural Resources (IUCN) (1980), *World Conservation Strategy: Living Resource Conservation for Sustainable Development*, 2nd edn, Gland, Switzerland.

Lakoff, Georg and Mark Johnsson (1980), *Metaphors We Live By*, Chicago, IL and London: University of Chicago Press.

Meadows, Donella H. (ed.) (1972), *The Limits to Growth: A Report for the Club of Rome's Project on the Predicament of Mankind*, London: Earth Island.

Mitcham, Carl (1995), 'The concept of sustainable development: its origins and ambivalence', *Technology in Society*, **17** (3), 311–26.

Nerlich, Brigitte and Richard James (2008), '"The post-antibiotic apocalypse" and the "war on superbugs": catastrophe discourse in microbiology, its rhetorical form and political function', *Public Understanding of Science*, **18** (5), 574–88.

O'Halloran, Kieran (2007), 'Critical discourse analysis and the corpus-informed interpretation of metaphor at the register level', *Applied Linguistics*, **28** (1), 1–24.

Parr, Adrian (2009), *Hijacking Sustainability*, Cambridge, MA: MIT Press.

Report of the World Commission on Environment and Development: Our Common Future (1987), transmitted to the General Assembly as an Annex to Document A/42/427, *Development and International Co-operation: Environment*, UN Documents.

Rydin, Yvonne (2003), *In Pursuit of Sustainable Development: Rethinking the Planning System*, London: RICS Foundation.

White, Michael (2003), 'Metaphor and economics: the case of growth', *English for Specific Purposes*, **22** (2), 131–51.

Victor, Peter A. (2008), *Managing Without Growth: Slower by Design, Not Disaster*, Cheltenham, UK and Northampton, MA, USA: Edward Elgar.

APPENDIX

Table 10.A1 Corpus: genres, periods and word tokens

Genre/instance	04-2008	10-2008	10-2009	04-2010	Sum
Political debate in newspapers and internet debate sites: DN, SvD, GP and Newsmill	14 109	34 667	25 441	30 894	*105 111*
Economical analyses in newspapers or internet sites: Veckans affärer, DN, e24	42 827	56 735	40 000	30 044	*169 606*
Reports by National Institute of Economic Research and the Swedish Riksbank	5 651	20 308	25 934	6 609	*58 502*
Political party blogs	8 543	60 730	28 912	46 797	*144 982*
Parliament debate	767 541	523 947	256 757	453 201	*2 001 446*
Sum: all corpus	*838 671*	*696 387*	*377 044*	*567 545*	*2 479 647*

Table 10.A2 Distribution of 'hållbar*' *(sustainable*) and* 'tillväxt*' *(sustainable*) in different periods (number of corpus hits)*

Genre/ instance	04-2008(838 671 w. tokens)	10-2008(696 387 w. tokens)	10-2009(377 044 w. tokens)	04-2010(567 545 w. tokens)
hållbar*	140	126	159	183
tillväxt*	446	478	429	376

Note: The asterisk is used in corpus searches to produce hits on terms and their variations (thus '*hållbar**' also renders '*hållbara*', '*hållbart*', '*hållbarhet*' etc.).

11. Macroprudential supervision and regulation – lessons for the next crisis

Lars Jonung

INTRODUCTION[1]

Every major financial crisis triggers a process of policy-learning. This is the case with the financial crisis that started in the United States in 2007 and rapidly spread to the rest of the world. This chapter summarizes the lessons on macroprudential supervision and regulation that are at present condensed from the global financial crisis. The chapter ends with a clear policy recommendation: the current framework for monitoring financial imbalances needs to be strengthened. Two options are considered. The first is to give the *central bank* greater responsibility for macrofinancial stability. The second is to establish a new authority, a *financial stability council*, with the remit to identify systemic risks in the financial sector and propose measures.

The recent international financial crisis, sometimes called the Great Recession, has inspired an intense debate about how future crises should be prevented. Those responsible for framing economic policies, as well as economists and financial economists at universities and international organizations such as the IMF and the OECD, grossly underestimated the systemic risks to the financial sector that had accumulated before the crisis.

A number of proposals for strengthening financial stability have been presented recently. True, financial stability was an economic policy goal in the past, but it has now emerged as an even more explicit one. Focus has fallen on macroprudential supervision and regulation targeting the *entire* financial system, unlike the traditional approach to financial regulation, concentrating on individual financial firms, individual financial instruments or individual markets.[2]

At present an international effort is under way to establish appropriate forms of macroprudential supervision and regulation. One difficult challenge is to define the boundaries of responsibility for financial stability between the central bank and the supervisory authority.

The first section discusses how the financial crisis has impacted on the way economists view the proper design of stabilization policies. The second section provides a framework for analysing financial stability. The third describes the instruments available to achieve the goal of financial stability. The fourth describes how the institutional framework for maintaining financial stability could be designed. The final section provides a concluding discussion.

THE FINANCIAL CRISIS AND THE RECIPE FOR STABILIZATION

A lively debate has taken place as to what caused the global financial crisis that began in 2007.[3] From this debate, it is evident that those responsible for stabilization policy underestimated the risk of financial imbalances. This neglect may be partly explained by the view of monetary and fiscal policies that prevailed before the Great Recession started.

Before the current crisis, the prescription for a successful monetary and fiscal policy was roughly as follows. Monetary policy should concentrate on maintaining low and stable inflation through the use of the short-term interest rate. This task had been delegated to central banks which were made independent of the political system. Fiscal policy should primarily be based upon automatic stabilizers. Discretionary fiscal policy, that is measures taken on a case-by-case basis, should be avoided. Fiscal policy should instead be rule-based. Over a business cycle, the general government budget should be balanced or show a surplus.[4]

This consensus on the design of macroeconomic policies, which emerged in the second half of the 1980s and in the 1990s, rested in part on the perception that there was a strong temptation for politicians in power to engage in expansionary short-term fiscal and monetary policies. Their focus on the short term was seen as the cause of rising deficits in public finances and high inflation in the 1970s and 1980s.

Before the recent crisis, most macroeconomists regarded the economy as a dynamically stable system that was not prone to end up in crisis. The financial sector was seen as an important engine of economic growth. The many innovations in the financial system – including those that followed in the wake of financial deregulation in the 1980s and 1990s – were seen as beneficial both for the financial system and for the economy in general. Financial instability and financial crises were not on the economic policy agenda in the United States and Europe, and barely on the agenda for researchers in macroeconomics. It was mostly economists interested in developing countries or in financial history who were engaged in these issues.

The stabilization policy prescription, as summarized above, was expected to lead to monetary and fiscal stability – and thus to macroeconomic balance. Macroeconomic developments from the mid-1980s until the current crisis – the Great Moderation – with low inflation, relatively good growth and small cyclical swings compared with the pattern of high inflation and stagnation in the 1970s and early 1980s were taken as evidence that the prescription worked.

Mainstream macroeconomic theory as it developed in the 1980s and 1990s was consistent with this interpretation of economic developments. Equilibrium models built on assumptions of rational expectations, and rational behaviour occupied a dominant position in macroeconomic research.

The global financial crisis showed in a forceful way that the established view of stabilization policy was fraught with weaknesses. It shut its eyes to the risks developing in the financial markets. It did not see how excessive expansion of credit to households and businesses combined with speculation in rising real-estate prices laid the foundation for the most serious recession since the 1930s.

Criticism has been directed at central banks around the world for allowing excessive credit growth. In this way, they contributed to the financial imbalances that triggered the global crisis. When central banks in addition had to resort to acute crisis management with the help of extremely low interest rates, unconventional monetary policy (quantitative easing) and various forms of assistance to financial institutions, they ended up in a political sphere outside traditional central bank policy. They no longer appeared independent of other economic policies. The crisis has therefore weakened the credibility of the monetary policy strategy based on inflation-targeting and on independent central banks that prevailed before the crisis.[5]

The crisis also undermined fiscal stability. Automatic stabilizers contributed to a growing gap between tax revenue, which fell as a result of the crisis, and public expenditure, which grew because of the crisis. Discretionary measures were introduced on a large scale to protect businesses and jobs. The Keynesian approach, which had lost credibility in the 1980s and 1990s, soon received attention again at the international level. Fiscal frameworks – such as that in the EU – were swept aside. The consequence has been large budget deficits and growing government debt throughout much of the Western world and in some cases acute fiscal crises.

Governments chose to support the financial system with enormous subsidies to avoid bank failures. Private debts were transformed into public debt – a process that was immediately registered in the rising government debt. Those in charge of both monetary and fiscal policy had to act as lenders and buyers of financial assets on a large scale. Thus, they abandoned the existing stabilization policy prescription based on rules and automatic stabilizers.

The global financial crisis has also unleashed a controversy in the academic world.[6] Many researchers are questioning what they consider to be fair-weather models in macroeconomic theory, which proved to be misleading. The economics profession, with few exceptions, paid insufficient attention to the risks posed by the financial imbalances that led to the global crisis. Established models in macroeconomics and financial economics – and thus the prevailing stabilization policy prescription – have therefore come under strong criticism.

A THEORY OF FINANCIAL CRISES

There is currently no generally accepted theory of financial crises in the same way as there are models of monetary and fiscal policy in introductory economics textbooks. But there is a significant consensus on some key elements in the analysis which provides sufficient basis for economic policy recommendations. This consensus is a generalization of the historical experience of financial crises.

A common feature of research on financial crises is the emphasis on the volume of credit.[7] The expansion and contraction in the amount of credit, particularly in that part channelled via bank loans, is the key to understanding financial crises.

The driving forces behind a financial crisis are best discussed with the help of the boom–bust pattern of a financial crisis. A positive impulse triggers the process. It may be financial deregulation, a more expansive monetary or fiscal policy, technological developments that create expectations about high productivity growth and high profits or a combination of these factors. The impulse sparks increased demand for credit. The financial system responds by expanding the supply of credit. In this phase, financial innovations generally contribute to the credit expansion.

The growing credit volume leads to rising real-estate and share prices. Rising asset prices increase the wealth of households and businesses. Balance sheets in the private sector swell. Households and businesses feel richer. These positive wealth effects contribute to increased optimism and increased appetite for risk. Households and businesses have more opportunities to take out loans thanks to the increased value of assets that can serve as collateral. Leverage increases. The demand for credit grows even more, which in turn feeds the increase in asset prices. This yields further positive wealth effects, more optimism and exorbitant expectations. The process becomes self-perpetuating. Psychological factors such as growing optimism and greater acceptance of risk-taking contribute to this cumulative streak. Credit volume grows in this phase at a pace far above its trend. At the same time, the perceived real interest rate, i.e. the nominal rate adjusted for expected inflation, is low, which pushes up the demand for credit and contributes to rising asset values.

The self-reinforcing forces are supported by the procyclical behaviour of the financial system. The prevailing optimism leads to underestimation of credit risk and poor credit assessment. Banks reduce their capital ratios when they become more risk-prone. They rely more than before on short-term borrowing to finance long-term lending during the boom phase.[8]

The rapid growth in the credit volume spreads from the financial system to the real economy. The positive wealth effects lead to an overheated economy with overfull employment. Households reduce their savings and increase their consumption. At the peak of the upturn phase, the savings ratio is low and sometimes negative. In an open economy, the export sector is crowded out when price and wage increases reduce its competitiveness internationally. Growth in the domestic sector, particularly in the construction sector, is fuelled by the credit-driven upturn.

The upturn is broken by a negative impulse that spreads through the financial system. It may come from a tightening of monetary or fiscal policy, leading to a sharp increase in the real rate of interest, a large-scale bankruptcy, or an external shock stemming from the global economy.

Boom is now followed by bust, with interest rates rising and credit growth slowing. Asset price inflation turns to asset price deflation. Falling asset prices lead to shrinking wealth, while the real value of bank loans rises as loans are given in nominal terms. In this phase, households and businesses try to reduce their leverage. Pessimism grows. Loans turn bad. Balance sheets in the private sector are undermined when equity is wiped out. The downturn, like the upturn, is propelled by self-perpetuating forces. Savings rise while investment and consumption fall when households and businesses face problems paying interest and amortization. The real economy is drawn into depression with bankruptcies and rising unemployment.

As noted earlier, the boom–bust cycle has a strong impact on the financial position of the public sector. During the upswing, government finances strengthen. During the downturn, the government's task is to take measures to soften the impact of the wealth losses that are created when the value of assets in the private sector is falling, thus weakening government finances.

The boom–bust cycle is not a new phenomenon. It has existed as long as there has been a credit system. Recently Iceland, Ireland, Spain and the United States have undergone this process. Similar processes took place in Finland, Norway and Sweden in the early 1990s.[9] The volume of credit is thus the key factor in all financial crises. The demand for credit, as well as the supply, is affected by the real rate of interest. Thus, monetary policy has an important role to play in the course of each crisis.

The history of financial crises does not suggest any precise pattern of growth in credit; not all episodes of rapid credit expansion end in deep recessions. Sharp swings in the volume of credit are thus a necessary but not a sufficient condition for a financial crisis.[10]

The boom–bust theory provides clear recommendations for economic policy. Stabilization policy should restrain the swings in the credit volume, in the real rate of interest and in asset prices. These swings are not due solely to faulty monetary policy and bad financial regulation. They are also created *within* the financial system through its procyclical behaviour. In brief, the task of economic policy is to dampen the procyclical pattern of the financial sector to avoid both boom and bust.

HOW TO ACHIEVE FINANCIAL STABILITY

Financial Regulation and Financial Stability

The traditional political response to a financial crisis is to strengthen the regulation of the financial sector. Most banking regulations have developed in this way. This response can also be observed now. A key lesson from the recent crisis is that more attention should be paid to *systemic risks* in the financial sector.[11] These risks were created by close, but underestimated, links between different institutions, between different assets in the financial system, and between different national financial systems. In this area, the existing financial supervision and regulation were the weakest. For this reason, macroprudential supervision and regulation are emphasized in the current debate as means to reduce the systemic risks that might contribute to future crises.[12]

The macroprudential approach is sometimes distinguished from the microprudential approach. The first focuses on the entire financial system, whereas the second focuses on individual financial firms, financial instruments and financial markets. Most of the current financial regulation is microprudential, although it is difficult to make a clear distinction

Table 11.1 Stylized comparison of the macroprudential and microprudential approaches

	Macroprudential approach	Microprudential approach
Intermediary objective	Limit risks of imbalances in the entire financial system (general equilibrium approach)	Limit risks of imbalances in individual financial institutions, instruments or markets (partial equilibrium approach)
Final objective	Prevent financial crises that undermine the macroeconomic balance	Protect consumers/depositors/investors/other financial institutions
Sources of shocks	Shocks are primarily seen as created endogenously in the financial system	Shocks are primarily seen as exogenous
Co-variation of risks and interdependence among financial institutions	Important	Less important or unimportant
The design of regulatory measures	Regulation addressing the entire financial system	Regulation addressing individual financial institutions, instruments or markets

Source: Borio (2008).

between the two types of regulation. Table 11.1 gives a simplified overview of the differences between macro- and microprudential regulation.

A large number of proposals for re-regulation are currently under discussion internationally, such as regulations of derivatives trade, bank capital adequacy ratios, transparency, accounting principles, supervision of credit rating agencies, deposit insurance, liquidation funds, hedge funds, short selling, and liquidation of financial institutions. Most of these proposals are basically of a microprudential character.

Many analysts are of the view that additional microprudential regulation is unlikely to prevent future imbalances. By focusing on individual firms or parts of the financial system, these regulations do not take into account the interdependence between markets and between financial institutions, which made the financial system so vulnerable. Experience shows that microprudential regulation often creates strong incentives for individual financial institutions to develop techniques aimed at circumventing regulation. The whole system of shadow banking in the United States grew up outside the regulated system to enable greater risk-taking than would otherwise have been possible. When the crash came, the shadow banking system was one source of the depth of the crisis.

The criticism of microprudential regulation should not be interpreted as implying that this kind of regulation is unnecessary. It is needed and there are reasons for improving it in a number of respects. But microprudential regulation is insufficient for ensuring financial stability. It should therefore be supplemented with macroprudential measures.

The proposals for macroprudential regulation include two kinds of recommendations: those that concern macroprudential supervision and those that concern regulation using macroprudential instruments.[13] The strongest consensus seems to be about supervision.

Macroprudential supervision

One possibility in this area is to establish special authorities or bodies (*macrofinancial stability councils*) with the task of supervising financial stability. The idea is that financial stability councils should assess the total risk, i.e. the systemic risk, for various financial imbalances. These authorities should focus their attention on links between the financial system and other parts of the economy. They should be able to propose measures if the risk of disruption looks threatening.

How stability councils should be positioned in relation to the central bank and the traditional regulatory authority is an open question. There are different solutions. Macroprudential supervision could be the responsibility of the central bank or of the supervisory authority. It could also be run by an independent authority outside existing institutions. There is also a discussion about the appropriate composition of a macrofinancial stability council.[14]

Macrofinancial stability councils have been set up in the EU and the United States. The European Systemic Risk Board (ESRB) was established in January 2011 with responsibility for macroprudential supervision in the EU as a whole. The ESRB is to monitor financial sector risks in all EU member states and risks associated with cross-border financial links in the EU. The board is also to survey risk in global developments. In case of potential shocks, which could affect the real economy, the ESRB is to issue warnings and make recommendations. These should be actively followed up. The ESRB consists of representatives from central banks and supervisory authorities in the EU and from the ECB and the EU Commission.[15]

In July 2010 the Financial Stability Oversight Council (FSOC) was established in the United States. Its primary objective is to monitor and ensure financial stability. The FSOC is to be consulted on most issues concerning financial supervision and regulation. The Dodd–Frank Act, the basis for the FSOC, also established other regulatory authorities and defined the areas of responsibility for existing regulatory bodies. The Act's objectives are to create a better system for the liquidation of large financial institutions, to protect consumers and investors, to increase transparency, to prevent excessive risk-taking and generally to strengthen the powers of supervisory authorities.

The United Kingdom has recently made two changes to its framework for macroprudential supervision. In 2009 the Bank of England, the Treasury and the Financial Services Authority (FSA) were given joint responsibility for financial supervision by way of the Financial Stability Committee (FSC). Shortly thereafter, this arrangement was criticized. It was viewed as weak and ineffective. In 2010, the law was amended. The Bank of England received full responsibility for financial stability when the FSC was associated with the Bank of England. Like the ESRB and the FSOC, the FSC has the task of identifying developments that may threaten financial stability.

Macroprudential regulation

There are a large number of proposals for macroprudential instruments.[16] A common characteristic of these proposals is their link to the stage of the business cycle or the credit cycle (the financial cycle). The aim in constructing them in this way is to make regulation more 'dynamic' in order to counteract the procyclical behaviour of the financial system.

Banks and other financial institutions could be required to take the cyclical situation into better account in their risk assessments. Supervisory and regulatory authorities could calibrate their assessments in a similar way. Dividend policies could be made more long-term, so that profits in an upturn could be set aside for reserves, to be used in a downturn.

Counter-cyclical capital requirements for banks have been recommended as a macroprudential instrument. The idea is that the capital requirement, i.e. the ratio between a bank's capital and its assets (lending), should be raised in times of strong credit growth. In a downturn, the requirement would instead be lowered. This would moderate the procyclical pattern in the growth of credit. Counter-cyclical capital requirements may be justified by the theory of externalities: each lender that changes its lending underestimates the impact of its behaviour on other lenders.[17]

Several proposals concerning household demand for credit have been presented, aimed at reducing the risk of imbalances, primarily in the housing sector. They include rules for amortizations, self-financing in home purchases, deductibility of interest on mortgage loans, etc. Such rules may in principle be made dependent on the stage of the business cycle. But in many countries, there is a strong political will to make it possible for households to buy and own their homes. If so, it would be desirable for household expenditure on home ownership to be easy to predict. That would not be the case if expenditure changes with the cyclical situation – except for variations caused by interest rate changes.

Other proposals aim at reducing the procyclicality in the supply of credit. They include the financial sector's remuneration systems. Bonuses, for example, can be based on long-term profits. The bonus payments can be made contingent on long-term ownership of shares. The idea is to extend the planning horizon of the management of financial institutions. Another option is to require owners of bank shares to shoulder a heavier responsibility in a banking crisis.

Challenges to macroprudential supervision and regulation

There is currently widespread optimism about the macroprudential approach.[18] But there are also objections. There is a risk that macroprudential supervision and regulation would be based on more or less arbitrary case-by-case judgements as there is no solid theory about when the threats to financial stability have become too great. There are no obvious threshold values indicating when a credit expansion, a mortgage leverage ratio or indebtedness has reached dangerous levels. The same applies to asset prices. We do not know at what point they have deviated too much from values, which should be considered fundamental. Assets prices tend to change rapidly, which could be interpreted as a sign of an unsustainable development – without necessarily being that. These difficulties explain to some extent why central banks so far have been disinclined to take asset prices into account in framing monetary policy.

Counter-cyclical regulation is based on the view that it is possible to acquire good knowledge about the cyclical situation and that the responsible decision-makers use this knowledge with precision, i.e. that they are able to take the right measures at the right time and with the right dosage. This argument takes us back to the longstanding discussion about discretionary fiscal and monetary policy, which so far has led to a rather sceptical view of discretionary policies.

Some proposals on macroprudential regulation might lead to direct controls on the composition of balance sheets in the financial sector, both on the asset and the liability side.[19] In that case, there is a risk that we would end up with a regulatory system similar to what Nordic countries experienced from the early 1950s to the early 1980s, i.e. before the process of financial deregulation. The regulatory system of that time, which included liquidity ratios, interest rate controls and foreign exchange controls, did result in a high level of financial stability, but it was also associated with arbitrary implementation and efficiency losses. The financial regulations of that time severely curbed financial innovations.

The main argument for expanded macroprudential supervision and regulation is that the costs of new financial crises are so great that the risk of creating new inefficiencies must be taken to avoid such crises. The alternative of not reinforcing macroprudential supervision and regulation is too risky. Also, a new macroprudential approach can be evaluated only after it has been tried in practice. It is hard to predict how effective it will be.

Institutions for Macroprudential Supervision and Regulation

Two basic approaches for improving macroprudential supervision and regulation have emerged in the international discussion. The first is to assign the responsibility for macrofinancial stability to central banks. In this case, a central bank should also be equipped with additional instruments to carry out its new task.

The second approach is to create a new agency in charge of monitoring systemic risks to the financial system. Such an authority, a *macrofinancial stability council*, should serve as a watchdog, signalling when the risks of financial crisis have reached a threatening level. The proposal of such a new authority raises a number of questions regarding the relationship between monetary policy and financial stability.

Monetary policy and financial stability

Why would a separate authority be needed for monitoring macrofinancial stability when central banks usually see themselves as guardians of financial stability and often have been required to fulfil that function? In addition to ensuring monetary stability, many central banks have a mandate regarding financial stability. Central banks also have the option of raising short-term interest rates enough to prevent rapid credit growth. Is there not a risk that a macrofinancial stability council would be a second-best solution, which would try to correct an inadequate central bank policy? Could we not get two central banks – one independent, the other one controlled by the government? In principle, there are two answers to these questions.

The first answer is that monetary policy should focus on only one objective: to keep inflation low. This should be the primary objective. It must not be diluted by financial stability considerations, such as asset price developments. A prominent advocate of this view is Alan Greenspan, the former chairman of the Federal Reserve Board. In his view, financial bubbles cannot be predicted. He therefore argues that a financial crisis should be handled only after it has erupted. In this view, the responsibility for financial stability should not rest with the central bank.

The second answer is that central banks should and can take asset prices and financial imbalances into account without compromising their fundamental task of keeping inflation low. Economists holding this view use the financial crisis in the United States as an argument that the Greenspan strategy is mistaken. The crisis demonstrates the danger of a policy that takes only consumer prices into account and neglects asset prices. It resulted in an overly expansionary monetary policy in the United States based on low interest rates. According to this view, the Federal Reserve under Greenspan's chairmanship contributed to pushing US housing prices upwards, thus creating large financial imbalances. Had monetary policy paid attention to housing prices, it could have mitigated the forces which eventually led to the crisis.

Economists have argued that there could be a conflict between monetary stability and financial stability objectives.[20] It becomes obvious when overall inflation is low while at the same time there is a rapid increase in asset prices. Financial market developments during the last decade are used as evidence of this conflict. This interpretation has been advocated by economists at the Bank for International Settlements in particular.[21]

The view that those responsible for monetary policy should take the impact of their actions on credit volumes and on asset prices into better account has gained stronger support after the crisis. However, there is no agreement on how this insight should be transformed into practical policy. One way would be to include asset prices among the targets of central banks. Another approach is to view financial stability as a constraint on monetary policy. A third alternative is to give an authority other than the central bank a mandate to monitor macrofinancial stability.

Fiscal policy and financial stability

As was pointed out initially, there are strong links between fiscal policy and financial stability. In business cycle upturns, tax revenue grows strongly, potentially hiding underlying weaknesses in government finances. It is therefore important to base fiscal policy on relevant estimates of the cyclical adjusted budget balance which take into account temporary tax revenue generated by unsustainable financial market developments.[22] This problem is currently illustrated by developments in countries such as Spain and Ireland.

The crisis has also strengthened the arguments for a tight fiscal policy in upturns, which would build room for manoeuvre which can be used to mitigate extreme downturns due to financial crises as well as other types of economic crisis.

Fiscal policy has an impact on financial stability via the design of the tax system. Rules for the taxation of capital income, including deductions for interest costs, for the taxation of property and wealth and for the taxation of income from renting dwellings have direct effects on the demand for credit. These rules may be designed to take account of the situation in the financial sector, i.e. they can be given a macroprudential component.

CONCLUDING DISCUSSION

The global financial crisis has taught us a new lesson: financial stability should be a more prominent economic policy objective. Many countries have now strengthened, or are in the process of strengthening, their macroprudential frameworks. Even though the financial system in some countries was hardly affected by the crisis, there are strong arguments for paying attention to the international lessons about macroprudential supervision and regulation.

Financial stability is not a new policy goal in most countries. Still, we see a recurrent weakness in existing arrangements: there is no public authority with primary responsibility for supervising the systemic risks in the financial sector and with the remit to propose measures when such risk approaches a critical level. The lesson is thus that the current framework for financial stability should be strengthened. We see two alternative routes to reach this goal.

The first is for the central bank to be given greater responsibility for macrofinancial stability, possibly with an expanded arsenal of instruments to safeguard this objective. The second is to establish a new authority, a financial stability council, with the remit to identify risks to the financial system and propose measures. We see arguments for both these solutions.

The following arguments support giving the central bank more authority. With its traditional monetary policy instruments, it has effective tools for managing developments in the financial markets. It is in direct contact with banks and financial institutions. It already has a responsibility for financial stability. It has the best analytical capacity.

There are also objections to giving central banks more powers. A conflict could arise between their objective of maintaining a low and stable level of inflation and the objective of ensuring financial stability. Their independence is to a large extent based on their having one single clear and unambiguously defined purpose, namely monetary stability as measured by a low rate of inflation. Should central banks be given increased responsibility for macrofinancial stability, it will be more difficult to evaluate whether they meet this goal.

The other option is to establish a financial stability council, which is a new public authority with responsibility for macroprudential supervision.

Such a council should have the remit to analyse the developments in the domestic and international financial system that might threaten financial stability. The authority should be required to publish its analysis on a regular basis. It should have the right to address its recommendations to the central bank, the Financial Supervisory Authority and the Ministry of Finance as well as to other public authorities and to financial institutions and financial companies. The recommendations would not be binding. In our opinion, a stability council should not have any policy tools of its own. A financial stability council should be independent of other authorities working on financial stability.

There are a number of advantages to this solution. There would be an authority focusing only on systemic risks in the financial sector. It could actively warn of financial dangers and publicly take the initiative in proposing measures. It would provide an additional voice in the economic policy debate.

One objection to a new authority is that there would be a duplication of analytical capacity. The central bank and the Financial Supervisory Authority already work on financial stability issues. Another disadvantage could be that the central bank might not feel the same degree of responsibility for macroprudential issues if a financial stability council was established.

We thus see two possible options for strengthening macroprudential supervision. The problem is hardly a lack of instruments – even though new instruments should be considered. The problem is to identify the growing risk of financial imbalances in good times. Here current international experience, as well as history, proves that existing institutions have lacked the capacity to react in time.

Achieving and maintaining financial stability is a new challenge for economic policy after the recent global crisis. Financial stability is not as easy to operationalize as monetary stability and fiscal stability. But current crisis experience demonstrates that financial stability should be given higher priority. The deepest depressions in many countries have been created by financial imbalances. Of course, the future will not be crisis-free even if a new framework for monitoring financial risks is established. But the risks of the next financial crisis may be reduced.

NOTES

1. This chapter builds upon ch. 5 in Fiscal Policy Council (2011).
2. Macroprudential policy covers two aspects: macroprudential supervision (surveillance) and macroprudential regulation. See for example Davis and Karim (2010).

3. The literature about the causes of the recent crisis is summarized by Davies (2010), among others. He provides a general discussion of some 30 explanations.
4. See for example Blanchard et al. (2010).
5. See for example Leijonhufvud (2010).
6. See for example Buiter (2009), Caballero (2010), Krugman (2009) and Leijonhufvud (2011) for different perspectives.
7. See for example Reinhart and Rogoff (2009) for descriptions of the boom–bust sequence in which the demand for and supply of credit play the central role.
8. The maturity transformation, which is one of the basic functions of the banking system, becomes more risky when short-term borrowing, particularly via market financing, is the predominant source of long-term lending.
9. See for example the various contributions in Jonung et al. (2009) for analyses of the Nordic pattern during the 1990s crisis.
10. The dynamics behind financial crises can also be described using the credit multiplier, expressing the ratio of bank loans to the reserves of the banking system. The multiplier is strongly procyclical. During a boom, the ratio of bank lending to bank reserves increases, while during a bust it decreases.
11. See for example Englund (2009).
12. See Davis and Karim (2010), Galati and Moessner (2010) and Hanson et al. (2011) for arguments in favour of macroprudential regulation.
13. See for example Davis and Karim (2010) for an overview.
14. Sibert (2010) proposes five members for a macrofinancial committee, all of whom should come from outside the public sector and international organizations, in order to get an independent opinion. Sibert explicitly excludes people from supervisory authorities. The committee is to gather information in order to warn of financial imbalances.
15. Sibert (2010) is of the view that the ESRB has been designed to achieve 'maximum inefficiency'. The board is too large, its composition is too homogeneous, it has no independence and its members already have more than enough to do elsewhere. See also Andersson (2010) for an overview of EU supervision of the European financial system.
16. See for example Davis and Karim (2010) and Galati and Moessner (2010).
17. This argument is taken from traditional welfare theory, where taxes and subsidies are used to equalize the private cost to the individual decision-maker with the cost to society (Jeanne and Korinek 2010). Externalities (network effects, etc.) in the financial system, which drive a wedge between the social and the private costs and benefits, are surveyed by Wagner (2010).
18. Representatives of the BIS, for example, argue strongly for macroprudential regulation. See BIS (2010), Borio (2008) and White (2009).
19. The same could be said about some proposals for new microprudential regulations.
20. See for example Bordo and Jeanne (2010).
21. See for example Borio (2008).
22. See also Jaeger and Schuknecht (2004).

REFERENCES

Andersson, T. (2010), 'EUs framtida tillsyn, kommer den att fungera?', *Penning- och valutapolitik*, **2**, 46–70.

BIS (2010), 'Macroprudential instruments and frameworks: a stocktaking of issues and experiences', report submitted by the Committee on the Global Financial System, Basel, May.

Blanchard, O., G. Dell'Ariccia and P. Mauro (2010), 'Rethinking macroeconomic policy', IMF staff position note, SPN/10/03, Washington, DC.

Bordo, M. and O. Jeanne (2010), 'Monetary policy and asset prices: does "benign neglect" make sense?', in C. Crowe, S. Johnson, J. Ostry and J. Zettelmeyer (eds), *Macrofinancial Linkages: Trends, Crises, and Policies*, Washington, DC: IMF, pp. 371–94.

Borio, C. (2008), 'The search for the elusive twin goals of monetary and financial stability', in L. Jonung, C. Walkner and M. Watson (eds), *Building the Financial Foundations of the Euro: Experiences and Challenges*, London: Routledge, pp. 404–30.

Buiter, W. (2009), 'The unfortunate uselessness of most "state of the art" academic monetary economics', *Financial Times*, 3 March, available at: http://blogs.ft.com/maverecon/2009/03/the-unfortunate-uselessness-of-most-state-of-the-art-academic-monetary-economics/.

Caballero, R. (2010), 'Macroeconomics after the crisis: time to deal with the pretense-of-knowledge syndrome', MIT Department of Economics working paper 10-16, Cambridge, MA: September.

Davies, H. (2010), *The Financial Crisis: Who Is to Blame?*, Cambridge: Polity.

Davis, P. and D. Karim (2010), 'Macroprudential regulation – the missing policy pillar?', *National Institute Economic Review*, **211** (1), 67–80.

Englund, P. (2009), *Systemic Risks in the Financial System*, Stockholm: Globalisation Council Report no. 36.

Fiscal Policy Council (2011), *Swedish Fiscal Policy, Finanspolitiska rådets rapport 2011*, Stockholm.

Galati, G. and R.Moessner (2010), 'Macroprudential policy – a literature review', De Nederlandsche Bank working paper no. 267, Amsterdam, the Netherlands.

Hanson, S., A. Kashyap and J. Stein (2011), A macroprudential approach to financial regulation, *Journal of Economic Perspectives*, **25** (1), 3–28.

Jaeger, A. and L.Schuknecht (2004), 'Boom–bust phases in asset prices and fiscal policy behavior', IMF working paper 04/54, Washington, DC.

Jeanne, O. and A.Korinek (2010), 'Managing credit booms and busts: a Pigouvian taxation perspective', CEPR discussion paper no. 8015, London.

Jonung, L., J. Kiander and P. Vartia (eds) (2009), *The Great Financial Crisis in Finland and Sweden: The Nordic Experience of Financial Liberalization*, Cheltenham, UK and Northampton, MA, USA: Edward Elgar.

Krugman, P. (2009), 'How did economists get it so wrong?', *New York Times*, 6 September, available at: www.nytimes.com/2009/09/06/magazine/06Economic-t.html?_r=1&pagewanted=all.

Leijonhufvud, A. (2010), 'Makroekonomi och krisen: en personlig tolkning', *Ekonomisk Debatt*, **38**, 40–5.

Leijonhufvud, A. (2011), 'Nature of an economy', CEPR policy insight no. 53, London.

Reinhart, C. and K. Rogoff (2009), *This Time Is Different*, Princeton, NJ: Princeton University Press.

Sibert, A. (2010), 'A systemic risk warning system', VoxEU, 16 January, available at: www.voxeu.org/index.php?q=node/4495.

Wagner, W. (2010), 'In the quest of systemic externalities: a review of the literature', *CESifo Economic Studies*, **56** (1), 96–111.

White, W. (2009), 'Should monetary policy "lean or clean"?', Federal Reserve Bank of Dallas Globalization and Monetary Policy Institute working paper no. 34, available at: http://www.dallasfed.org/institute/wpapers/2009/0034.pdf.

12. Recovered imaginaries, imagined recoveries: a cultural political economy of crisis construals and crisis management in the North Atlantic financial crisis

Bob Jessop

Crises are multifaceted phenomena that invite multiple approaches from different entry-points and standpoints. This chapter deploys a cultural political economy approach to explore how the current crisis in the North Atlantic economies has been construed from the viewpoint of different economic imaginaries.[1] Of particular interest is the shock that crises gave to the prevailing economic wisdom and dominant policy paradigms, leading to the recovery of other economic perspectives as well as a search to imagine alternative economic and political paths to economic recovery. Key aspects of the retrospective interpretation and prospective envisioning of economic performance are actors' differential capacities for lesson-drawing and asymmetrical abilities to refuse to learn from their mistakes. Accordingly the following analysis considers the multifaceted nature of the so-called global financial crisis, the selection of some construals rather than others as the basis for economic responses and crisis management, and the transformation of a crisis that originated in private credit relations and securitization into a crisis of public finances and sovereign debt. Of special interest are two issues. One is the contestation between hegemonic neo-liberal economic imaginaries and those that had been consigned to oblivion in recent decades as scientifically outmoded, historically superseded, politically disproven, or ideologically unacceptable. The other is the capacity of economic and political elites committed to neo-liberalism to reject alternative, possibly more accurate or adequate, readings of the crisis and maintain a neo-liberal course in the face of economic and political resistance. Addressing these issues reveals the limits of a purely constructivist approach to political economy and the advantages of a more materialist cultural political economy (or CPE) account.

CULTURAL POLITICAL ECONOMY

This approach integrates the cultural or, better, a broader semiotic turn (a concern with the social production of intersubjective meaning) into the analysis of instituted economic and political relations and their social embedding. It does not add 'culture' to politics and economics to create a three-dimensional analysis. Instead, arguing that all social phenomena have semiotic *and* material properties, it studies their interconnections and coevolution in constructing as well as construing social relations. This enables CPE to avoid both a structuralist Scylla and a constructivist Charybdis. A significant feature of CPE regarding this 'third way' is the distinction between the sedimentation and repoliticization of discourses (cf. Glynos and Howarth 2007; Jessop 2009). These processes are contingent aspects of all social relations, with sedimentation giving rise to the appearance of their structural fixity and repoliticization in turn suggesting their socially arbitrary nature. Crises are particularly important moments in the general dialectic of sedimentation and repoliticization and my contribution explores this regarding struggles to interpret the 'global financial crisis' and to formulate and pursue alternative paths to recovery. Another significant feature, also important in crisis dynamics and crisis management, is the role that learning plays in the variation, selection and retention of competing economic imaginaries (including recovered as well as extant and new imaginaries) and paths to economic renewal.

CPE studies semiosis and structuration as potentially complementary but possibly contrary or disconnected mechanisms of complexity reduction in social relations. The world is too complex to be understood in all its complexity in real time and not so open that all possible combinations of social relations can be realized in the same time-space. For social agents to be able to 'go on' in the world, they must reduce complexity by selectively attributing meaning to some of its features rather than others and also set limits to compossible sets of social relations through processes of structuration. Accordingly, CPE explores the interpenetration and coevolution of semiosis and structuration in regard to the emergence, consolidation and transformation of the instituted features of what it regards as an inevitably improbable, contradictory and crisis-prone ensemble of economic and political relations in specific historical contexts. This short contribution cannot present CPE in the round but focuses instead on four basic sets of categories for studying economic and political crisis. These comprise: social imaginaries and lived experience; the 'economy' as an imagined ensemble of social relations; the instituted nature of the economy; and the contradictions, crisis tendencies and counter-tendencies of the capitalist mode of production (see Jessop 2002, 2009, 2011).

First, an imaginary is a semiotic ensemble (without tightly defined boundaries) that frames individual subjects' lived experience of an inordinately complex world and/or guides collective calculation about that world. There are many such imaginaries and they are involved in complex and tangled relations at different sites and scales of action (see also Althusser 1971; Taylor 2000). Without them, individuals cannot 'go on' in the world and collective actors (such as organizations) could not relate to their environments, make decisions, or pursue more or less coherent strategies.

Second, because the totality of economic activities is so unstructured and complex, it cannot be an object of effective calculation, management, governance, or guidance. Such practices are always oriented to 'imagined economies'. These comprise subsets of economic relations (economic systems, subsystems, networks, clusters etc.) that have been semiotically and, perhaps organizationally and institutionally, fixed as appropriate objects of intervention. They are discursively constituted and materially reproduced on many sites and scales, in different spatio-temporal contexts and over various spatio-temporal horizons. Economic imaginaries have a crucial constitutive role here in so far as they identify, privilege and seek to stabilize some economic activities from the totality of economic relations. They give meaning and shape thereby to the 'economic' field but are always selectively defined. As such they typically exclude – usually unintentionally – elements vital to the overall performance of the subset of economic (and extra-economic) relations that have been identified. The recursive selection of semiotic practices and extra-semiotic processes tends to secure the 'requisite variety' (constrained heterogeneity rather than simple uniformity) behind the structural coherence of economic activities. Indeed, if they are to prove more than 'arbitrary, rationalistic, and willed' (Gramsci 1971, pp. 376–7), economic imaginaries must have some significant, albeit necessarily partial, fit with real material interdependencies in the actually existing economy and/or in the relations among economic and extra-economic activities.

Third, when an imaginary has been operationalized and institutionalized, it transforms and naturalizes these elements into the moments of a specific, instituted economy with specific emergent properties. Structuration sets limits to compossible combinations of social relations and thereby contributes to the institution of specific political economies. However, there are always interstitial, residual, marginal, irrelevant, recalcitrant and plain contradictory semiotic and extra-semiotic elements that escape any attempt to identify, govern and stabilize a given 'economic arrangement' or broader 'economic order'. These can disrupt the smooth performance of instituted economies. However, they also provide a reservoir of semiotic and material resources to be mobilized in the face of instability or crisis (see below).

Fourth, while a critique of political economy must address the categories that belong to the dominant imaginaries and that shape the institutionalization of economic relations, a CPE approach must also identify the structural contradictions and strategic dilemmas inherent in these relations and their extra-economic supports. While it may be possible to displace and/or defer these contradictions and to resolve strategic dilemmas in the short to medium term, they are generally incompressible in the longer term and, through the interaction of specific crisis-tendencies in specific conjunctures, create crises that destabilize economic imaginaries, disrupt crisis management routines, and provoke a search for new imaginaries and new ways to manage or overcome crises.

ON THE VARIATION, SELECTION AND RETENTION OF IMAGINARIES

CPE semiotic analysis integrates the evolutionary mechanisms of variation, selection and retention already familiar in institutional economics. It studies the coevolution of semiotic *and extra-semiotic* factors and processes in the contingent emergence, subsequent privileging, and ongoing realization of specific discursive and material practices. Crises are interesting here because they often produce profound cognitive, strategic and practical disorientation by disrupting actors' sedimented views of the world. They disturb prevailing meta-narratives, theoretical frameworks, policy paradigms and/or everyday life and open the space for proliferation (*variation*) in crisis interpretations, only some of which get *selected* as the basis for 'imagined recoveries' that are translated into economic strategies and policies – and, of these, only some prove effective and are *retained.*

Given this volume's concern with crises, I will explore how semiosis and extra-semiotic factors vary in importance across different stages of economic crisis.[2] I suggest that semiosis becomes more important in path-shaping when crises disrupt taken-for-granted discourses and generate unstructured complexity, provoking multiple crisis interpretations. Its scope is more restricted in the selective translation of some imagined paths to recovery into specific social responses. Extra-semiotic mechanisms matter most in the retention of some strategic responses as the basis for new, sedimented routines, organizations and institutions.

Figure 12.1 depicts the interrelations among these hypotheses. One of the purposes of this heuristic schema is to suggest how to avoid the twin temptations of the constructivist Charybdis and structuralist Scylla by

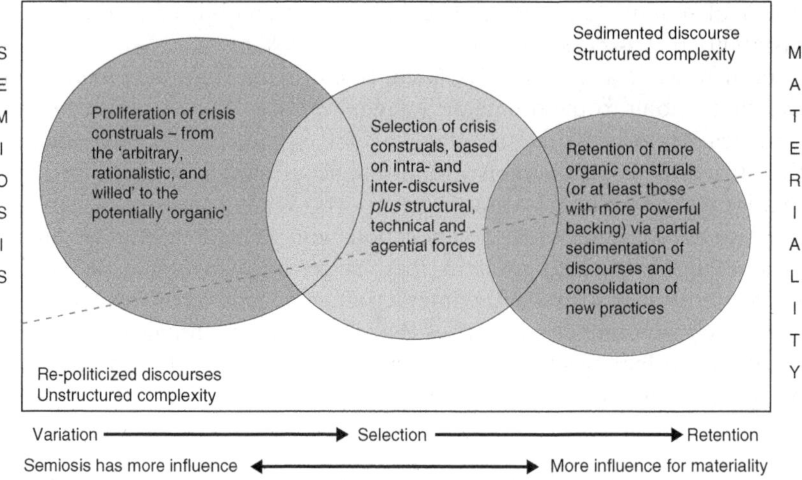

Figure 12.1 Schematic representation of variation, selection and retention

avoiding overemphasis on the role of construal due to a one-sided focus on variation (where semiosis matters most and might be thought to be determinative) or on the structural determination of crisis responses due to a one-sided focus on retention (where the sedimentation and structured coherence achieved in part through specific technologies of power) matter most. It represents an overlapping sequence of variation, selection and retention of crisis interpretations triggered by a crisis that sees the repoliticization (contestation) of sedimented discourses and the breakdown of established patterns of structured complexity (relative institutional coherence). The dotted diagonal line indicates that the semiotic and material are always co-present but their relative weight changes across the three stages. As one crisis interpretation and its imagined recovery trajectory are selected, discourse is sedimented again and new forms of structured complexity are established (or old patterns restored). If stage three is not reached because the proposed response is impractical, the sequence will restart at stage one or two.

The first phases of a crisis generally prompt massive *variation* in construals of its nature and significance, opening a space for the (re)politicization of sedimented discourses and practices. Many early accounts are short-lived, disappearing in the cacophony of competing interpretations or lacking meaningful connections to the salient phenomenal forms of the crisis. This holds for religious readings of the crisis as signs of divine retribution for moral degeneration, for example, as well as for the equally fanciful claims that the terminal crisis of capitalism was close. Overall, the plausibility of interpretations, strategies and projects depends on their resonance (and hence their capacity to reinterpret and mobilize) in an 'intertextual' field with its own discursive selectivities. Relevant aspects include the lived experiences of members of key classes, strata, social categories, or other crisis-hit groups, diverse organizational or institutional narratives, and meta-narratives (see Somers 1994).

What matters in CPE terms is which of these many and diverse interpretations get *selected* as the basis for private and public strategic and policy initiatives to manage the crisis and/or move beyond it through imagined recoveries. This is not reducible to narrative resonance, argumentative force, or scientific merit alone (although each has a role in certain contexts) but also depends on diverse extra-semiotic factors associated with structural, agential, and technological selectivities. This involves, inter alia, the prevailing 'web of interlocution' (Somers 1994) and its discursive selectivities (Hay 1996), the organization and operation of the mass media, the role of intellectuals in public life, and the structural biases and strategically selective operations of various public and private apparatuses of economic, political and ideological domination. That some institutional and meta-narratives resonate powerfully does not validate them. All narratives are selective, appropriate some arguments rather than others and combine them in specific ways. So we must study what goes unstated or silent, repressed or suppressed, in specific discourses. Moreover, while some narratives (and their narrators) need to convince only a few key policymakers or strategists to be acted upon, others are effective only through their capacity to mobilize significant support from a broader range of social forces.

A third phase begins when some accounts are *retained* and undergo theoretical, interpretative and policy elaboration, leading eventually to sedimentation and structuration. However, there is many a slip between the discursive resonance of old, reworked or new imaginaries in a given conjuncture and their translation into adequate policies, effective crisis-management routines, durable new social arrangements and institutionalized compromises to support accumulation. It is one thing to (re)politicize discourses in the context of the unstructured complexity associated with crisis, it is another to move to sedimented (taken-for-granted) discourse and seemingly structured complexity. This raises the key issue of the (always limited and provisional) fit between imaginaries and real, or potentially realizable, sets of material interdependencies in the economy and its embedding in wider sets of social relations. Proposed crisis strategies and policies must be (or seen to be) effective within the spatio-temporal horizons of relevant social forces in a given social order. Generally, the greater the number of sites and scales of social organization at which resonant discourses are retained, the greater is the potential for institutionalization.

This in turn should lead to relative structured coherence across institutional orders and modes of thought and to relatively durable patterns of social compromise among key actors (Jessop 2004; Sum and Jessop 2001). If this proves impossible, the new project will seem 'arbitrary, rationalistic and willed' and the cycle of variation, selection and retention will restart.

A CULTURAL POLITICAL ECONOMY OF CRISIS

Crisis conjunctures are unbalanced: they are objectively overdetermined and subjectively indeterminate (Debray 1973, p. 113). Because they are never purely objective, extra-semiotic events or processes that automatically produce a particular response or outcome, crises offer a real-time laboratory to study the dialectic of semiosis and materiality. Thus a CPE approach examines: (1) how crises emerge when established patterns of dealing with structural contradictions, their crisis-tendencies, and strategic dilemmas no longer work as expected and, indeed, when continued reliance thereon may aggravate matters; and (2) how contestation over the meaning of the crisis shapes responses through processes of variation, selection and retention that are mediated through a changing mix of semiotic and extra-semiotic mechanisms. Here I focus largely on the second set of questions.

Imaginaries shape the interpretation of crises and the responses thereto. At one pole of a continuum, some crises appear 'accidental', that is, are readily (if sometimes inappropriately) attributable to natural or 'external' forces (for example, a volcanic eruption, a tsunami, a crop failure). At the other pole, there are form-determined crises – that is, crises rooted in crisis tendencies or antagonisms associated with specific social forms (for example, capitalism). Another useful distinction is that between crises *in* a given social configuration and crises *of* that configuration. Crises '*in*' occur within the parameters of a given set of natural and social arrangements. They are typically associated with routine forms of crisis management that restore the basic features of these arrangements through internal adjustments and/or shift crisis effects into the future, elsewhere, or onto marginal and vulnerable groups. This is exemplified in alternating phases of unemployment and inflation in the postwar advanced capitalist economies and their treatment through counter-cyclical economic policies. Crises '*of*' a system are less common. They occur when there is a crisis of crisis management (that is, normal responses no longer work) and efforts to defer or displace crises encounter growing resistance. Such crises are more disorienting than crises 'in', indicating the breakdown of previous regularities and an inability to 'go on in the old way'. They can cause social stasis or regression, attempts to restore the old system through *force majeure*, fraud, or corruption; efforts at more radical social innovation for good or ill, leading in some cases to exceptional regimes (for example, military dictatorship, fascism) or to attempts to break the power of such regimes. This is seen in the crisis *of* the postwar mode of growth, reflected in the declining effectiveness of Keynesian economic policies, which created the conditions for a neo-liberal regime shift and a transition to a finance-dominated mode of growth.

In short, a crisis is a moment for contestation and struggle to construe it and inform individual and collective responses. This involves, among other issues, delimiting the origins of a crisis in space–time and its uneven spatio-temporal incidence; identifying – rightly or wrongly – purported causes (agential, structural, discursive and technical – in various senses of this last word) at different scales, over different time horizons, in different fields of social practice and at different levels of social organization from nameless or named individuals through social networks, formal organizations, institutional arrangements, specific social forms or even the dynamic of a global society; determining its scope and effects, assessing in broad terms whether it is a crisis '*in*' or '*of*' the relevant arrangements; reducing its complexities to identifiable causes that could be targeted to find solutions; charting alternative futures; and promoting specific lines of action for socially identified forces over differently constructed spatio-temporal horizons of action.

To have reached consensus on interpretations about the crisis (or crises) and its (their) most salient features is to have framed the problem. Successfully to blame one set of factors and/or actors distracts blame from oneself and sets the stage for efforts to resolve crisis. For example, limiting crisis management to the search for correct policies, however wide-ranging, implies that the crisis is due to incorrect policy or inadequate regulation rather than being rooted in deeper structural causes linked to patterns of economic, political and social domination that demand more radical solutions (Wolff 2008). Whether the crisis is defined as a crisis *in* or *of* a given set of social relations, conflicts occur over how best to resolve it and allocate its costs. Other things being equal, more resonant interpretations will get selected as the basis for action, whether this takes the form of restoration, piecemeal reform or radical innovation. But other things are rarely equal. Power matters. Powerful narratives without powerful bases from which to implement them are less effective than more 'arbitrary, rationalistic and willed' accounts that are pursued consistently by the powerful through the exercise of power. Indeed, periods of crisis illustrate forcefully that power involves the capacity *not to have to learn from one's own mistakes* (Deutsch 1963, p. 111). Asymmetries of power are especially significant in the selection of crisis interpretations and their translation into crisis responses and imagined recovery scenarios. This helps to explain the reassertion of key elements in the neo-liberal project despite the initial shock to that project from the form, timing, location and incidence of the current crisis.

CRISIS MANAGEMENT AND LEARNING

Learning has a critical role in crises (including crises of crisis management), affecting the capacity to formulate imagined recoveries. It has the same selectivities (semiotic, structural, technological and agential) as semiosis more generally and also undergoes variation, selection and retention. A crisis does not automatically lead to learning: cognitive capacities may be lacking or the situation may be too unstructured (chaotic); or, again, lessons learnt are irrelevant because the situation is too turbulent to apply them. Learning depends on a dialectics of *Erlebnis* and *Erfahrung* that has its own temporalities, shaped by crisis dynamics. *Erlebnis* refers to *immediate experience* in the face of disorientation and associated attempts to make sense of disorienting events and/or processes. *Erfahrung* refers to the lessons learned from this disorientation and sense-making. Importantly, it typically includes an element of the objective dimensions of the crisis – lessons must be adequate to the crisis, not just idiosyncratic reactions.

When crises throw established modes of learning into crisis, three stages in learning can occur: learning in crisis, learning about crisis and learning from crisis (Ji 2006). Each stage is likely to involve different balances of semiosis and structuration (see Figure 12.1). It can also involve different degrees of reflexivity, i.e. learning about learning. This requires that actors recognize the need for new imaginaries, because inherited approaches have not worked well in crisis situations, and that they reorganize information collection, calculation and embodied and/or collective memory. Shifts in strategic learning and knowledge production often require a shift in the balance of forces in wider social relations.

Crises of a given system, hence crises of crisis management, are especially likely to disrupt learned strategic behaviour and lead to an initial trial-and-error, 'muddling-through' approach. *Learning in crisis* occurs in the immediacy of experiencing crisis, considered as a moment of profound disorientation, and is oriented to the phenomenal forms of crisis. It involves attempts to make sense of an initial disorientation (at some level of everyday life, organizational and/or institutional and/or policy paradigms, disciplinary or theoretical framing, and meta-narrative) in order to 'go on' in the face of the crisis as it is experienced (*Erlebnis*). Three points merit attention here. First, social actors have different social, spatial and temporal positions, as well as reflexive capacities and pasts, and will live the crisis in different ways. In this sense, actors' strategic learning does not come directly from the crisis as a whole, but from their own circumstances and crisis experiences. This can lead to different strategic responses (strategic variation); and their results vary in terms of success or survival under certain structural and conjunctural conditions (strategic selection). Second, actors vary in their capacities to 'read' the crisis and to respond to it in the 'short term'. At one extreme we find wilful blindness or repeated bouts of 'crying wolf' that lead to the dismissal of real crises; at the other extreme, crises may be manufactured (or crisis construals may be deliberately biased) to force decisions favourable to one's own interests. Lastly, in critical realist terms, learning in crisis is more likely to address the empirical and actual dimensions of the crisis than to deal with its real causes (especially in terms of their spatio-temporal breadth and depth).

Learning about crisis occurs as a crisis unfolds, often in unexpected ways, with lags in real time as actors begin to interpret the crisis in terms of underlying mechanisms and dynamics. It goes beyond the 'phenomenal' features of a crisis to its 'essential'[3] features in order to develop more effective initial responses and a more effective mid-term strategy. It is most likely where the routine crisis management procedures adopted by actors prove, or seem to be, inadequate or inappropriate, with the result that policymaking and implementation must engage in experimentation. This stage differs from learning in crisis because it takes more time to dig beneath phenomenal features (if it did not, then this would not be a 'crisis' that is disorienting at the level of theoretical or policy paradigm, and it would be possible to engage in routine crisis-management routines) and/or to scan the environment for analogous events in past or present. Social actors learn through 'trial-and-error' in specific conditions and, in this sense, through 'learning about crisis' they also embark on learning from crisis.

Learning from crisis occurs after a crisis is (temporarily) resolved (or changes its form, e.g. from liquidity crisis to sovereign debt crisis or fiscal crisis) and includes preventive or prudential actions to prevent repetition, to improve crisis management routines, and so on. It may lead to revisions in imaginaries, whether these take the form of meta-narratives, theoretical frameworks, policy paradigms, or everyday expectations and routines. In this phase, strategic lessons are retained after the surviving social actors have had time to reflect on the new, post-crisis realities. Only then is overall strategic reorientation and path-breaking likely to be accomplished.

Lessons from the past are often invoked in the course of all three learning types. This involves the use of history to make history or, put differently, the effort to define appropriate historical parallels as a basis for responding effectively to the crisis in real time. Such lessons often interact with 'spatial' dimensions, such as policy transfer across different fields, sites, levels and scales of policymaking.

CONSTRUING THE FINANCIAL AND ECONOMIC CRISES (2007–11)

The 'global financial crisis' (GFC) offers a good opportunity to test this approach. The GFC is far more complex, multidimensional and multiscalar than its simple label implies and has unfolded very unevenly around the globe – to such an extent, indeed, that one might ask whether it is truly global or whether this label merely offers an alibi to actors in the economic spaces where it emerged before spreading elsewhere through contagion. The GFC began to develop well before it attracted general attention in 2007–08 and is a product of the interaction of at least five processes:

1. the global environmental, fuel, food and water crisis;
2. the decline of US hegemony, dominance and credibility in the post-cold-war geopolitical order;
3. the crisis of a global economy organized in the shadow of ongoing neo-liberalization;
4. a range of structural or branch crises in important sectors (such as automobiles and agriculture); and
5. the crisis of finance-dominated accumulation regimes that emerged in a few but important economic spaces.

Each process has its own spatio-temporal and substantive logic, each interacts with the others, and, collectively, they are overdetermined by specific local, regional, national and macroregional factors that ensure that crisis-tendencies are always spatio-temporally and substantively specific rather than simple instantiations of global crisis tendencies. Lastly, there are unevenly distributed capacities for crisis management.

The crisis has passed through different stages and spread unevenly, whether through contagion and/or endogenous causes, leading to different phases in its interpretation and different learning processes. Indeed, this unfolding raises an important theoretical question: is a crisis a single event (and, if so, how would one identify its beginning and its conclusion), a contingent series of events distributed in time and space that are connected, if at all, because of earlier crisis responses that could have taken a different turn, or a series of events with an underlying tendential logic that therefore unfold as a relatively predictable process? This question can be answered, and often is, in terms of alternative crisis construals. In other words, the crisis is defined through its construal and has no reality outside that construal. In contrast, for a CPE approach, contradictions, crisis tendencies, strategic dilemmas and material interdependencies also matter. Nonetheless, to avoid the structuralist Scylla as well as the constructivist Charybdis, CPE emphasizes that these features exist only in so far as they are reproduced through particular social practices.

This poses the twin issues of (1) the resonance of construals and (2) their material adequacy. Thus, as the crisis became more visible from mid-2007 (however far back its causes may be traced) and unfolded as a series of events that were regarded as a connected process, its extent, depth and complexities grew faster than economic and political leaders could grasp, let alone find time to agree upon a coherent, coordinated response to them. This was most remarkable in September–November 2008, with countless competing interpretations, explanations, strategic plans and specific policy recommendations. Early accounts ranged from claims that this was the terminal crisis of capitalism to the equally bizarre belief that it was a blip in an otherwise sound, self-correcting free-market system. Even 'mainstream' interpretations, explanations, blame and proposed solutions reflect different regional, national and macroregional economies' experiences of 'the' global financial crisis and its broader repercussions. This is linked in turn to uneven *learning in crisis*, as the GFC seems to have transmuted from an allegedly containable crisis in the subprime mortgage market in a few economies into a broader liquidity crisis in the financial sector affecting more economies, next to a solvency crisis affecting many financial institutions and the 'real economy',[4] then to a fiscal crisis requiring major austerity packages to reduce public debt and/or a sovereign debt crisis requiring international rescue packages at the cost of more or less grudgingly accepted austerity programmes implemented through exceptional measures and policed by external economic and political bodies.

This has been accompanied by important disputes about the character, material causes and agential responsibility for the crisis as different actors seek to draw *lessons from the past* and/or from elsewhere – does it involve a normal business cycle, a normal recession, an epic recession, a great depression and so on? Further, are the parallels to be found, for example, in Weimar Germany, the depression years in the US, the crisis of the Atlantic Fordist accumulation regimes that became visible in the late 1960s and 1970s, Japan's 'lost decades' (1990–2010 and continuing), the so-called Asian crisis in 1997–98, the bursting of the irrationally exuberant dotcom bubble in 2000 and its wider repercussions, or in yet other cases of crisis? This illustrates the role of historicity, i.e. efforts to identify historical parallels, construe the crisis in their terms, and thereby frame the correct business and policy responses. Moreover, as various official and unofficial inquiries into earlier features and dynamics of the crisis report and seek to understand and draw lessons, we can see efforts to *learn from the crisis* and shape how recovery may be conceived in future.

The crisis means different things to different actors and its interpretation beyond immediate lived experience is heavily mediatized, i.e. filtered through information from various communication media. To labour the obvious, the crucial sites for crisis interpretation and crisis management following the outbreak of crisis in 2006–08 have been the United States and the international financial institutions that it dominates with the UK and European Union as its junior partners. Much mainstream commentary has read the crisis from the viewpoints of capital accumulation rather than social reproduction, the global North rather than the global South, and the best way for states to restore rather than constrain the dominance of market forces. Such commentaries reflect government responses to the crisis, especially in the global North. They have been slower to respond to the needs of 'social reproduction' in daily, life course, and intergenerational terms; and to take effective action on impending environmental, food and fuel crises.

The disorienting effects of crisis can be seen in the now well-known confession by Alan Greenspan, chair of the Federal Reserve (1987–2006), that he was in 'a state of shocked disbelief' over the crisis because it contradicted the efficient-market hypothesis, a key element in neoclassical economics, and the basis of his conviction that markets should be left to manage themselves (Greenspan 2008). This disorientation was widely shared in the economics profession and led many, in a state of denial, to blame the crisis on one or another form of state intervention rather than on predatory or imprudent activities enabled by deregulation. Putting aside such blinkered, self-serving reactions, the crisis certainly opened the space for the recovery or reassertion of other economic imaginaries. These include:

- Marx's critique of the capitalist mode of production and its crisis tendencies, including his observations on the distinctive features of financial crises as well as the crisis tendencies inherent in the circuits of productive capital.
- Reassertion of different variants of Marxism, with conflicting interpretations focusing more or less one-sidedly on specific features of capitalism, imperialism and/or neo-liberalism.
- The general Keynesian critique of 'casino capitalism' and the revival of the case for a government role in contra-cyclical demand man-

agement to avoid a spiral into recession and/or prevent a second downward dip.

- The rediscovery of Hyman Minsky, a financial Keynesian, whose most famous dictum is that 'stability is de-stabilizing'. Several commentators declared the crisis to signal a 'Minsky moment', i.e. a point in financial cycles when even interest payments on loans could not be met from income because borrowers had gambled on continued asset appreciation. This reflects Minsky's account of a transition from prudent hedged finance to speculative and then Ponzi[5] financing and is exemplified in (without being confined to) the role of subprime mortgages.
- The reassertion of Ordoliberalism, based partly on Austrian economics, with its emphasis on the necessity of a strong state (and/or strong regulatory framework) for the smooth operation of free and competitive markets. Ordoliberalism survived largely intact in the European Union's Rhenish heartlands and, indeed, on this basis, Germany initially experienced *Schadenfreude* over the Anglo-Saxon crisis. Conversely, in the US, Ordoliberalism was revived through calls to return to New Deal regulatory principles, especially the desirability of separating retail from investment banking.
- Developmental-state models also saw a revival because the East Asian economies had recovered from their own crisis through a careful mix of fisco-financial prudence, neo-liberal reforms in selected parts of the private and public sectors, long-term investment and renewed competitive export-oriented growth. In addition, the charge of 'crony capitalism', once levelled against the Asian economies by the advocates of neo-liberal reform, was redirected towards the Anglo-Saxon economies and the practices of their predatory financial and industrial capitalist institutions and tightly interwoven economic and political elites.
- Other recovered economic imaginaries have restated mutualist or cooperative visions about how to organize a sustainable economy based on solidarity rather than the anarchy of exchange or top-down planning. Ecological imaginaries have also been mobilized, focusing on various forms of 'green recovery' with a more or less strong commitment to de-growth rather than the renewal of the treadmill of competitive accumulation.

Most of these recovered imaginaries have been ignored by dominant (trans)national economic and political elites as the basis for pursuing imagined recoveries. Marxist readings have won some intellectual attention and have shaped some responses within some radical left-wing parties, among some labour union militants and from some social movements. But they remain marginal in the global North. The critique of casino capitalism has proved more resonant but proposals to limit the scope for financial speculation and risk-taking have been diluted during the legislative process and are being further undermined through wars of attrition by vested financial interests, clever legal and accounting tricks, and continued expansion of shadow banking. Minsky had his own 'moment' in the early stages of the crisis but it has passed as far as mainstream economics is concerned and the policy responses advocated by Minsky and his followers (financial regulation, government spending, a state role as 'employer in the last resort' at the minimum wage, and community development banks) have been largely ignored or rejected. Ordoliberalism has enjoyed a revival in Europe's coordinated market economies but Germany has applied these principles to its domestic economy in continuation of its neo-mercantilist, export-oriented policies while choosing to back a neo-liberal fiscal compact for the European Union as a whole and to impose austerity packages on southern Europe in exchange for loans that are intended primarily to rescue insolvent or illiquid financial institutions in the wider North Atlantic region. The developmental-state model has been re-evaluated, especially in the light of the continued competitiveness and quick recoveries of the East Asian economies, but it has not been translated into policies at supranational or national level in the North Atlantic economies. Mutualism and cooperation have also gained greater attention but are still largely confined to the margins of the leading economies as flanking or supporting mechanisms to soften the impact of the GFC rather than operating as agents of radical transformation. Finally, although ecological imaginaries have become more influential outside Australia, Canada and the US (where climate change denial has powerful economic and political backing), pursuit of green recovery remains marginal and/or is being integrated into neo-liberal crisis packages through the commodification of green policy measures.

IMAGINED RECOVERIES

Looking beyond the revival of economic imaginaries that had been marginalized as neo-liberalism became hegemonic, the GFC has also been construed in the global North in one or both of two ways:

1. As a crisis *of* finance-led accumulation, prompting efforts to limit the influence of the financial sector through more radical re-regulation,

restrictions on the size and activities of banks, and greater investment in the 'real economy'.

2. As a crisis *of* neo-liberalism more generally, requiring efforts to roll back neo-liberalism at home and impose more controls on market forces in supranational and international contexts, notably regarding finance and credit.

Even in more neo-statist or neo-corporatist advanced capitalist economies, however, calls are being made for stricter regulation of *financial* markets in various supranational and international contexts. But this has not yet prompted leading forces to question the broader commitment to world market integration through free trade in goods and services or to take seriously sub- or counter-hegemonic proposals from subaltern nations, institutions, agencies and social forces. In this sense, the neo-liberal economic imaginary remains dominant and continues to shape imagined economic recoveries.

Overall, surveying responses across the broad spectrum of advanced capitalist economies, economic and political elites have proposed variable combinations of the following solutions in response to the renewed recognition that markets can fail:

- The restructuring, recapitalization and nationalization of banks, as well as isolating toxic assets in state-owned or state-supported 'bad banks'. This is a core plank of crisis management in all advanced economies and has been pursued behind a veil of secrecy through emergency legislation and executive discretion. It resulted in the nationalization and/or recapitalization of 'impaired' banks (notably in Iceland, Ireland, the US and the UK plus those Baltic states and eastern and central European economies that took a radical neo-liberal turn and, inter alia, experienced real-estate booms). It is especially significant in the recent efforts to manage the sovereign debt crises in Europe.
- A turn to the typical state powers of sovereignty, command, planning, nationalization and subvention, taxation and public spending to restore stability, to stimulate growth, and to restructure public finances through a mix of modest tax rises and more or less savage spending tax cuts. This is reflected in a partially recovered Keynesian economic imaginary and in the shift, nationally, regionally or globally, from 'private Keynesianism' – where consumer debt sustained demand despite declining real wages – to the provision of short-term stimuli to some hard-hit industrial sectors plus massive quantitative easing in the North Atlantic economies most affected

by the crisis. Such responses are handicapped because deregulation and liberalization have weakened state capacities ideationally and materially. This explains the resort to 'printing money' through quantitative easing, which, in the absence of public outcry, is one of the least demanding of state responses, and through continued reliance on historically low interest rates. These measures are nonetheless proving ineffective because of deficient demand for productive investment in a context of economic austerity. This is reflected in the accumulation of reserves by productive capital or their investment in emerging markets and in the recycling of freshly minted money capital into the purchase of government debt and/or speculation.

- Efforts to redesign and re-regulate markets so that they are less prone to predictable kinds of market failure. This is the preferred approach of neo-liberal organic intellectuals and think tanks, financial lobbyists and unrepentant neo-liberal politicians. This applies particularly to a medium-term strategy of restructuring the international financial architecture. Here we find echoes of Bretton Woods as another recovered imaginary. This is proving hard to realize in a concerted and coherent way even with the expansion of the G8 to the G20, at first informally, then formally. It appears easier to introduce new institutions than reform old ones, which leaves the latter in place and in power. The opportunity for tighter regulation seems already to have been lost as the semblance of 'business as usual' was restored in 2009–10 in the financial sector and as financial interests have blocked or weakened measures to restrict their activities.
- Another imagined path of recovery is through the G20. This self-elected group of 19 key industrial and emerging market economies (plus the European Union, the IMF, World Bank and other major IFIs) has become the *de facto* global crisis committee. This reflects growing recognition of the actual and potential influence of the BRIC economies (Brazil, Russia, India and China) and the creditor position of major East Asian economies (see Sum, this volume). Thus, the G20 Summit in November 2008 expanded the Financial Stability Forum to incorporate creditor nations, including China; and in April 2009 it established a Financial Stability Board with a wider remit. This has integrated the leading 'southern' economies into problem-solving and burden-sharing, thereby strengthening the leading IFIs, and has also reinforced an unsustainable growth-oriented global economy. But the informal, self-selected status of the G20 means that it cannot replace the United Nations, IMF, WTO and other official bodies in crisis management with their capacities for significant strategic intervention (Bello 2009). The rise

of the BRIC economies has seen their redefinition as an exit strategy for mobile capital and a source of strength and hope for a global recovery (Sum, this issue). A sometimes favoured alternative is the G77, which is a loose union of developing nations. Despite its ties to China, however, it lacks clout in international policy forums.

- Measures to introduce further flanking and supporting mechanisms to maintain the momentum of neo-liberal reforms – a sort of re-invigorated Third Way approach. This approach concedes that there are some problems with neo-liberalism, especially in its earlier celebration of greed and its creation of distorted incentives as well as in its polarizing redistributive effects, with broad swathes of the middle classes as well as the industrial working class and 'under-class' losing out to financial elites, transnational capital and political insiders (see below). But Third Way policies are not intended to stop the further extension of a hopefully *remoralized* neo-liberalism. Instead they are meant to provide greater compensation to those who lose from that extension within national frameworks or, in the EU case, in a European framework that nonetheless visibly reproduces centre–periphery relations.
- The 'Tea Party' and 'Occupy' movements represent two responses to these changes. But the former is more of an artificial, 'astroturf' movement manipulated by monied interests than an effective grass-roots party; and the latter, though it has certainly shifted the political agenda with its slogan of the '99 percent' against the '1 percent', is subject to authoritarian policing and has hitherto had a largely local and weak economic impact.
- Another imagined route to recovery is the remoralization of capitalism in tune with corporate social responsibility (CSR) and responsible, even 'green' competitiveness (Sum 2009). This remains largely rhetorical and has had limited impact on the operation of the real economy and even less on the still-dominant financialized sectors of regional, national and global economies.

CONCLUSIONS

Although the crisis has opened space for sub- and counter-hegemonic discourses, projects and practices, the overall trend emerging from crisis interpretation and practical response has been further strengthening of the neo-liberal project at the cost of some modest (and capitalistically necessary) limits on finance-dominated accumulation. With some differentiation reflecting specific economic, political and institutional locations and interests, the leading economic and political actors in neo-liberalized economies have defined this as a crisis *in* finance-led accumulation or, at most, *in* neo-liberalism. In the short-term, generous (and often ill-defined) discretionary powers were granted to the executive, or its nominees, to solve the crisis (Scheuerman 2002). The authorities reacted quickly without much consultation and with timely, targeted and temporary emergency measures to safeguard the monetary, banking and credit systems and stimulate demand in vulnerable industrial sectors. In particular the aim was to rescue financial institutions that were deemed too big (or too interconnected) to be allowed to fail. These emergency measures were accompanied by recapitalization of the biggest (but not all) of the vulnerable banks, (promises of) tighter regulation, and proposals for a reformed (but still neo-liberal) international economic regime. In addition, and crucially, excessively leveraged and indebted private giant industrial and financial concerns were enabled through crony capitalist connections to offload toxic assets to the state based on the capacity of states to create fiat money backed formally by their powers of taxation and monopoly of organized coercion. Because the amount of toxic assets far exceeded the immediate revenue-generating capacities of the states concerned, however, this has opened the space for demands that government spending on 'entitlements' and social welfare be drastically cut. In this context the manufactured 'deficit hysteria' is an excellent (but disastrous) example of how economic imaginaries can shape crisis management. Attention has thereby been redirected from the crisis in the financial sector and the real (but private) economy to the public sector, framed in terms of accumulated government debt, unsustainable public spending and public sector employment. Another effect was the concentration and centralization of political power in the hands of economic and political elites, and the extent of agreement among the leading political parties has narrowed the space for democratic debate and accountability to a limited set of alternatives. This diverted attention from more basic questions of institutional design and, more radically, of the basic social relations that reproduce crisis tendencies and shape their forms.

This said, sub- and counter-hegemonic projects have proved significant sources of local and regional resilience, have put social and environmental protection on the agenda away from the mainstream forums, and provide a reservoir of alternative economic imaginaries and alternative paths to recovery that offer a standing critique of neo-liberal and mainstream theoretical and policy paradigms. There is widespread evidence that local solutions can be developed to address the short-term effects of the crisis in its various local manifestations, and the challenge is to establish ways to exploit this real-time experimental laboratory to find what works, for whom, when and why, as a basis for mutual learning and policy transfer among subaltern groups. Developments in the European Union in 2010–12 and the more general signs of a great recession around the world indicate that the global economic crisis has not disappeared, and that emergency measures have produced only a temporary illusion of business-as-usual while downgrading the urgency of other moments of the multiple crises confronting global capital.

NOTES

1. This chapter derives from research conducted during an ESRC-funded Professorial Fellowship on the Cultural Political Economy of Crises of Crisis-Management (RES-051-27-0303). It has benefited from dialogue with Norman Fairclough, Joo-Hyoung Ji, Amelie Kutter and Ngai-Ling Sum. All errors are, of course, mine.
2. Similar arguments hold for other types of crisis.
3. The scare quotes warn against a simple, fixed distinction between appearance and essence. At stake is strategic, not ontological, essentialism.
4. The real economy has long been monetized and depends on credit–debt relations.
5. Minsky (1986) distinguished three types of financial transaction: *hedging* occurs when payment of interest and repayment of principal are funded from routine business activities, *speculation* when interest payments are met from business activities but capital repayment depends on asset appreciation, and *Ponzi finance* when even interest payments depend on asset appreciation.

REFERENCES

Althusser, Louis (1971), 'Ideology and ideological state apparatuses', in *Lenin and Philosophy and Other Essays*, London: New Left Books, pp. 127–87.

Bello, Walden (2009), *G20: Form, Not Substance*, 24 September, Washington, DC: Foreign Policy in Focus.

Debray, Régis (1973), *Prison Writings*, London: Allen Lane.

Deutsch, Karl W. (1963), *The Nerves of Government*, New York: Free Press.

Glynos, Janos and David Howarth (2007), *Logics of Critical Explanation in Social and Political Theory*, London: Routledge.

Gramsci, Antonio (1971), *Selections from the Prison Notebooks*, London: Lawrence & Wishart.

Greenspan, Alan (2008), Evidence given on 23 October 2008, House Committee on Oversight and Government Reform, Washington, DC.

Hay, Colin (1996), 'Narrating crisis: the discursive construction of the "Winter of Discontent"', *Sociology*, **30** (2), 253–77.

Jessop, Bob (2002), *The Future of the Capitalist State*, Cambridge: Polity.

Jessop, Bob (2004), 'Critical semiotic analysis and cultural political economy', *Critical Discourse Studies*, **1** (2), 159–74.

Jessop, Bob (2009), 'Cultural political economy and critical policy studies', *Critical Policy Studies*, **3** (3–4), 336–56.

Jessop, Bob (2011), 'Rethinking the diversity of capitalism', in Geoff Wood and Christel Lane (eds), *Capitalist Diversity and Diversity within Capitalism*, London: Routledge, 209–37.

Ji, Joo-Hyoung (2006), 'Learning from crisis: political economy, spatio-temporality, and crisis management in South Korea, 1961–2002, PhD thesis, Lancaster University.

Minsky, Hyman P. (1986), *Stabilizing an Unstable Economy*, New Haven, CT: Yale University Press.

Scheuerman, William E. (2002), 'Rethinking crisis government', *Constellations*, **9** (4), 492–505.

Somers, M. (1994), 'The narrative constitution of identity: a relational and network approach', *Theory and Society*, **23** (5), 605–49.

Sum, Ngai-Ling (2009), 'The production of hegemonic policy discourses: "competitiveness" as a knowledge brand and its (re-)contextualizations', *Critical Policy Studies*, **3** (2), 184–203.

Sum, Ngai-Ling and Bob Jessop (2001), 'Pre-disciplinary and post-disciplinary perspectives in political economy', *New Political Economy*, **6** (1), 89–101.

Taylor, Charles (2001), *Modern Social Imaginaries*, Durham, NC: Duke University Press.

Wolff, Rick (2008), 'Policies to "avoid" economic crises', *MR Zine*, 6 November, available at: http://mrzine.monthlyreview.org/index061108.html (last accessed 30 June 2012).

Index